The Cabinet and Political Power
in New Zealand

OXFORD READINGS IN NEW ZEALAND POLITICS: No. 5

General Editor: Martin Holland

The Cabinet and Political Power in New Zealand

Elizabeth McLeay

Auckland
OXFORD UNIVERSITY PRESS
Melbourne New York Toronto

Oxford University Press, Walton Street, Oxford OX2 6DP
Oxford   New York   Toronto
Delhi   Bombay   Calcutta   Madras   Karachi
Kuala Lumpur   Singapore   Hong Kong   Tokyo
Nairobi   Dar es Salaam   Cape Town
Melbourne   Auckland   Madrid
and associated companies in
Berlin   Ibadan

Oxford is a trade mark of Oxford University Press

ISBN 0 19 558312 4
ISSN 0967-4144

Cover designed by Nikolas Andrew
Typeset in Adobe Times by Egan-Reid Limited
Printed through Bookpac Production Services, Singapore
Published by Oxford University Press
540 Great South Road, Greenlane
PO Box 11-149, Auckland, New Zealand

For my parents,
Molly and Rod McLeay

CONTENTS

SERIES INTRODUCTION

Elizabeth McLeay's *The Cabinet and Political Power in New Zealand* is the fifth title to appear in the Oxford University Press series *Oxford Readings in New Zealand Politics*. The book, like the previous four titles, has been written to meet a specific need within the discipline of political science in New Zealand—namely, to provide a contemporary analysis of a key decision-making area, the cabinet. The book is a much needed and long overdue contribution to our knowledge of the New Zealand political system. Together with the previous titles (which encompassed the topics of electoral behaviour, the state and the economy, environmental policy, and health policy), the series has redressed some of the substantive gaps in our domestic literature, and has provided a core body of New Zealand political science that both complements the international literature and distinguishes New Zealand from it.

This latest contribution to the series also demonstrates the broad spread of expertise in New Zealand. Despite the comparatively small size of the discipline in New Zealand, the series has underlined the active research ethic that permeates all New Zealand Departments of Politics and the collaborative nature of much of our work.

Lastly, as General Editor, I would like to express my thanks to Oxford University Press for supporting political science research and publication in New Zealand.

Martin Holland
General Editor

ACKNOWLEDGEMENTS

I should like to acknowledge the generous financial assistance granted to me by the Internal Affairs Committee, Victoria University of Wellington. Jacqueline Owens, Tim Bollinger, and Grant Klinkum were admirable part-time research assistants, and Julia Craven transcribed tapes efficiently and perceptively. Both Julia and Adrienne Nolan were patient with my numerous requests for secretarial assistance while I was working on this book. Maurice and James Goldsmith both put up with me during the writing process, and Maurice added to his chores by helping with the proof-reading and word-processing. Keith Jackson contributed valuable ideas and criticisms, and this work also benefited from some early discussions with Jonathan Boston. Simon Cauchi staunchly edited the work. The faults are, as always, mine. My colleagues in the Department of Politics were invariably supportive, and I should particularly like to thank Paul Harris and Margaret Clark, departmental chairpersons. I should like to thank all the MPs and ministers who were so generous with their time and help. Finally, I wish to thank Robert Chapman, who set me off into the area of cabinet studies many years ago.

Elizabeth McLeay
January, 1995

Abbreviations

AJHR	*Appendices to the Journals of the House of Representatives*
CE	Chief Executive
CO	Cabinet Office
FPP	'First-Past-the-Post' (electoral system)
GST	Goods and Services Tax
MD	Managing Director
MEC	Member of the Executive Council
MP	Member of Parliament
MMP	Mixed Member Proportional (electoral system)
NDC	National Development Conference
NZLP	New Zealand Labour Party
NZPD	*New Zealand Parliamentary Debates*
PLP	Parliamentary Labour Party
PM	Prime Minister
PMC	Department of the Prime Minister and Cabinet
PMD	Prime Minister's Department
PMO	Prime Minister's Office
SOE	State-Owned Enterprise
SSC	State Services Commission

1

INTRODUCTION

Since the middle of the 1980s the New Zealand cabinet, the central organ of government, has been poised between two major movements of political and constitutional change: sweeping state sector reform; and an equally radical shift from a simple plurality to a proportional electoral system. By 1990 the public service had been both shrunk and remodelled; and the party system has been changing since the 1970s. Undoubtedly, the cabinet's functioning has been affected by the transfigurations surrounding it. Cabinet will have to adapt still further after the introduction of proportional representation. The basic system of cabinet government itself has, however, so far remained intact, appearing to be largely unaffected by the transformations cabinet itself has either stimulated or initiated. Thus the contemporary cabinet is in a curious position; the pincer-like movements of political change appear to hold cabinet semi-paralysed in their grasp.

Much has been written about recent political events in New Zealand, naturally focusing upon change. Even so, with all the structural, economic, and political alterations that New Zealand has undergone in the past couple of decades, it seems surprising that scant attention has been paid to the functioning of cabinet and the roles of ministers, outside their relationships with their government departments and corporations. This is all the more strange since part of the explanation of why there has been discontent with the political system lies with the behaviour of successive cabinets; New Zealand's elected governments have attempted to reshape the political culture with only partial success, producing voter resentment. Nonetheless, the remedies for policy failure have almost all been sought outside the 'black box' of cabinet decision-making, through reform of the public service, reduction of the scope of government, attempts at improving the accountability of top public servants, and constraining executive power through changing the electoral system to represent more fairly political parties in Parliament, thus making it almost impossible for single-party majority governments to be formed. The effects of this latter transformation of the party system and of Parliament upon the structure and functioning of the New Zealand cabinet have yet to be seen.[1]

Whether single-party or coalition cabinets are created in the future, and whether minority or majority governments are formed, the essential characteristics of cabinet government will remain: Prime Ministers with their cabinets will have to retain the support of Parliaments in order to retain power. So, for constitutional and political reasons, collective cabinet responsibility will continue to be a dominant characteristic of our present system of government, and either all or most of the ministers will be drawn from Parliament. Only this last feature has attracted the attention of reformers.[2] But this proposal has been received with no enthusiasm so far, perhaps for the reason that Walter Bagehot put forward in 1867: 'Those who wish to remove the choice of Ministers from Parliament have not adequately considered what a Parliament is. A Parliament is nothing less than a big meeting of more or less idle people. In proportion as you give it power it will inquire into everything, settle everything, meddle in everything.'[3]

Hence, as the New Zealand political system continues to be changed, it is timely to ask some questions about the core political executive itself: whether cabinet too has been quietly modifying itself, or whether perhaps it has been undergoing some sort of metamorphosis. Furthermore, there has never been a book on cabinet itself, although there have been scholarly works on Parliament, on government administration, on the selection of cabinets, and on particular governments.[4] It seemed time for this gap in our literature to be at least partly remedied.

The guiding assumption of this analysis of cabinet government in New Zealand is that institutions and structures, their formal rules and behavioural norms, play the major role in shaping political action. This might seem to be a somewhat anodyne claim given that people argue about the shapes of constitutions precisely because they believe that institutions and rules make a difference to behaviour. The contemporary debates about the problems of the New Zealand political system and the nature of the constitution are about how power can best be shared and constrained.

Compare an institutional focus, however, with other sorts of possible approaches. Cabinet is, after all, about the personalities within it, and the relationships between those individuals. This work might have concentrated upon those politicians, telling how they rose to and fell from power, and the influences upon and development of their personalities. Such an approach to cabinet situates the individual as the central unit of analysis, and concentrates upon psychological theories about leadership and political behaviour. Of course the personalities of individuals can make a great deal of difference to policy outcomes and the ways in which institutions work, especially those institutions which are as vulnerable to personal style as is the New Zealand cabinet. But, while not avoiding discussion of the individuals who have shaped our political system, this book is about structures and processes, and the ways in which individuals are shaped by those structures and processes and in turn help to shape them. Thus, for example, the story of how cabinets have been chosen fits into this sort of approach, as does the discussion of cabinet committees and the accountability issue.

A second approach is that based upon the assumptions of rational choice theory. This school of analysis, the single most important influence on contemporary political science, in its purest (or perhaps rawest) state assumes a uniformity of motivation of political men and women whereby the goals of particular behaviours are construed as individualistic and self-serving rather than dependent upon context. The public choice school has indeed taught us much, particularly concerning the positioning of political parties on the political spectrum, the processes of coalition formation, the problems of collective action (why people join organizations and work for them when they could be 'free-riders'), and the adverse effects of some aspects of bureaucratic behaviour. But public choice has had to recognize its explanatory shortcomings when it comes to altruistic and group-oriented behaviour. Here we need to understand the part played by the values of community and society, the behavioural norms inculcated by political and social structures. It is not really surprising that public choice theory has been modified to encompass context, alternative goals, and the part played by institutions. Indeed, in the USA and Britain there has arisen the 'new institutionalism' that combines the impact of structures with some assumptions about 'rational' behaviour.[5] In this work I sometimes use public choice-type explanations, but always within the institutional context, remembering that ideology can often form as powerful an incentive for acting in a particular way as does the incentive to gain power for its own sake. It is salutary to note that theorists of cabinet formation in coalition situations have had to consider the impact of the policy goals of potential coalition partners as well as parties' urges to share the fruits of office.[6]

More concretely, I assume that in order to understand the New Zealand cabinet and the extent of its power we need to consider three factors: party, Parliament, and the historical institution of cabinet itself. Each contributes towards constraining and shaping the opportunities and actions of the political actors. Individuals can be presumed to be ambitious for power, that is, to pursue self-interest. Yet party ideology and policy goals, as well as the norms of behaviour within the central political organizations, all affect individual political behaviour. Nevertheless individuals are not like pieces of driftwood dependent upon wind and the ocean currents; they also alter the direction and shape of the institutions of which they are part. Every Prime Minister, for example, has influenced the way in which cabinets have operated.

I examine the contemporary cabinet using primarily a thematic approach.

The next chapter positions the New Zealand cabinet within the context of theories and approaches to cabinet government, and then examines the New Zealand cabinet within the domestic, constitutional context. Chapter Three, also contextual, discusses cabinet both in relation to the changing nature of the party system and in relation to parliamentary representation and behavioural patterns. I continue to develop the contextual theme in the fourth chapter, which briefly traces the histories of the development of cabinet selection in the National and Labour parties. This provides some understanding of how the ideologies of the political parties and the behaviour of the party leaders in the cabinet selection process have contributed to the development of norms of political behaviour within the institutional context. Next, in Chapter Five, I shift focus to concentrate upon the structure and operations of cabinet and cabinet committees, moving from there to analyse in Chapter Six the roles of the ministers themselves. From this point, the focus again expands outwards, to look at the public service and advice to the Prime Minister in Chapter Seven, and in Chapter Eight at the extent to which ministers consult outside interests, and at the types of interests and groups that are thereby involved in the political process. The last substantive chapter takes up a normative theme: the extent to which ministers and cabinet in New Zealand take responsibility for and are made accountable for their actions. The book concludes with a short discussion of the nature of cabinet power in New Zealand. I said above that this work analyses cabinet government thematically but, since political scientists are trained to look for patterns and comparisons, I use examples and developments from New Zealand's past cabinets as well as very brief illustrations from other cabinet systems.

There is perhaps more political sociology than public administration in this book. My early work was on parliamentary careers and the selection of cabinets.[7] It reflected a long-standing and continuing fascination with political élites and issues relating to representation, especially the interrelationship between representative systems, the exercise of political power, and the presence or absence of women, ethnic minorities, and economic interests. But in part this emphasis relates also to my appreciation of (and dependence upon) the rich literature now available on New Zealand's public service, especially the more recent changes to public and state sector developments, and my awareness as both a teacher and a researcher of the very wide gaps in our political knowledge.

The sources upon which this analysis is based are the orthodox ones of political science. The primary sources include the *New Zealand Parliamentary Debates* (*NZPD*), Parliamentary Papers and other official papers, published biographies and autobiographies, and newspaper reports. The other main data source has been my own interviews of politicians (see Appendix I).

Between 1971 and 1974 I interviewed over one hundred MPs and ministers on the subject of parliamentary careers and cabinet selection. Most of the interviews took place in 1971 and 1972, before and after the 1972 general election. I have drawn on the relevant portions of the thesis for this book, twenty years later. Then in 1991 and early 1992 I interviewed almost all the ministers of the fourth National Government led by Jim Bolger, and three National Party caucus chairpersons. The more recent round of interviews concentrated upon the role of the minister rather than the career process. The literature of cabinet studies has scarcely ever been based upon qualitative data of this sort,[8] and longitudinal élite studies are not usually attempted. Thus this New Zealand work is a modest attempt to add to our knowledge of the behaviour of political élites in a democratic, liberal state.

The concentration upon the membership of one contemporary cabinet (rather than, say, interviewing a range of representatives from the two different administrations within the past decade) was deliberate. Talking to a range of ministers within the Bolger Government allowed me to discern patterns of behaviour and policy formulation within the cabinet. Besides, much had been written on the fourth Labour Government. I also believed that there was a great deal to be learned from studying the operations and style of one cabinet in some depth. Material from these interviews has been used throughout the book. Whenever possible, the views of the ministers have been put in their own words.[9] In order to allow them to speak freely, the ministers have not been named. Additionally, anonymity encourages a search for patterns and insights rather than a fixation upon the politics of personality—the focus of most of the New Zealand mass media. The concentration on a National administration is an innovation for New Zealand political science; all the recent studies have been about Labour governments, reflecting, perhaps, social scientists' interest in reforming regimes rather than those which are perceived as preserving the *status quo*. My focus on National, however, given its untraditional reforming zeal, permitted me both to break ranks with my colleagues and indulge in a political scientist's natural fascination with political change.

This book has also been informed by numerous informal conversations with political scientists, politicians, public servants past and present, and seminars and talks given by political participants. Where possible I attribute my material, but in order to preserve confidentiality this has not always been possible. My knowledge of how cabinet works and interacts with the public service has been enlightened by practical experience. Between 1974 and 1976, and again between 1989 and 1991, I served as one of the outside, part-time directors of the Housing Corporation, and I have utilized my experiences and observations where appropriate.

Finally, I have been enormously indebted to the recent books and articles published on the New Zealand political system. There has been an incomparably better choice of material available for this work in the 1990s than there was in the 1970s, in terms of both primary sources and secondary analysis. Newspapers, too, are better informed. This is partly because of the Official Information Act 1982 but also, perhaps, because New Zealand has caught up with the rest of the world in terms of the 'leak'; information now emerges with much greater regularity from caucus meetings, public servants, and even cabinet itself—for which political scientists, if not governments, can be thankful.

Despite the attention given to the wider context of cabinet government and political power in New Zealand—the constitutional context, the political parties, the public service, the representativeness of cabinet, and the policy communities—the central focus is upon the institution of cabinet itself. The New Zealand cabinet is powerful. The only formal constraint upon its power has been the triennial general election. A political executive untroubled by challenges to its hegemony by an interfering and retarding upper house, by federal components to the political system with their own sources of power and authority, by judicial review of its decisions, or (until the new system of proportional representation is instituted) by troublesome, multi-party parliaments, deserves its own analysis.

2

WESTMINSTER AND WELLINGTON: CABINET AND THE CONSTITUTION

New Zealand and the Westminster System of Government

Arend Lijphart once wrote that 'New Zealand has a special status among the world's democracies as the purest example of the Westminster model of government'.[1] Lijphart defined the Westminster model in terms of two clusters of characteristics. First there is: (i) the simple plurality electoral system, (ii) a two-party system in which the parties are divided primarily on socio-economic issues, and (iii) a cabinet composed of a single majority party which dominates the legislature. The second cluster of structural character-istics comprises: (i) a unitary and centralized government, (ii) either a unicameral legislature or a bicameral legislature with a very weak upper house, and (iii) an unwritten constitution. New Zealand demonstrates all these features in their most extreme form.[2]

Lijphart has since further refined his analysis, arguing that the majoritarian model—where pre-proportional representation New Zealand has been situated—is not necessarily the best possible type of democracy, and that the consensus (multi-party, federal, coalition-governed) variety is the most suitable type of government for a divided society.[3] Lijphart has correctly argued that a shift to a proportional system of representation in New Zealand will make minority or coalition governments likely, will change the nature of the party system so that socio-economic issues are not the primary division between the parties, and may well decrease the power of cabinet over Parliament. One cannot quarrel with these predictions. Indeed, the Royal Commission on the Electoral System recommended proportionality precisely because it would produce those outcomes.[4] The 'purity' of New Zealand's Westminster version of majoritarian democracy is one of the reasons why the Royal Commission was appointed by the fourth Labour Government, why there has been a stream of criticisms from commentators, lawyers, and political scientists about the political system, and why the perceived failings of the system were sufficient to persuade voters to choose change when offered the opportunity to vote on the issue. In 1993 New Zealanders voted in a referendum to adopt the 'Mixed Member Proportional' electoral system (MMP).[5] The country was split between preferring to retain the 'First-Past-the-Post' (FPP) system, with two parties dominating Parliament and the ability to deliver (generally) single-party majoritarian governments, and preferring to shift to a proportional system of government which would radically alter both those conditions. The verdict was for MMP: governments had been widely perceived to be unfettered, uncontrolled, and unrepresentative, thus discrediting the majoritarian model.

Even after MMP is instituted, New Zealand will continue to have 'responsible government'. Lijphart's categorization of the Westminster system is founded upon key structural features. Many writers, however, seize upon the most significant part of the process of Westminster government by highlighting the consequence of drawing ministers from Parliament and having to retain support from that body. Commentators have focused upon the feature that ministers, themselves responsible for advising the Queen or her representative, are responsible to the legislature for their actions. As a New Zealand constitutional lawyer has put it: 'In theory, the House of Representatives controls the political executive. Under responsible government, Cabinet is collectively accountable to Parliament and constitutional convention commands the government's resignation should it lose its working majority. However, no modern government has been defeated on a confidence motion.'[6]

Ministers are singly as well as jointly responsible for their actions. In fact (because of the development of cohesive parliamentary parties), ministers in New Zealand scarcely ever resign for their own actions and never resign for the actions of their public servants (see Chapter Nine). This means that here, as in Australia, 'responsibility' has come to mean simply that 'ministers, the political leaders of the government, though legally appointed by the head of state, *hold office* by virtue of the parliamentary majority, as tested by significant votes in the legislature'.[7]

Thus the advent of cohesive parliamentary parties, together with a two-party system which has allowed the formation of single-party majority governments (albeit with occasionally very slender majorities), made those governments secure from votes of no-confidence in the House. Rather, governments have been 'responsible' to the electors because citizens have voted for and against parties rather than for individual candidates.[8] So we have two interpretations of 'responsible' government, one emphasizing the domination of Parliament over the executive, and the other stressing the control of the voters over the executive. And this shift to plebiscitary control[9] entails the domination not of Parliament over cabinet but vice versa. The classic doctrine of responsible government has also been muddied by the very close relationship between New Zealand cabinets and the other members of their parliamentary parties; caucus is often deeply involved in the policy process. It is an irony of the recent reforms of the electoral system that, while the adoption of proportional representation seeks to shift the New Zealand polity back to working as a 'responsible government' by increasing the power of MPs over the political executive, the Citizens Initiated Referenda Act 1993 better fits the plebiscitary model.

This whole notion of 'responsible government' is, however, conceptually and practically problematical, as can be seen from this very brief treatment, not least because the same word is used for different aspects of the system of accountability that 'responsible government' has come to signify. As G. A. Wood has succinctly put it, 'To confuse students of New Zealand politics there are (a) "responsible government", which means the Queen or Governor-General acts on the advice of "responsible advisers", (b) "Cabinet responsibility" which means Cabinet speaks with one voice, and (c) "ministerial responsibility" which means a minister is in charge of his or her department.'[10]

When the single-party majority government characteristic of New Zealand's version of responsible government changes with the introduction of proportional representation, New Zealand's political system may well shift towards a more consensual one based upon notions of shared executive responsibility. Another characteristic of the Westminster system of cabinet, the idea and institutionalization of 'The Opposition', the government-in-waiting, may also disappear. With a multi-party Parliament there will almost certainly be more than one opposition party—although, of course, it is quite possible that all parties except one might form a government, thus leaving one party in opposition. More importantly, parties will either have to form coalitions in order to command a majority in the House or else will have to develop ways of governing as minority governments. New Zealand will no longer be the very model of Westminster Government. But it is important to realize that there will still be cabinet government; that part of the system will continue, not unaltered but essentially run on similar principles to those of the past.

Cabinet Government

The one continuous feature of the New Zealand polity will be, therefore, that it is characterized by having cabinet government. Unfortunately we again run into definitional problems. As Patrick Weller has observed, there is no general consensus on what cabinet government is. Agreeing with Patrick

Dunleavy and Rod Rhodes that most descriptions of cabinet have prescriptive aspects to them, Weller argues that the structural characteristics of cabinet government should be kept analytically separate from the normative aspects.[11] He does say that there are certain descriptive characteristics that cabinet governments possess in common with one another. Cabinet government

> is a group of ministers, including the elected heads of the main departments of state, who meet regularly, in part or in whole, to act as the highest authority for the making of decisions; it is a forum where political and administrative interests intersect. The ministers will be members of one of the Houses of Parliament, and are held collectively responsible for all cabinet decisions.[12]

Weller goes on to argue that it is difficult to go beyond this. Procedures vary through time and between countries; cabinets are never constitutionally recognized and defined; and we cannot even define the outer limits of 'cabinet government' because of the various systems of cabinet committees and support agencies that exist in different political systems.

Citing in particular Peter Hennessy's critique of Margaret Thatcher's cabinet, Weller derives from the literature three normative statements about cabinet government:

> First, there should be 'collective deliberation by the cabinet' for which ministers are then held collectively responsible. Second, there should be due process, rather than a system of ad hoc meetings and *faits accomplis*. Third, the emphasis should be on the *collective* nature of decision-making in formal structures and with established agenda, rather than merely working with those most closely involved, that is, a need for proper consultation with ministers.[13]

These principles were derived from the debate that has dominated British cabinet studies: the question of whether or not cabinet government has become prime ministerial government. This dispute has been detrimental to proper understanding of cabinet government. And Weller argues that, when tested against the data, these normative propositions are then demonstrated to constitute more the product of nostalgia than anything else. Cabinet government cannot be neatly described. Rather it is better to understand it as a 'pattern of meetings and opportunities than as a distinct set of procedures which, if followed, will constitute some proper balance of powers (however defined)'. And researchers need to look at how prime ministers have changed their participation in the various arenas in order to assess their influence.[14] We need to look at the Prime Minister in cabinet, in the context of the decision-making process, to see how well systems actually work.

New Zealand political analysis has on the whole avoided the undue concentration upon prime ministerial versus cabinet power characteristic of the British studies, perhaps less because our political scientists have been peculiarly liberated from received British doctrine and debates than because they have neglected to analyse cabinet in any great detail.[15] As well, political commentators, constitutional lawyers, and political scientists have all stressed the collective nature of cabinet government. This feature can certainly be over-emphasized if one is examining how cabinets actually operate, given the personal authority of particular Prime Ministers, the roles and responsibilities of cabinet committees, and the extent of unilateral decision-making by individual ministers.

Yet Weller rushes too rapidly to dismiss the significance of collective decision-making as a persistent and persuasive ideal, and the connection between this ideal as a process and the constitutional convention of collective cabinet loyalty—a fairly persistent theme in studies of the Westminster model and, indeed, in this study of the New Zealand cabinet. Whether or not cabinet *per se* actually makes the decisions in joint committee, it is its task (here and elsewhere) to stamp its approval upon major decisions and, simultaneously, to bind cabinet members together to support these decisions in public. Party loyalty, shored up by the shared political incentives of gaining and keeping power, also supports the collective imperative. Walter Bagehot, writing before party dominated the cabinet and the House of Commons, opined that 'The English Constitution, in a word, is framed on the principle of choosing a single sovereign authority, and making it good; the American, upon the principle of having many sovereign authorities, and hoping that their multitude may atone for their inferiority.'[16] Leaving aside Bagehot's anti-Americanism, his emphasis on the 'single sovereign authority' is as relevant today as it was when he wrote.

What Bagehot did not discern about cabinet government, however, is that, at the same time as it forms this unitary function, it is pulled in the other direction by its representative and pluralistic character. This is an essentially conflictual model. Cabinet government is not only consensual and unitary; it is also competitive in nature and pluralistic in composition and direction, as some of my interview data on the contemporary New Zealand cabinet will show. (These tensions are more persistent and powerful than is the tension between the prime minister and the cabinet.) The fact that unity as an issue, and the effect of prime ministerial power upon that unity, have been recognized, whilst competitiveness, representativeness, and pluralism have not, testifies to the persuasive force of the convention of cabinet collective loyalty in the Westminster system of government.[17] It is also an indication of the character of the political histories of Westminster-type systems. Because simple plurality, single-member constituency electoral systems exaggerate the seats gained in Parliament by the two major parties at the expense of the minor parties, single-party majority government has become the norm. If coalitions had been more usual, although collective cabinet loyalty would still have been a guiding principle (because of the political necessity of cabinets commanding the legislature), there might have been more recognition of the elements that divide cabinets and set ministers in competition with one another. (An exception is the Australian federal Government's coalition between the Country (later National) Party and its larger partner, the Liberal Party. But this relationship is more like that of a long-married couple than a series of temporary arrangements of desire and convenience.)

The 'purity' of the New Zealand version of the Westminster system of cabinet government is essentially due to its simplicity. Because New Zealand is a centralized state with a unicameral legislature, and because single-party government and not multi-party coalitions have existed since the Coalition Government went out of power in 1935, the structure of cabinet is also, on the face of things, simple. Local government is weak, the upper house (the Legislative Council) was abolished in 1951, and the two major political parties, Labour and National, have alternated in government between 1935 and 1993. Whereas in Britain some ministers are appointed from the House of Lords in order to have the Lords represented in government and to achieve a wider choice, and some ministers are chosen from the Australian Senate for the same reasons, in post-1951 New Zealand ministers have come only from the one place. Nor does federalism place its representative demands upon cabinet composition, although there has been some recognition that ministers should come from a spread of geographical areas.

This simplicity is however only surface-deep. For many years now cabinet has operated a complex system of committees. And the relationship between ministers and the parliamentary party from which the ministers are drawn can also be complex. Moreover, nearly all New Zealand ministers hold several portfolios, usually comprising one (or even more than one if the minister is senior) important portfolio and one or more less important ones. Important offices are labelled 'Minister of' the area or department concerned, whilst less important offices are entitled 'in charge of' or 'for' the area or department. Ministers without portfolio have been called 'Member of the Executive Council', or 'Minister of State', as was Sir Keith Holyoake, for example, in John Marshall's 1972 cabinet and in Robert Muldoon's 1975 cabinet. Other offices which are not department-based or area-based are, of course, the positions of Prime Minister and Deputy Prime Minister, although there is now a Department of the Prime Minister and Cabinet. Also there have been 'assistant' and 'associate' ministers whose tasks will be discussed later. Some ministers have held their portfolios outside cabinet, but until recently the two-tier ministry was not the norm. As can be seen, New Zealand's version of cabinet government has its own distinctive and complicated features.

The New Zealand Cabinet and the Constitution

Documents and Conventions
One of the most striking characteristics of New Zealand's inherited, Westminster-style political system is that cabinet, the single most important committee of government, appears nowhere in the written parts of the constitution. In this, at any rate, New Zealand faithfully follows the British model.

The New Zealand constitution is a scattered, haphazard series of statutes and conventions. Apart from the Treaty of Waitangi of 1840, the founding document of New Zealand, the major constitutional documents are the Electoral Act 1993 (formerly 1956), the Letters Patent Constituting the Office of Governor-General in New Zealand 1983 (part of the common law), and the Constitution Act 1986. These together establish that New Zealand is governed by Parliament which consists of the Sovereign and the House of Representatives, determine how the members of the House of Representatives are elected and for how long, and stipulate that the members of the Executive Council (the advisers to the Queen's representative, the Governor-General) must be Members of Parliament. The acts themselves are ordinary statutes: the only constitutional features protected by entrenchment are the reserved provisions: the three-year limit to the term of Parliament (New Zealand does not have a fixed parliamentary term), the voting age (18), the methods of determining the boundaries and number of electorates, and the method of voting. Section 268 of the Electoral Act 1993 follows the 1956 statute and states that these provisions cannot be altered unless 75 per cent of the MPs agree or, alternatively, a majority of the valid votes cast at a referendum on the issue favours a change. The entrenching clauses themselves are not entrenched; they could be changed by simple majority vote in the House. This has not so far happened, and it seems that it has become a convention of the New Zealand constitution that the protected clauses should be respected in accordance with the intent of the original legislation. It should be noted that the title 'The Constitution Act 1986' is somewhat misleading, for it is a short document that clarified some aspects of New Zealand's constitution and incorporated a few key provisions of earlier statutes, most notably the (UK) New Zealand Constitution Act 1852. It is only of limited help in the pursuit of 'the New Zealand constitution'.

The rest of the constitution is found in the conventions of New Zealand government—the unwritten rules that through time became the traditional and legitimate way to conduct political affairs. 'Conventions, not being laws, are unenforceable in the courts. They are obeyed for a variety of reasons: sheer inertia, habit, the desire to conform, or the belief that it is right and proper to obey them, or because politicians wish the machinery of government to go on.'[18]

The most important conventions are, first, that the Governor-General assents to the bills placed before him or her, heeding the advice of the Prime Minister. Joseph argues that this convention is more important than the Governor-General's power to withhold consent but notes that the Constitution Act did not abolish this latter power. Section 16 states, 'A Bill passed by the House of Representatives shall become law when the Sovereign or the Governor-General assents to it and signs it in token of such assent.'[19] Second, there is the doctrine of collective cabinet responsibility whereby the advice given the Governor-General by her ministers must be unanimous. This doctrine is shored up by political necessity, that is, the need for governments to retain a majority of the votes in Parliament in order for their legislation to be passed. Third, individual ministers are responsible to Parliament for their own actions and those of their public servants.[20] Fourth, a government resigns when defeated at a general election. Fifth, 'The Governor-General must appoint as Prime Minister the member of the House most likely to command a majority of its members.'[21] And sixth, the Governor-General accepts the Prime Minister's nominations of the members of the ministry. Some conventions have been clarified in bodies of rules established by the governing institutions, namely Parliament's *Standing Orders* and the *Cabinet Office Manual*.[22]

It is noticeable that political parties—the private organizations which contest power at elections, control governmental power through dominating Parliament, and provide a measure of policy coherence and stability—are at best shadow players in New Zealand's constitution. The conventions assume their existence and the statutes generally ignore them. The Electoral Act 1956, however, set out some rules concerning parties' behaviour at election time. Its successor, the Electoral Act 1993, goes further with its requirement that parties must be registered in order to be eligible to put forward party lists (Sections 62–70). Parties are also now required to use democratic means of selecting their candidates (Section 71). The Electoral Act 1993 established an independent Electoral Commission which, among other tasks, will be registering the parties. Most proportional methods of representation assume that modern politics is about parties competing for power, so it is hardly surprising that these organizations appear more prominently in the contemporary legislation than they ever did before.

Other significant, 'quasi-constitutional' statutes are, first, a cluster concerned with individual and group rights: the Treaty of Waitangi Act 1975, the Ombudsmen Act 1975, the Official Information Act 1982, the Maori Language Act 1987, the New Zealand Bill of Rights Act 1990, the Privacy Act 1993, the Human Rights Act 1993 (consolidating previous race relations and human rights legislation and expanding the anti-discrimination legislation), and the Citizens Initiated Referenda Act 1993.[23] Of these statutes the Ombudsmen and Official Information Acts have had the most impact upon cabinet government in New Zealand. These acts together have made the policy process very much more democratically open than in the past.[24] They are ordinary statutes and are thus subordinate to the sovereignty of Parliament. Even the last-mentioned piece of legislation does not substantially challenge the sovereignty thesis, since the verdicts of the referendums are advisory rather than mandatory upon governments.[25]

It is worth noting at this point that the human rights legislation was enacted during a period when there were moves world-wide to attempt to protect individual and group rights through national and international codification. New Zealand is a signatory to a whole range of international conventions— on individual rights, women's rights, and labour law, for example.[26] To this extent New Zealand cabinets have increasingly been bound by their international obligations.

Second, there is a group of legislative measures enacted during the term of the fourth Labour Government that set out the basic structure and processes of the public sector: the State-Owned Enterprises Act 1986, the State Sector Act 1988, and the Public Finance Act 1989. Because these statutes codified a number of key political arrangements in the course of altering the nature of the public sector, they must be regarded as part of the constitution. In so far as cabinet is concerned, the legislation defined the responsibilities of ministers and chief executives respectively, making the former responsible for defining 'outcomes' (policy goals) and the latter responsible for governmental 'outputs' (policy implementation). Chief executives are appointed to limited-term contracts and have written performance agreements with their ministers about agreed departmental outputs. Also the whole nature of financial reporting and accounting has been modified. Trading organizations were corporatized, in the process freeing them from day-to-day ministerial control. The net impact of the changes was to destroy the old concept, inherited from Westminster, of the 'unified' political service with its security of tenure for all employees and its relatively closed system of appointments and promotions.

A fourth piece of legislation, the controversial Reserve Bank Act 1989, also ought to be mentioned at this point because of its implications for monetary policy in particular and the limitations upon the policy flexibility of cabinets in general. The Reserve Bank is New Zealand's central bank whose primary function is 'to formulate and implement monetary policy directed to the economic objective of achieving and maintaining stability in the general level of prices' (Section 8). As well as clarifying and making more transparent the accountability relationships between government and Bank, the Act requires the Governor of the Reserve Bank and the Minister of Finance to fix economic targets, particularly relating to an agreed maximum rate of inflation. The policy targets must be tabled in Parliament. The Bank also carries out other functions, such as ensuring that there are adequate prudential guide-lines for banks and seeing that these are respected. However, the most important aspects of the legislation, as the Bank itself has stated, is that 'monetary policy is explicitly recognized as the primary function of the Reserve Bank' and that 'monetary policy must be targeted at the objective of maintaining a stable price level', as well as the mechanisms enshrined in the legislation for implementing and monitoring these goals.[27] Significantly, the 1989 legislation refers only to the price stability objective: 'All references to the social welfare of New Zealand, and to production, trade and employment, have been removed from the statutory objectives.'[28] Thus, as it stands, the Reserve Bank Act 1989 restricts the economic flexibility of government, but of course, like the public sector legislation, it could be simply changed by a future government.[29]

Rather than working through each of the statutes, conventions, and rules that affect cabinet government in New Zealand, I shall now discuss the relevant constitutional framework under the following headings: the appointment and definition of cabinet and the prime minister; sources of power and limitations on authority; cabinet size and composition; dissolution, tenure, and government succession; and Parliament, caucus, and cabinet.

The Appointment and Definition of Cabinet and Prime Minister
The 'Letters Patent Constituting the Office of Governor-General of New Zealand (1983)'[30] declares the Governor-General to be the Queen's representative in New Zealand. The document goes on to say:

> VII. And We do by these presents constitute an Executive Council to advise Us and our Governor-General in the Government of Our Realm of New Zealand.

> VIII. The Executive Council shall consist of those persons who, having been appointed to the Executive Council from among members of Parliament in New Zealand, are, for the time being, Our responsible advisers.

The Governor-General is authorized to appoint, among other officers such as overseas representatives, 'all such Members of the Executive Council' and 'Ministers of the Crown'. And,

> XVI. Our Ministers of the Crown in New Zealand shall keep Our Governor-General fully informed concerning the general conduct of the Government of Our said Realm, so far as they are responsible therefor, and shall furnish Our Governor-General with such information as he may request with respect to any particular matter relating to the Government of Our said Realm.

So, the Governor-General is advised by an Executive Council and by her ministers, who must also be MPs. This feature of New Zealand's political arrangements is spelt out further in the Constitution Act 1986, Section 6. The requirement that ministers must also be MPs had earlier in New Zealand history been convention rather than statute. Before it was included in the 1986 statute, the necessity for ministers to be drawn from Parliament had been 'first codified under s. 6(1) of the Civil List Act 1950 and re-enacted as s. 9(1) of the Civil List Act 1979'[31] providing for salaries to be paid to ministers.

Thus the formal parts of the Constitution provide for an Executive Council and Ministers of the Crown, but not for 'cabinet'. As K. J. Scott explained, the Executive Council has existed since 1841 and the cabinet since 1856 when responsible government was introduced. The Executive councillors, newly appointed in 1856, 'immediately adopted the British convention of meeting privately, without the Governor, as Cabinet'.[32] These two bodies, cabinet and Executive Council, have had identical or nearly identical memberships but have different constitutional functions. 'The function of Cabinet is to decide policy, the function of the Executive Council to tender advice to the Governor-General when the law requires advice to be tendered in this way, for instance when advice is tendered that an Order-in-Council be issued.'[33]

As indicated in the Letters Patent, appointment to the Executive Council is by the Governor-General. In fact, and by constitutional convention, the Governor-General acts on the advice of the Prime Minister and follows his or her advice on the composition of the Executive Council which, in turn, depends upon the composition of the cabinet. Because cabinet itself is not a legally created body, there is no formal procedure for appointing to cabinet, and this task is managed by the parliamentary parties. The practice has been for the National Party Prime Minister to appoint the cabinet and for the parliamentary Labour Party to elect it. These differing practices 'are important parts of our constitutional arrangements'.[34]

Although the Prime Minister is the Governor-General's chief adviser, this position is mentioned in neither the Letters Patent nor the Constitution Act.

Prime Minister and cabinet are creatures of convention in so far as their existences are concerned. 'Convention dictates that the leader of the party with the support of the House is chosen as Prime Minister, although the Governor-General is not bound to follow anyone's advice in this matter.'[35] The Governor-General therefore has some flexibility in a situation where a Prime Minister dies or is ill, or where there is an uncertain situation after a cabinet loses a vote of confidence after an election, or if an election result does not deliver an obvious winner or winners. In fact, however, the practice has been for the political parties to make all these decisions.

Writing three decades ago, Scott was able to say that 'Appointment to the Executive Council is an indirect indication of appointment to Cabinet.'[36] The situation never was as clear as suggested by Scott; and since 1987 the memberships of the two bodies have certainly not been identical. Although the membership of the Executive Council has always been obvious, simply because of the stipulated appointment processes, the membership of cabinet has not always been as apparent. Until 1987 members of the Executive Council who were Ministers of the Crown with portfolio responsibilities were always also members of cabinet. There were two groups of office-holders, however, whose precise status was indistinct, although the first group causes less definitional difficulty than does the second.

The first group comprised those called Members of the Executive Council but who did not hold portfolios. They were typically entitled Member of the Executive Council without portfolio or, in the case of Maori members, Member of the Executive Council without portfolio representing the Maori Race. Until the Legislative Council was abolished, there were also members of the Executive Council representing the upper house. Three members of the Legislative Council were appointed to the Executive Council in the first Labour Government and one in the first National Government. None of the three (initially, anyway) was a minister holding a portfolio.[37] Their primary function was, of course, to represent the Legislative Council in the executive and to provide a link through the executive between the two chambers. Also in this first group were those whose main function was to represent Maori interests in the executive. Two members of the Executive Council were in this position between 1935 and 1975.[38] Hilda Ross had analogous status as a member of the House of Representatives who was a Member of the Executive Council without a portfolio during part of Sidney Holland's prime ministership. Thus women, with Maori, were granted their token representation. Hilda Ross was in this position from November 1954 until September 1957 when the new Prime Minister, Keith Holyoake, gave Mrs Ross a full portfolio. Until then her function (although not her official title) was to look after the interests of women and children. Since then there have been other ministers without portfolio entitled Ministers of State: Keith Holyoake, former Prime Minister, 1975–77; and Jonathan Hunt, also Leader of the House, 1987–88. (I have excluded examples of Ministers of State who also held specific portfolios.) Despite their lack of portfolios all the Members of the Executive Council listed above appear to have been regarded as members of cabinet and to have attended cabinet meetings.

Unlike those ministers just discussed, categorization of the second group is more difficult because a formal announcement was made concerning their status and then not followed in practice. Three appointments to the Executive Council were made by the National Prime Minister, Sidney Holland, of members who held no portfolios. Holland said that they were to be outside cabinet and were to attend cabinet meetings only when their own responsibilities were discussed.[39] It seems that these members did in fact usually attend cabinet meetings although Holland did not announce their transition to full cabinet membership.[40] The tradition of appointing some members without full ministerial portfolios has been continued until the present, but generally the title 'Member of the Executive Council without portfolio' has been dropped in favour of the less equivocal term 'Minister without portfolio'.

Assistant and associate ministers used always to be in cabinet. Since the 1987 Lange government, however, there have been ministers with either full or associate portfolio status appointed to the Executive Council, some of whom have been outside cabinet itself. The two bodies, cabinet and Executive Council, are certainly not now identical. This has relevance for the legality of the actions of associate ministers. In 1990 the Cabinet Office sought the opinion of the Solicitor-General on whether associate ministers could exercise the powers of their principals (usually necessitated by absence overseas or illness). The legal opinion was that Section 7 of the Constitution Act 1986 allowed associate ministers to exercise the powers of their principal ministers provided that the associates were members of the Executive Council: 'Any function, duty or power exercisable by or conferred on any Minister of the Crown (by whatever designation that Minister is known) may, unless the context otherwise requires, be exercised or performed by any member of the Executive Council.'[41] Any ministers (not only ministers in the same portfolio areas) who are members of the Council may act for a period of time for any other ministers. No additional legislative authority is necessary. This of course allows prime ministers a great deal of flexibility, although it would be constitutionally undesirable were these sorts of arrangements to be more than temporary measures.

To summarize, the relationship between cabinet and the Council seems to have moved through three stages. First, the memberships were somewhat indistinct. The abolition of the Legislative Council, the shift by Labour governments towards putting at least one Maori into cabinet with a full portfolio, and, perhaps, the lack of success of Holland's attempt to appoint ministers outside cabinet, all contributed to a decline in attempting to distinguish between two classes of minister. Consequently there was a second period in which cabinet and Executive Council were identical. The one exception between 1957 (when Hilda Ross assumed the responsibility of a full portfolio) and 1987 was the appointment in the Rowling Ministry (1974– 75) of Hugh Watt whose full title was 'Member of the Executive Council, Minister Without Portfolio, Resident in London', reflecting his absence from cabinet meetings whilst preserving his cabinet status. The third phase that began in 1987 has seen the regular use of ministers in the Executive Council but outside cabinet itself. This is a marked shift in the structure of New Zealand cabinets, indicating clearly that prime ministers wish to distinguish between levels of calibre and experience within their ministries. This phase also shows the extent of flexibility possessed by New Zealand prime ministers when shaping their cabinets, organizing ministerial hierarchies, and expanding their executives.

For Labour ministries, there is a further complication with levels of ministers because 'cabinet' is composed of those members of the parliamentary party who have been elected to cabinet post by their caucus colleagues; the positions outside cabinet are appointed by the Prime Minister. In Labour, therefore, inner and outer ministers owe their appointments to two different sources of authority: the collective vote of caucus on the one hand, and the personal patronage of the Prime Minister on the other.

Under-secretaries, although appointed by the Governor-General, are not Members of the Executive Council and do not attend cabinet meetings unless requested to do so by the Prime Minister (to contribute to a matter that directly concerns their aspect of administrative responsibility). Like full ministers, the appointment of under-secretaries is authorized by statute in the Constitution Act 1986, Section 8.

What then, is a 'ministry'? All ministers, in or out of cabinet, with or without portfolios, have been included in the ministry lists of the *New Zealand Parliamentary Record*. Scott was unclear as to the precise meaning of 'ministry'. He wrote,

> It might seem appropriate that the term 'the ministry' should be used as a collective term for only such members of Cabinet and the Executive Council as are also ministers of the Crown, but the term is always used either as a collective term for the full membership or as a synonym for either 'Cabinet' or 'the Executive Council', and never with the narrower definition.[42]

Recent developments affirm the utility of the broader interpretation of 'ministry' rather than Scott's implied preference, for the more sweeping term allows the distinction to be made between cabinet—meetings of those members of the Executive Council who are also cabinet ministers—and the full ministry, comprising all ministers whose warrants of appointment to ministerial portfolio have been signed by the Governor-General.

Sources of Power and Limitations on Authority

> In a broad sense it is the Ministry or Government of the day which governs. The members of the Ministry as a whole have the support of the House and must stand behind and take collective and individual responsibility for their decisions, the decisions that are taken in their name, and the measures which they propose. That is the position in law and in convention. The responsibility and the power to take decisions results from the electoral process and the political contest.

Sir Kenneth Keith next distinguishes between 'real power and legal form': cabinet takes decisions that are then taken in a legal sense either by the Governor-General, or the Governor-General in Council, or a particular minister.[43] Cabinet itself is an informal institution, without statutory basis or obligations. This means that the actions of cabinet are free from the supervision of the courts.[44]

It is useful to distinguish between power and authority as well as between power and legality. In the case of the New Zealand cabinet, its political power comes from its ability to control Parliament and thus secure the resources and ensure the legislation necessary to implement its policies. Cabinet can either control Parliament by dominating it through force of numbers, either with a single-party majority administration or a coalition of parties which together command a majority of legislative votes, or, in the case of a minority-party government, by obtaining the acquiescence of sufficient MPs in the House to support the Government in votes of confidence, thus enabling it to continue in office. Much of cabinet's power depends on its collective solidarity. Thus one of the conventions of our system of cabinet government is founded upon sheer political survival.

Cabinet's authority to govern, on the other hand, derives from two sources. First, authority is indirectly and collectively acquired through the electoral process, since ministers must both be MPs and also have the confidence of the rest of the House. Second, authority is granted directly and individually because, as we have seen, ministers are appointed by the Crown who also must acquiesce in the actions of the Executive Council, 'the highest formal instrument of Government'.[45] 'Usually all Ministers are members of the

Executive Council and because Cabinet is coincidental with the Executive it derives much of its authority from that identity.'[46] Thus the bases of political power and authority in a democratic state are essentially grounded in the processes of election and appointment, one of the reasons why these important informal processes receive so much attention in this cabinet study.

'Cabinet' may not have explicit legal powers, but the 'Crown' does. Crown prerogative over certain issues is confirmed in the Constitution Act 1986: the House 'shall not pass any Bill providing for the appropriation of public money or for the imposition of any charge upon the public revenue unless the making of that appropriation or the imposition of that charge has been recommended to the House of Representatives by the Crown' (Section 21). Various parliamentary standing orders confirm executive dominance of the parliamentary processes both in terms of public expenditure and taxation and priority of government business.[47] Conversely, under Section 22, the Crown cannot levy taxes, raise loans, or spend public money without parliamentary approval.

There are opportunities granted to the Opposition in the *Standing Orders* to raise issues concerning government policy formulation and implementation. New legislation is debated as it goes through the House; the Address in Reply debate allows the Opposition to debate general policy areas; members can request time for debates on matters of urgent public importance; ministers are required to answer questions concerning their portfolios; select committee reports are sometimes debated; and a miscellany of issues can be raised in the general debates held each Wednesday. The Prime Minister also is held responsible for government decisions in question time. Thus there are some institutionalized mechanisms by which cabinets can be held collectively responsible for their actions and omissions. But constitutional and parliamentary rules alike confirm the dominance of the political executive in the policy process.

Individual ministers' powers, according to the *Cabinet Office Manual*, derive from common law powers of the Crown and from statute. Ministers have extensive executive powers which have been supervised by the Regulations Review Committee of Parliament since the reforms of the select committee system in 1985. Unusually, this committee has been chaired by a member of the Opposition. Under the doctrine of ministerial accountability, ministers are responsible to the House for their own conduct and that of their departments. Ministers must answer for their actions and defend their policies in parliamentary debate and, especially, through written and oral questions. The *Manual* states,

> Ministers are accountable to Parliament for ensuring that the departments for which they are responsible properly and efficiently carry out their functions.

On occasion, this may require a Minister to account for the actions of a department when errors are made, even when the Minister had no knowledge of or involvement in those actions. The question of subsequent action may be a matter for the State Services Commissioner (in the case of Chief Executives), or for Chief Executives if any action to be taken involves members of their staff.[48]

As has been frequently noted in works on New Zealand politics, the development of cohesive parliamentary parties has meant that it is impossible for MPs to force ministers to resign, for they are protected by their party's majority. This does not mean that they are not answerable for mistakes but it does mean that ministers individually are almost never punished for their errors. Cabinet collective loyalty prevails; and cabinet as a whole will take responsibility, hoping that voters have short memories. This whole issue, with examples, is discussed in Chapter Nine. At this stage, however, it should be noted that the 1984–90 public sector reforms reduced the scope and depth of ministerial responsibility at the same time as they endeavoured to clarify it. First, the State-Owned Enterprises Act 1986, designed to improve the efficiency of government trading organizations, removed their operations from direct ministerial responsibility. The Act now makes only a very small aspect of the activities of these organizations subject to the responsibility of the 'shareholding ministers' to Parliament. Second, the State Sector Act 1988 hastened an already expanding public knowledge about the identity of top public servants by changing the processes of and criteria for appointment. Chief executives are now appointed on fixed-term contracts by the State Services Commission, but the Commission's nomination can be rejected by the Executive Council which can then appoint an alternative candidate. Further, the chief executives are responsible for staff appointments within their ministries and departments. Third, the Public Finance Act 1989 made ministers responsible for policy 'outcomes' and chief executives for the 'outputs'.

> 'Outcomes' means the impact on, or the consequences for, the community of the outputs or activities of the Government;
> 'Outputs' means the goods or services that are produced by a department, Crown Agency, Office of Parliament, or other person or body (Public Finance Act, Section 2, Interpretation).

Part of the rationale of the conventional doctrine of ministerial responsibility was to protect the anonymity of public servants in order that they might equally loyally serve the ministers from any political party. This sentiment was well expressed in the 1979 edition of the *Cabinet Office Manual*:

> It is part of a Minister's responsibility to ensure the efficient and proper discharge of the duties of his department. Moreover, the acceptance by Ministers of responsibility for the acts of officials is a recognized principle without which it would be impossible to have a Civil Service able to serve Ministers and Governments of different political persuasions with equal zeal and honesty.

The 1979 version went on to set out in detail the doctrine of ministerial responsibility, and finished by saying that, even where there was wrong behaviour of an official and the minister had not known about that behaviour, the minister 'must remain constantly responsible to Parliament for the fact that something had gone wrong. He alone can tell Parliament what had occurred and render an account of his stewardship.'[49] We can dismiss the inherent gender bias as typical of the era and praise the similarly old-fashioned notion of what constitutes proper behaviour.

Cabinet Size and Composition
There is no constitutional limit to the size of the cabinet, although theoretic-ally it is of course restricted by the provision that only MPs may be appointed to the Executive Council. In practice cabinet size is determined by the leader of the majority party. In New Zealand as elsewhere, the precisely desirable size of cabinet is arguable and argued about. In brief, smallness is primarily said 'to facilitate the deliberative and decision-making functions of the governing body, and to improve interdepartmental cooperation'.[50] Both social interaction and administrative co-ordination favour smaller rather than larger groups. As Leslie Lipson put it, 'It is a self-evident mathematical truth that, the larger the cabinet, the greater the difficulty in maintaining internal harmony.'[51] But ideal size depends also upon the personalities of the individuals involved, on political style, and the leadership capabilities of the head of government. And, of course, a cabinet is not only a working committee but also 'an organ of leadership' which needs breadth of support and must therefore be representative of parties, groups, and opposition to the leadership.[52]

One factor in the growth of New Zealand cabinets has been the growth of the state itself. The gradual increase in the size of the New Zealand cabinet for many years paralleled the growth of the public service and the number of public agencies, departments, and corporations.[53] From the 1890s until the 1970s the New Zealand cabinet grew from about eight members to twenty. Expressed proportionately, in 1890 those in cabinet (including the premier) comprised 10.8 per cent of the members in the House of Representatives; in 1935 it was 16.3 per cent of MPs; and by 1972 it had reached 23 per cent. Jim Bolger's 1990 cabinet of twenty was 20.6 per cent of Parliament (by then containing ninety-seven seats), and the whole ministry of twenty-five was 25.8 per cent. Because of the latitude allowed New Zealand cabinet-makers in terms of cabinet size it is tempting for them to control their caucuses through exercising their patronage widely, thus assuring a majority or near-majority of the parliamentary party. This is of course easier when governments command a bare majority of parliamentary seats. In 1993 the National Government only just managed to retain power with its fifty out of ninety-nine seats. The Prime Minister appointed a cabinet of twenty (including himself), four ministers outside cabinet, and three under-secretaries. Add a couple of whips, whose task it is to ensure that the executive gets its policies through the parliamentary party and Parliament itself, and over half the caucus is bound by collective loyalty to support the decisions of cabinet. Even in Bolger's 1990 ministry—when National won the huge number of sixty-seven seats, with a cabinet of twenty, five ministers outside cabinet, and three whips—well over one-third of all National MPs were in executive, or executive-supporting, positions. (Not that this prevented all dissent for, by the time of the next general election, three National MPs had left the party.) The absence of a constitutional limit upon cabinet, therefore, plus the drive to make cabinet both representative and dominant, are factors which have contributed towards creating large ministries.

The unicameralism of the present New Zealand Parliament now simplifies the composition of cabinets, but for a large part of New Zealand's history the legislature was bicameral. The Legislative Council, composed of political appointees, was abolished by the first National Government when it amended Section 32 of the 1852 Constitution Act.[54] The Council had played a minor part in the cabinet formation process. First, for legislative co-ordination, it was necessary for the Council to be represented in cabinet and for at least one government representative in the Council to hold a full portfolio. This was important 'not only because it implied a more detailed contact with certain government departments, but also because it usually involved a more continuous participation in the process of policy-making'.[55] The second reason for Legislative Council representation in the government was that, although at times it was evidently difficult for a prime minister to find a suitable Council minister, at other times it enlarged the choice allowed the prime minister. Angus McLagan, for example, was made a member of the Legislative Council on 30 June 1942 and on the same date he became Member of the Executive Council and Minister of Industrial Manpower in the War Administration, an appointment agreed to by the Opposition because of McLagan's knowledge of industrial law and his experience in the Federation of Labour. In 1946, though, McLagan moved to the House of Representatives.

The other requirement for cabinet composition deriving from the shape of the constitution is of a rather different nature. Maori representation in cabinet has been an informal requirement for governments whenever there have been eligible Maori in the majority political party. The nature of the electoral system has provided an impetus for this to happen, although personal ability, electoral imperatives, and, now, the belief that Maori as tangata whenua deserve a greater share of political power, all work towards Maori representation in cabinet. Since 1867 Parliament has consisted of two categories of members—General ('European' until 1975) and Maori. After the 1993 general election there were 99 seats, four of them being Maori seats, a total which has been fixed—unlike the general seats which have increased according to population.[56] At the time of the two referendums on electoral reform in 1992 and 1993, there was extensive debate about the future of Maori representation and it became obvious that Maori preferred to retain their separate Maori electorates. The 1993 legislation allowed Maori to choose whether to register on the Maori or the General roll. The total number of Maori on the Maori roll would determine the number of Maori electorates. This, in turn, would also affect the total number of general electorate seats. The result was that there would be five Maori electoral districts for the next, MMP, general election.[57] In the future, a Maori party might provide ministers in a coalition cabinet.

There is a further factor about cabinet composition that will certainly be more salient in the future. First-past-the-post generally delivers single-party majority governments. Hence it is not surprising that New Zealand has not had a coalition government since the Depression. When New Zealand entered the Second World War there were demands from the press and from members of the Opposition for a coalition government. There had been a coalition during the First World War. This precedent was cited by those who favoured one in 1939. The Labour Party did not want a coalition and, as a compromise, in July 1940 a War Cabinet was formed. It consisted of the Prime Minister, Peter Fraser, the Deputy Prime Minister, Walter Nash, the Minister of Defence, Dan Sullivan, the National Party leader, Adam Hamilton, and a former leader of the Reform Party, J. G. Coates. In November 1940 Sidney Holland replaced Adam Hamilton as leader of the National Party but Holland would not enter the War Cabinet on the grounds that the National Party could more effectively oppose the Labour Government if the National leader remained outside the War Cabinet. Then, in June 1942, a War Administration was formed. There were thirteen members of the War Administration, six of them (including Holland) from the National Party. Although the War Cabinet lasted until the war ended, the War Administration survived four months only. The National Party members resigned from the War Administration because they disagreed with the way the Labour Party treated a miners' strike. However, Coates and Hamilton, perhaps accustomed to surviving coalitions, remained in the War Cabinet in a non-partisan capacity. Sid Holland, having made his point about the necessity for national unity by his participation in the War Administration, also managed to preserve his image as untainted by the austerities and controls of wartime New Zealand.

No coalition has been necessary between that time and the present, although some cabinets have had to govern on precariously tiny majorities. Between 1981 and 1984 the National Government had forty-seven seats, Labour forty-three and Social Credit two. National, having provided the Speaker and then having experienced some dissent amongst its members, at times had to rely on the Social Credit members not to ally with Labour and bring down the Government. In 1993 the immediate future was secured for the National Government (which had won fifty seats out of ninety-nine) by the publicly expressed intention of the two Alliance MPs to support whichever party won the most seats in the election, and the agreement of the newly elected Labour leader, Helen Clark, to allow Peter Tapsell to become Speaker of the House. (Tapsell was the first Opposition member and the first Maori to hold the position of Speaker of the House.) This latter example has to be seen in the context of the systemic insecurity of the post-1993 period, with a polity hovering between two sorts of electoral systems. No political party wanted a general election soon after the 1993 contest; the costs were too high, both financially and in terms of the constitutional and legitimacy difficulties of holding a general election under a set of rules rejected by New Zealand voters. The 1993 general election, which came very close to producing a hung Parliament, thus did not in the end produce either the minority-party cabinet or the majority coalition cabinet characteristic of proportional systems of representation and undoubtedly important to the patterns of cabinet government in New Zealand's future.

Dissolution, Tenure, and Government Succession
Single-party majority governments are generally stable in terms of the duration of particular regimes. Even then, however, these sorts of governments may not last their full terms; prime ministers may recommend dissolution of Parliament and the calling of an early general election.[58] In New Zealand, although governments are able to dissolve Parliament with the permission of the Governor-General and call a general election at a time suitable to the Prime Minister within the permitted maximum three-year term, the triennial time-limit discourages early dissolutions. Three years allow little enough time for governments to achieve their goals; and the disruption and risks of elections provide disincentives to going to the polls

early.[59] Only twice this century has Parliament been dissolved before reaching full term. When National first took office in 1949 it called a general election after two years. The Government was embroiled in a major industrial dispute with the watersiders. The Labour Party was internally divided over the issue, the Federation of Labour was itself disunited, the economy was in a satisfactory position, and so Sid Holland, the Prime Minister, went to the country to secure a mandate for his draconian measures against the strikers.[60]

Whereas Holland increased his parliamentary majority, the next Prime Minister to call an early dissolution lost power altogether. The National Prime Minister, Robert Muldoon, who had been in office continuously from 1975, in 1984 called a general election some months before the end of the three-year term. In June 1984 Marilyn Waring, a National back-bencher, resigned from the party because the Government had insisted that she vote against the Labour Party's 'nuclear free' bill. This left the Government with a majority of one. Muldoon consulted his caucus (or informed it, perhaps) and, against the advice of Sue Wood, then party president, immediately went to the Governor-General to request a dissolution on the grounds that he could no longer be sure of retaining a majority in the House.[61] (Marilyn Waring has another perspective, arguing that the real reason the election was called was that it was felt that 'the tide was going out so fast' that if the Government waited until November marginal seat MPs might lose seats they could otherwise retain.)[62] Despite the fact that the Government's majority had not been tested in a vote of confidence in the House (and, indeed, Waring has said publicly that she told the Prime Minister that in those circumstances she would not bring down the Government), the Governor-General assented to the dissolution; and the July 1984 election returned the Labour Party after almost twelve years in opposition.

It is clear that the prime ministers in both cases effectively exercised the right to choose to have Parliament dissolved and a general election called. The Constitution Act 1986 (Section 18) gives the Governor-General the formal right to dissolve Parliament, but convention dictates that, as with policy issues, the Governor-General acts according to the advice of the Prime Minister.[63] It can be argued that these two episodes confirmed the convention that the Governor-General assents to the Prime Minister's request for a dissolution, since in both cases the 'crises' were political rather than constitutional in nature; in neither case was it demonstrated either to the Governor-General or the country that the Government could not continue to govern.

In general, New Zealand has been remarkable for its orderly and fairly leisurely transitions of power from one government to another, the process taking up to a fortnight. In part the delay is to allow special votes to be counted and final results declared. (In Britain, where the process is similarly orderly, the pace is quite different. Defeated governments are replaced within 24 hours.) Writing in the middle 1970s, Keith Jackson argued that there are merits to the fortnight transition since the ministers of the old order have time to clear their desks, the process of cabinet-making can be undertaken without undue haste, and there is time for public servants to brief the members of the new order and for those ministers to consider their priorities before they have to take up the reins of office.

Jackson strongly criticized, on the other hand, the time that frequently lapsed between an election and calling Parliament together, for this was a practice that 'favours governments at the expense of oppositions and reduces the influence of Parliament as an institution'.[64] Indeed, ministers, without having to seek the sanction of Parliament, could make major policy decisions through the use of executive orders and, especially, by using the Economic Stabilisation Act 1949 (passed by the first Labour Government and not repealed until 1987 by the fourth), which sanctioned a wide variety of economic mechanisms.[65] Although new governments can and do still implement policy decisions without putting them to Parliament, under the Constitution Act 1986, Section 19, 'After any general election of members of the House of Representatives, Parliament shall meet not later than 6 weeks after the day fixed for the return of the writs.'[66]

The other significant change concerning government succession is that in recent years the process has become increasingly bureaucratized. First, public servants, having familiarized themselves with Opposition party manifestos, now as a matter of course prepare briefing papers for incoming ministers (whether there has been a change of government or not). Some briefing papers (or summaries of them) are released to the public.[67] Second, clear guide-lines have been developed on the access to the cabinet records of previous governments. Since the 1957 general election, there has been a convention that, whenever there has been a change of government, the Prime Minister and the Leader of the Opposition have exchanged letters concerning the use of cabinet records. Obviously it would be detrimental to administrative continuity and policy coherence were new ministers not permitted to examine the cabinet records—the submissions, minutes, memorandums and so forth. These records are held by the Cabinet Office. The 1979 *Cabinet Office Manual* nicely summarized the behavioural convention governing this process: 'The Cabinet record of one administration is available to the other provided that the confidentiality of that record is respected. Release of such information therefore depends on consultation and good manners.'[68] By convention also ministers may retain cabinet minutes and submissions but not departmental papers and files.[69] Cabinet papers are not protected under the Official Information Act 1982.

Not only must Parliament now be called within a certain time. Incoming ministers must not anticipate Parliament's confirmation of their actions; retrospective legislation is unconstitutional. This was made clear by the decision in *Fitzgerald* v *Muldoon and Others* (1976).[70] After the 1975 general election the Minister of Finance, Robert Muldoon (also Prime Minister) made a press statement announcing the abolition of the previous government's superannuation scheme, saying that the compulsory requirement for employee and employer deductions to the scheme would cease after the end of the month (December). A private citizen challenged Muldoon's actions. The legal decision went against Muldoon, on the basis of the Bill of Rights 1688: the suspension or execution of laws without the approval of Parliament was illegal. Retrospective legislation could not overturn this fundamental constitutional precept.

It has been a convention of government succession that 'the outgoing Government must not undertake any action that will embarrass the incoming Government'.[71] In 1984, Robert Muldoon (again) initially refused to agree to the new Government's decision to devalue the dollar in response to the rapidly developing drain of finance out of the country.[72] Muldoon, until he capitulated on the advice of his colleagues and public servants, was acting in contravention of this convention.

The 1984 crisis revealed a further problem: when do ministers start and finish in their posts after a general election? How quickly can a new government take office, given that ministers must be Members of Parliament? The term of ministerial appointment had been clear enough for most purposes, dating from formal appointment by the Governor-General and finishing with the acceptance by that person of a minister's resignation. But there was a obviously a grey area concerning the conditions of ministerial appointment and resignation when an election handed power from one party to another. This was related to the question of whether the House of Representatives continues in formal existence despite dissolutions.[73] The Constitution Act 1986 (Section 6(2)) tidied up the problem of the continuity and certainty of government on changes from one administration to another. The Act provided that ministers who are not Members of Parliament may be appointed as ministers and members of the Executive Council if they have been candidates for the immediately preceding general election, but they must resign after 40 days if they are not elected. This allows for a transfer of power as soon as the results are known. When ministers or members of the Executive Council lose their seats they may continue to hold their executive positions for 28 days. Thus they may continue in office until the electoral results are clear and a new government can be formed.

Like many of the country's rules the initiation and formulation of the

Constitution Act 1986 had been stimulated by an immediate political problem. The usefulness of the constitutional clarification was demonstrated after the 1993 general election when the election night results indicated that a hung Parliament might be the result and that the final results could not be declared until all the special votes had been counted. Despite a certain amount of media panic, it was quite clear that New Zealand still had a government whatever the final results, which, in the event, confirmed the National Government in power. That Government respected the convention that new and controversial decisions should not be made in what could have been an interregnum period.

Parliament, Caucus, and Cabinet
The nature of the constitutional relationship between the legislature and the political executive has already been indicated above. In short, the Constitution Act and the *Standing Orders* document the Westminster system of cabinet dominating the legislative process, a dominance confirmed by the development of government by party.[74] Two further aspects concerning the nature of New Zealand's version of cabinet government need to be discussed: the relationship between the parliamentary select committees and cabinet, and the links between cabinet and the governing parliamentary party. One further issue will not be discussed here. The 1992 changes to the *Standing Orders* reformed the previously highly unsatisfactory nature of the parliamentary scrutiny of financial measures. These changed procedures have not, however, been in operation for long enough for comment to be made on their impact upon cabinet–Parliament relationships.

In 1985 the select committee system was reformed, creating a set of functional committees 'related loosely to the main functions of government'.[75] There are also several committees relating to House business. The select committees have the power both to examine the administration, policy, and expenditure of government agencies as well as to carry out the functions of scrutinizing legislation. The second function has by far dominated the activities of the committees, partly because of their legislative workloads but also because the committees are constructed so that they have a majority of MPs from the governing party. Although much legislation is altered as a result of submissions and committee scrutiny, the principles of bills are seldom changed, especially when the legislation is contentious (the subject of partisan disagreement) and is for the government a non-negotiable issue. Executive domination is confirmed by the practice of appointing committee chairs from amongst the government back-benchers (except for Regulations Review and, in 1994, Maori Affairs). The chairpersons, again, have usually also chaired the associated caucus committees, thus ensuring still further that cabinets achieve their legislative goals. Furthermore, the advisers to the committees have been the associated government departments, not inclined to provide criticism of government policy or to support the independence of the committees from the executive arm of government.

Ministers do not sit on select committees, thus signifying some separation of powers between legislature and executive. This helps ministers with their workloads, but also ensures that they do not themselves hear the evidence produced in submissions on legislation. Ministers, however, can be summoned to committee hearings. A major step forward was that the 1985 reforms made the select committees more accessible than previously. The hearings are far more open to public submissions than they were before 1985. Moreover, the potential of the New Zealand committees to exert their powers and demonstrate their independence is certainly there. Under MMP there might well be a quite radical change, with the policy balance shifting much more to Parliament and away from cabinet, especially if minority-party governments become frequent.

The New Zealand parliamentary parties are highly organized, a characteristic of the political system. The informal aspects of caucus behaviour are discussed in the next chapter, but the development of the system of caucus committees in New Zealand has raised an interesting problem of the proper constitutional relationship between those committees, which are often deeply involved in the policy process, and the ministers and the public servants.

Where Opposition committees are concerned there is no real problem, since here there is no difficulty in distinguishing between executive and legislature. As M. C. Probine has pointed out, although it does not frequently happen, public servants might be asked to brief members of the Opposition. This should only happen with the approval of the minister of the department concerned, and within guide-lines set down by that minister.[76] Nor should there be a problem where caucus committees of the governing party are concerned. The relationship is still quite clearly that between the legislature and the executive; public servants serve ministers, not back-benchers, whatever their party affiliation; and the guide-lines for government committees are exactly the same as those for the Opposition. The use made of caucus committees by ministers, however, has tended to blur the constitutional separation of powers, not least, as Probine explains, because of the different views on this matter:

> In the eyes of some, the appearance of public servants before caucus committees smacks of involving the Public Service in party politics. Others regard it as a healthy and useful link between the work of the Public Service and members of Parliament. There is no doubt that there is advantage in

having caucus members participating in policy development and in their being well informed on all aspects of a new measure.[77]

The different views on this issue have meant that the guide-lines are certainly not always obeyed; the distinction between legislature and executive, always somewhat unclear in cabinet systems of government, is even more blurred in the New Zealand Parliament.

Conclusion

This chapter has shown that the fundamental normative principles of the Westminster version of cabinet government exist in New Zealand. But it has also demonstrated that the Wellington model has its distinctive constitutional characteristics. This is unsurprising, given the largely uncodified nature of the cabinet system of this small state; prime ministers, in particular, have a great deal of flexibility in how they construct their cabinets and, indeed, exercise power over these cabinets. But, as the rest of this book shows, certain institutional and normative constraints, products of the constitution rather than parts of it, also exercise considerable influence on the nature of cabinet government in New Zealand. Before the detailed workings of cabinet are discussed, however, cabinet needs to be placed in its wider political context. Accordingly, the next chapter seeks to explain the characteristics of the changing party system and the parliamentary parties.

THE POLITICAL PARTIES, PARLIAMENT, AND CABINET

Party Government, the Changing Party System, and Political Discontent

Since 1935 two parties have shared political power between them. The Labour Party, founded in 1916, first formed a government in 1935. Labour began as a socialist party, moderating its policies in the long years of establishing its place in voters' allegiances, but retaining its formal links with the affiliated trade union movement. The National Party was formed in 1936 out of the conservative Reform and United parties to unite the rural and urban anti-socialist forces in order to defeat Labour. National first assumed office in 1949. (See Table 3.1.)

The leaders of the Labour and National parties automatically assume the prime ministership when their parties win a general election. Unlike the parties in some other similar sorts of states, Canada, for example, or the British Labour Party, New Zealand Labour and National leaders are elected to their positions by their parliamentary colleagues rather than having to submit themselves for approval by a larger, extra-parliamentary constituency. The Parliamentary Labour Party (PLP), like the Australian Labor Party, has also retained the right to elect the cabinet ministers whilst the National Party Prime Minister has the power to choose. In both parties the portfolios are allocated by the Prime Minister.

The simple plurality, single-member constituency electoral system in New Zealand (as elsewhere) has made it extremely difficult for minor parties to gain legislative representation. But although Labour and National have dominated Parliament and government since 1935, their grip upon voting allegiances is not so secure. During the 1950s Social Credit switched from being a pressure group to becoming a party contesting general elections, gaining 11.1 per cent of the total valid votes cast in 1954. After that its support dropped, then went up to 14.5 per cent in 1966, with one seat in Parliament. Down again it went until 1978 when it recovered to get 16.1 per cent of the valid vote (one seat), and in 1981 it gained 20.7 per cent, two parliamentary

Table 3.1: Parliamentary Parties, Prime Ministers, and Leaders
of the Opposition, 1935–93

Election Year	Parties and Seats		Prime Ministers	Leaders of the Opposition
1935	Labour	53	M. Savage	A. Hamilton
	United/Reform	19	(1935–40)	(1936–40)
	Ratana	2		
	Country	2		
	Others	4		
	Total	80		
1938	Labour	53	P. Fraser	S. Holland
	National	25	(1940–9)	(1940–9)
	Others	2		
	Total	80		
1943	Labour	45		
	National	34		
	Others	1		
	Total	80		
1946	Labour	42		
	National	38		
	Total	80		
1949	National	46	S. Holland	P. Fraser
	Labour	34	(1949–57)	(1949–50)
	Total	80		
1951	National	50		W. Nash
	Labour	30		(1951–7)
	Total	80		
1954	National	45	K. Holyoake	
	Labour	35	(Sept–Oct 1957)	
	Total	80		
1957	Labour	41	W. Nash	K. Holyoake
	National	39	(1957–60)	(1957–60)
	Total	80		
1960	National	46	K. Holyoake	W. Nash
	Labour	34	(1960–72)	(1960–3)
	Total	80		
1963	National	45		A. Nordmeyer
	Labour	35		(1963–5)
	Total	80		N. Kirk
				(1965–72)
1966	National	44		
	Labour	35		
	Social Credit	1		
	Total	80		

Table 3.1: Parliamentary Parties, Prime Ministers, and Leaders
of the Opposition, 1935–93 (*continued*)

Election Year	Parties and Seats		Prime Ministers	Leaders of the Opposition
1969	National	45	J. Marshall	
	Labour	39	(Feb–Dec 1972)	
	Total	84		
1972	Labour	55	N. Kirk	J. Marshall
	National	32	(1972–4)	(1972–4)
	Total	87	W. Rowling	R. Muldoon
			(1974–5)	(1974–5)
1975	National	55	R. Muldoon	W. Rowling
	Labour	32	(1975–84)	(1975–83)
	Total	87		
1978	National	51		
	Labour	40		
	Social Credit	1		
	Total	92		
1981	National	47		D. Lange
	Labour	43		(1983–4)
	Social Credit	2		
	Total	92		
1984	Labour	56	D. Lange	R. Muldoon
	National	37	(1984–9)	(July–Nov 1984)
	Social Credit	2		J. McLay
	Total	95		(1984–6)
1987	Labour	57	G. Palmer	J. Bolger
	National	40	(1989–90)	(1986–90)
	Total	97	M. Moore	
			(Sept–Oct 1990)	
1990	National	67	J. Bolger	M. Moore
	Labour	29	(1990–)	(1990–3)
	NewLabour	1		
	Total	97		
1993	National	50		H. Clark
	Labour	45		(1993–)
	Alliance	2		
	NZFirst	2		
	Total	99		

Sources: P. Harris and S. Levine et al. (eds.), *The New Zealand Politics Source Book*, 2nd ed. (Palmerston North, Dunmore Press, 1994), pp. 120–7; and G. A. Wood (ed.), *Ministers and Members in the New Zealand Parliament*, Supplement (Dunedin, Tarwode Press, 1992), pp. 38 and 42.

seats. After that Social Credit faded, losing votes in 1984 to the short-lived New Zealand Party. Subsequently Social Credit renamed itself the Democrats and then split into two parties, the Democrats and a splinter-group, Social Credit. Other parties to challenge Labour and National were the Values Party (a precursor of the Greens), which received 5.2 per cent of the valid vote in 1975, and Mana Motuhake (a Maori rights party), led by a former Labour MP and minister, Matiu Rata. The New Zealand Party gained 12.3 per cent of the vote in 1984, gaining no seats. This party drew its main support from disillusioned National voters. In 1990 the newly formed Greens won 6.8 per cent, with no seats, and NewLabour—created by a dissident Labour MP, Jim Anderton, who kept his seat in 1990—5.2 per cent. There has also been a plethora of other, very minor political parties over the years, such as the marvellously named McGillicuddy Serious Party, as well as the Blokes Liberation Front, the Natural Law Party, the Christian Heritage Party, the Socialist Unity Party and the Communist Party, to name just a small selection.

For a variety of reasons, including an increasingly educated population, a wider awareness of citizens' rights, the advent and spread of television, and the rise of new social movements such as feminism, Maori rights groups, and the environmental and the peace movements, the 1970s saw the weakening of party identification and some erosion of the traditional bases of support of the two major political parties.[1] New Zealand is not exceptional in this. Across liberal democratic states, 'even if few major realignments have occurred, party systems are no longer as static as they appeared to be in the 1960s'.[2]

Together with the shift of disillusioned electors away from Labour and National in New Zealand, there was a marked change in attitudes towards the political system itself, a mounting degree of adverse criticism both at the élite level and amongst voters. The rules by which MPs were elected seemed especially unfair: not only did minor parties find it nearly impossible to achieve parliamentary representation but also there was either scanty or non-existent representation of women, Maori, the migrant groups from the Pacific Islands, younger people, and the less affluent communities. Furthermore, the distortions of the electoral system were such that it was possible for a party (Labour, very narrowly) to win the most votes at two elections (1978 and 1981) but to gain fewer seats than its opponent. The new Labour Government in 1984 set up a Royal Commission on the Electoral System which advocated the adoption of MMP.[3] The story of the campaign to gain MMP, and the way in which both the Labour and National leaderships found themselves boxed in to commitments to take the issue to referendum, has been told elsewhere.[4] It is rare for parties in power to alter voting systems, for electoral laws 'facilitate the survival of established parties and the continuity of party systems'.[5]

Thus the first major political characteristic that needs to be understood is the interrelationship between the changing party system and citizens' perceptions about the strengths and weaknesses of the electoral system. But it was not only the workings of that system that were seen as increasingly creaky and outmoded. From the mid-1970s New Zealanders, like voters in other liberal democratic states, became disillusioned with the performances of their governments. After some years of steady growth and affluence, the period between 1967 and 1975 saw balance of payments problems, rising inflation, and mounting unemployment, caused, in part, by wildly fluctuating export prices for wool, meat and dairy products and also the rise of oil prices in 1973–74. Additionally, New Zealand was trying to adapt to the loss of a substantial part of its overseas markets caused by Britain's entry into the European Community. Diversification of products and the search for new markets were, and are, major goals for New Zealand's heavily export-dependent economy. Governments were inevitably blamed for failing to cope with New Zealand's economic ills.

Second, the policies and actions of cabinet itself stimulated many criticisms. Discontent with New Zealand's poor economic performance coalesced with criticisms from both the left and the right of the performance and costs of New Zealand's subsidized economy and welfare system.[6] In short, the considerable degree of consensus about the main directions of public policy that had existed amongst New Zealand's political, economic and bureaucratic élite disintegrated. Many facets of the New Zealand state were being questioned by the early 1980s: the acceptance of the essential correctness of Keynesian principles for government management of the economy; the commitment to the welfare state; the belief that government's main political goal was to retain full employment; and the state's direct role in such commercial activities as telecommunications, financial lending, insurance, transport, publishing, and so forth. Meanwhile, Maori were protesting against past and present injustices and vigorously arguing for the restoration of their rights and for Maori sovereignty (or at least bi-culturalism). And women too were demanding their right to take their part as full citizens of the New Zealand state.[7]

It is one thing, however, to blame governments for the country's economic and social problems but quite another to seek systemic remedies for what was going wrong. It is extremely unusual for a stable democracy to generate a widespread demand for constitutional reform. In New Zealand's case, a major explanatory ingredient can be found in the style of governmental performances. Ruling parties added to the sin of failing to deliver prosperity by behaving in ways seen as arrogant and dishonest. First, Robert Muldoon, Prime Minister of the National Government in power between 1975 and

1984, a controversial politician who stimulated strong support and even stronger hostility, was perceived to have acted at times dictatorially, particularly in the early 1980s. There was dissent within cabinet and between cabinet and the extra-parliamentary party. The disagreements were both to do with his personal style—abusive to colleagues and critics alike—and his increasingly interventionist economic policies.

The next shock for New Zealand voters and party supporters came from Labour. When that party defeated Muldoon at the snap general election of July 1984, the new government found itself with a currency exchange and balance of payments crisis. Labour not only floated the New Zealand dollar but also very swiftly moved to liberalize the economy generally, control inflation through monetary discipline, permit the internationalization of the economy, and in general transform New Zealand from being a highly regulated economy to an equally radically liberalized one. In particular, there was a dramatic reduction of agricultural support schemes, for example, the Supplementary Minimum Prices arrangements for meat and wool, subsidies for fertilizer, irrigation, and noxious weed control, and interest rate subsidies through the Reserve Bank for the producer boards and through the Rural Bank for farm purchases.

But agriculture was not the only sector affected. There was reduced support for the protection of industry, accustomed to such mechanisms as tariff protection for manufacturing industry, export incentives, and import licensing. Moreover, price controls were almost completely abolished and the financial sector was deregulated (floating the dollar, removing exchange controls, permitting the entry of foreign banks into the industry, and doing away with the controls on interest rates). Certain supplier and occupational monopolies were attacked (for example, in transport and dentistry). Labour also deregulated the labour market to some extent. Although welfare expenditure did not actually go down, for there was a great deal of support within the cabinet and caucus for the principles of the welfare state, changes were made to the welfare system. Labour also moved towards attempting to deal with Maori grievances, allowing Maori to appeal to the Waitangi Tribunal for claims back to 1840, and changing the structures and processes of state dealings with Maori.[8] The theoretical framework for Labour's programme was provided primarily by the New Zealand Treasury, vigorously supported by key ministers, especially Roger Douglas, Minister of Finance, and a pressure group called the Business Roundtable composed of about thirty representatives from the private corporate sector.[9] The principles for reform were drawn from neo-classical economics and public choice theory.

Not only the private sector was affected by Labour's zeal for radical change; the public sector was also remodelled. Commercialization was the outstanding characteristic of the changes, 'using private enterprise as the model on which to organize economic relations'.[10] Hence the state's commercial activities were corporatized and privatized. Private sector managerial practices were also strong influences, particularly 'agency theory', a version of the public choice school of economic and bureaucratic behaviour.[11] As we saw from the last chapter, three major pieces of legislation guided the transformation of the New Zealand Public Service: the State-Owned Enterprise (SOE) Act 1986, the State Sector Act 1988, and the Public Finance Act 1989. Nor did local government escape the reforming energy of the Labour cabinet, receiving the same treatment in terms of both its structures and its processes.

The policy communities that had developed between ministers, government bureaucrats and pressure group leaders during the years of National government—in agriculture, education, manufacturing, industrial relations, and so forth—were enormously dislocated by the changes in policy direction. Labour was hostile towards pressure groups. Pressure groups were regarded as special interests, by definition acting in their own interest; governments should act, in contrast, to safeguard the public interest. Doctrine went hand-in-hand with practicalities; the new Labour Government was anxious to push forward with its reforms of state and economy unimpeded by having to negotiate with almost certainly hostile, interested groups. Government–group relationships were further affected by the removal of subsidies and other state benefits. (See Chapter Eight.) The extra-parliamentary Labour Party was also regarded as a special interest, and there was much strain between members, who had campaigned for the old party values, and the Labour cabinet, caught up in pursuing the new agenda of economic liberalization and state reform. Matters came to a head after the 1987 general election, especially over the sale of state assets, when there was open hostility between party and government.[12]

Despite the shocks delivered to New Zealand's political culture, the electors permitted Labour's experiment further time to prove its efficacy by returning the government in 1987. In 1990, however, Labour was roundly punished by the voters.[13] The promised economic revival proved elusive, unemployment continued to rise, and there was public, bitter dissent within the cabinet and between the cabinet and the extra-parliamentary party. A dispute about pursuing further the neo-liberal economic agenda resulted in the departure of Roger Douglas from the cabinet (see Chapters Four and Nine). When the Labour caucus voted Douglas back into cabinet, the Prime Minister, David Lange, resigned. Geoffrey Palmer, Lange's successor, had less than a year as Prime Minister. He resigned nine weeks before the 1990 general election, to be succeeded by Mike Moore. Labour's private opinion polls had been indicating a disastrous defeat were Palmer to remain leader. The relationship between party and government, also, had been very poor; the party had lost many members because they disagreed with the policies of their government. By 1990 the fourth Labour Government had been perceived not only as torn apart by dissent but also as dishonest, having broken its election promises. Many New Zealanders were especially dismayed by its programme of state asset sales between 1987 and 1990, after it had promised that these would remain in public ownership.

When the new National Government also broke several of its promises, especially the pre-election commitments to remove the surcharge on superannuation and abolish students' fees, public reaction was hostile. The National Government, too, had found itself with a fiscal crisis and its response was to reduce state expenditures, primarily through the reduction of welfare benefits but also through the introduction of 'user pays' in health and tertiary education. Its other controversial move was to deregulate the labour market very much more extensively than Labour had done.

In 1993 the New Zealand public voted to change the electoral system in the referendum held at the time of the general election. It also punished the two major parties by awarding the minor parties a total of 30.3 per cent of the valid vote. The Alliance—a federation of NewLabour, the Greens, Mana Motuhake, the Democrats, and the Liberals—gained 18.2 per cent (two MPs); and New Zealand First, formed during the election year by Winston Peters (the dissident former Minister of Maori Affairs in the 1990 Bolger government) won 8.4 per cent (two MPs). National scraped through to continue in government, with 35.1 per cent and 50 MPs. Labour improved its parliamentary representation, moving up from 29 to 45, but gained only 34.7 per cent of the total valid vote. After the election Helen Clark, the deputy leader, replaced Mike Moore as leader of the Labour Party.

Thus, in addition to the faults of the electoral system, viewed by many as intrinsically unfair, governments were widely seen as unsuccessful, unrestrained and untrustworthy, and hence were punished at the polls. Whatever the constitutionality of the doctrine of the electoral mandate (that is, that political parties are bound to keep the promises they make at election time in their manifestos), New Zealand electors certainly have indicated by their behaviour and attitudes that they regard the failure to honour policy commitments as breaches of faith.[14] Unrestrained single-party cabinet government was seen to be failing. The lack of constraints upon governmental power could not only be discerned in the inability of Parliament, caucus or party organization to require governments to keep their pledges. The sweeping changes briefly outlined above were also seen as indications of systemic failure. The alternating governing parties had radically reversed each other's policy decisions. In the past, policy changes had been usually muted by a high degree of bipartisan, intra-élite consensus on the fundamentals of public policy. The new pattern of adversary politics, it has been argued, dates from 1972. Since then, a 'climate of stress', the unfavourable economic climate, plus the presence within the political system of politicians who are 'policy aggressors' helped to create a period of adversarialism.[15] The policy switches on superannuation policy provide an example. A more consensual style of policy-making was needed.

The rapidity of the transformation of New Zealand's economy, the public sector, and the welfare state had been made possible by the nature of the New Zealand political system. The first-past-the-post electoral system delivered the control of Parliament to the winning party which itself was controlled by cabinet. Cabinets, supported by strong collective cabinet responsibility and the highly disciplined, cohesive party system that has been characteristic of New Zealand's Parliament, were responsible for making the changes that, in the end, rebounded against them.

Parliament, Caucus, and Cabinet

Because New Zealand cabinets are products of Parliament they are linked with that body in terms of their behavioural norms and social composition. I shall discuss this latter aspect first.

The candidates who are elected to the New Zealand Parliament exhibit the characteristics of the winners of a competitive selection system; they have demonstrated their loyalty and their political skills through their experience in the extra-parliamentary party organization, in local government, and in the interest groups that have been associated with the two parties (trade unions with Labour, employer and producer sectoral interests with National). Labour, the older party and one which established itself outside Parliament, preceded National in establishing its apprenticeship system, and its rival soon followed. For many years now, both parties have demanded that their parliamentary candidates—at least those candidates who contest seats that are safe or winnable for their party—be politically experienced.

The two-party dominance over the voting behaviour of New Zealanders together with these apprenticeship requirements have combined to create a semi-closed system of recruitment to the New Zealand parliamentary élite. The Labour and National parties are open to those who wish to become party members. But only those who have been prepared to spend the time and effort proving their suitability for selection have been likely to be given the opportunity to become Members of Parliament. Although the introduction of MMP will widen the range of parties represented in Parliament and in cabinet, ministers will continue to be the products of an apprenticeship system that creates party politicians.

The two parties have demonstrated social biases in their selection processes. Each has historically leant towards its electoral strongholds. Labour's bias in representation was once towards the blue-collar workers, trade unionists, party officials, those in small businesses, and teachers, but since the 1960s it has become increasingly less representative of working-class people and trade unionists. National's bias has been towards farmers, those in business, and some professional people.[16] The parties differently represent the rural sector, with National having a high number of farmers (or MPs with farming interests), a result of the party selection preferences in the rural National strongholds. In so far as social composition is concerned (but not gender or ethnicity) there has been quite a wide spread of occupations and backgrounds in Parliament. Nevertheless, since the 1930s, the parliamentary parties have converged, with Labour selecting fewer trade unionists and manual workers for safe or marginal electorates, and both parties selecting more professional and tertiary-educated aspirants to contest elections. The tendency for members to be better educated in recent years is partly a consequence of the democratization of education and is thus a direct product of the changing social structure of New Zealand. Partly, also, the rise in the educational attainment of MPs is the consequence of the Labour and National parties selecting more professionally and administratively trained candidates. Here the parties may be responding to the increasing complexity of New Zealand society, its growing urbanization, cultural sophistication and social heterogeneity.

The changed pattern of recruitment and selection has had a two-fold impact upon the cabinets. Ministers are now mostly tertiary educated and increasingly from the professions (law, teaching, and accountancy) and management. Cabinets are now composed of ministers who, compared with past cabinets, are skilled and educated. At the same time the modern biases of recruitment and selection have meant that cabinets decreasingly represent the less-educated and poorer members of society. This might not matter if ministers represented the interests of those at the bottom of the heap through social conscience and awareness and consultation with colleagues and groups who are in touch with the poor and struggling. This touches upon wider debates about the nature of political representation and the extent to which the various interests in society must be represented by people like or similar to them.

Whether or not social and economic interests should be actually represented in legislatures and cabinets, there is a very strong case for the fair representation of ethnic and cultural minorities and women. This is because, although making a case for 'mirror' representation on the grounds of the pursuit of group interests is always problematical, since people once in power do not necessarily remember their origins and respond to their own group allegiances, making a case for group or gender representation on the grounds of democratic fairness is much less debatable. As the Royal Commission on the Electoral System argued, women and members of minority groups should have as much access to political power and influence as everyone else.[17] Unfortunately, like other colonizing powers the New Zealand state has ill-represented the indigenous people, the Maori, and their interests. And like every other polity with equivalent sorts of social and political cultures and FPP electoral systems, the New Zealand Parliament has also poorly represented women.[18]

As was mentioned in the previous chapter, the New Zealand Parliament has had four seats reserved for Maori. They have been controlled by Labour ever since an agreement of mutual support between Labour and the Ratana (Maori) church. From the defeat in 1943 of the National MP and minister, Sir Apirana Ngata, Labour has held every Maori seat in every election until, in 1993, Tau Henare, representing the New Zealand First Party led by Winston Peters, won the seat of Northern Maori. Only four Maori have represented National in Parliament between 1935 and 1993.[19] In 1993, Sandra Lee, an Alliance candidate (Mana Motuhake) won Auckland Central. No Maori has represented Labour in a general seat. Neither Labour nor National has made a determined effort to nominate Maori for their safe, general seats. In 1993 the first MP from a Pacific Islands (Samoa) background was elected, Phillip Field, representing Labour.

It follows that National has seldom had a Maori in cabinet. Ben Couch was Minister of Maori Affairs between 1978 and 1984, and Winston Peters also held that position between 1990 and his dismissal in 1991. There was no Maori in a Labour ministry until P. K. Paikea was put in as Member of the Executive Council in 1941. The first Labour PM held the Maori Affairs position himself: the patronising tone of the times was well captured by the following: 'In choosing the portfolio of Native Affairs for himself, Mr Savage is activated by a desire personally to safeguard the interests of the Native people, whose well-being he has closely at heart. It has been made clear to him that the Native people prefer a European to administer their affairs'.[20] After that, other Pakeha ministers held the position in Labour governments, despite the presence in the PLP of the four Maori MPs, and despite also Labour's dependence upon those four votes between 1946 and 1949 for its four-seat majority. In the second Labour Government, the PM, Walter Nash, held the portfolio with Eruera Tirikatene, Minister of Forests, as his associate. Under Norman Kirk, however, Matiu Rata held Maori Affairs (with Lands), and the portfolio was held by Koro Wetere between 1984 and 1990. During those two governments two of the four Maori MPs were elected to cabinet.

There has been a marked shift in attitude in New Zealand, not so much concerning the necessity of representing Maori in cabinet, but on the question of whether or not Maori should take the portfolio of Maori Affairs. Generally the notion of direct representation of interests varies according to one's own set of interests. In New Zealand the opinion has often been voiced that the Minister of Agriculture ought to be a farmer, that the Minister of Industries and Commerce ought to have had some experience in business, but the Minister of Maori Affairs ought not to be a Maori. In part this can be explained by Sir Apirana Ngata's career as Native Minister. While this was productive and distinguished it ended sadly when he resigned from the cabinet in 1934 after it was found that Maori of his own tribal area had been more generously treated than other iwi in the granting of money. Note the following:

> An even more questionable appointment is that of Mr Tirikatene as Minister of Forests. To have a Minister of the Executive Council representing the Maori race is one thing, but to entrust him with a portfolio in which his Maori sympathies may well run counter to the national interest is most assuredly another. With all respect to Mr Tirikatene, this is a risky appointment.[21]

This attitude displayed not only a deep-rooted paternalism mixed with distrust but an interesting view of the nature and role of representation in cabinet and how it interacts with interests. Both Koro Wetere and Winston Peters, although in a generally less outspokenly racist climate, suffered constant queries about the potential conflict of interests they faced.

Although women have been enfranchised since 1893 and have been eligible to stand for Parliament since 1919, both political parties have chosen men rather than women as candidates for their safe seats. However, Labour's record on gender equity is rather better than National's, especially from the late 1970s onwards when Labour feminists made a determined push to occupy key positions in the party, and to support the selection of women candidates. In 1975 there were only two Labour and two National women elected to the New Zealand Parliament; in 1984 there were respectively ten and two; and in 1990 there were eight women elected to each of the caucuses. The 1993 general election produced a record twenty-one women out of the ninety-nine MPs: one Alliance (Mana Motuhake), six National and fourteen Labour.[22] New Zealand has the highest proportion of women MPs in a first-past-the-post electoral system; but it has some way to go before reaching the thirty-to-forty per cent of Norway, Sweden, and Denmark.[23] Electoral reformers have hoped that MMP, with its party lists, will produce a more representative legislature. Some minor parties, including the Alliance, have also promoted women candidates.

With so few women MPs it is unsurprising that New Zealand cabinets have been overwhelmingly dominated by men in terms of both numbers and political style; women have found the combative parliamentary atmosphere difficult, and have suffered the whole range of discrimination, from being ignored to being verbally criticized and abused.[24] As numbers have risen the atmosphere in caucus and Parliament has, however, improved, thus giving credence to the theory that a 'critical mass' of a political minority in an institution has an impact upon that body's behavioural norms. Ten women have made it into cabinet, three National and seven Labour, whilst one from each party has become a minister outside cabinet. The two recent governments have had the highest ratios of women to men, Labour doing better than National. The early women ministers took the traditional 'womanly', caring portfolios (Health, Women and Children, Child Welfare). Since 1984, however, there have been women ministers of Police, Finance, Employment, Disarmament and Arms Control, and Labour, as well as heading the new Ministry of Women's Affairs established by the fourth Labour Government. Indeed, the fourth National Government saw women appointed to Finance and Social Welfare, not to succour the latter but to cut its size and generosity. The larger political élite is also undemocratically male; in 1993 only five out of thirty-six chief executives were women.[25]

The demands for geographical recognition in cabinet have historically been voiced noisily. The politics of geography are recognized by the structures of the parties; the National Party has had a divisional level of party organization since its inception, and Labour followed during the 1970s with its regional councils. Earlier research found that National and Labour spread their ministers fairly evenly through the divisional regions. The difference between the parties was mainly due to the more even spread of seats held by National. But both parties demonstrated an overall balance of geographical representation.[26] Localism, party and caucus demands for their areas to be recognized, the effort made by parties to appeal electorally as widely as possible, and the general desire for governments to appear nationally based, have tended to ensure geographically balanced cabinets. The daily newspapers, locally produced and locally oriented, have supported geographical spread. For example, 'The Auckland province will feel particular satisfaction over the promotion of Messrs. Smith, Eyre and Halstead. As private members they have all laboured energetically in Auckland interests, and they will, no doubt, continue to keep the government acquainted with the needs of the fast-developing northern constituencies.'[27] More recently some self-consciousness about such barefaced parochialism has crept in, but the old desires are present: in 1990 one report of the new National cabinet pointed out that there were no ministers from Wellington and that rural dominated over urban representation.[28] Nevertheless, the 1990 ministers came from throughout the country.

Sectional representation has also been demanded of cabinets. It has been felt that urban and rural areas should be directly and fairly balanced in cabinets. Often this is more simply expressed in a demand for farmer representation, as has already been shown, or in a demand that a city be represented. In this way the sectional divisions within New Zealand project themselves into the top political leadership. Sectionalism, like geography, is important in the shaping of cabinets, but it is more subject to the nature of the electoral bases of the two parties. Like the occupational composition of Parliament and cabinets, sectionalism has reflected the party-specific factors of ideology and voting behaviour. Perhaps selection or election to cabinet for geographical reasons, along with the more important criterion of seniority, not only satisfies New Zealand's parochialism but also makes it easier for selectors to justify their choices in the small confines of the New Zealand parliamentary party.

Parliament and cabinet have also over-represented the middle-aged. In Parliament in 1991 there were 3.1 per cent under 30 (compared with 28.4 per cent of the total voting-age population), 20.6 per cent between 30 and 39 (21.3 percent), 50.5 per cent between 40 and 49 (16.9 per cent), 22.7 per cent between 50 and 59 (12.3 per cent), and 3.1 per cent who were 60 and over (21.1 percent).[29] Nevertheless, parliaments (and cabinets) are younger than they were in the early years of the two-party system.

Selected entirely from the small number of MPs of one party in a single chamber house, the composition of cabinets naturally mirrors its source. There is some distortion in this representativeness, however, towards those who come from the party strongholds, the safe seats. This distortion has been exaggerated in times of rapid and extensive electoral movement where governments succeed each other after only brief periods of office. Marginal members, who have tended to be from the towns and from the socially mixed areas of the cities, as well as being younger, perhaps female, and from more varied backgrounds, have been defeated. When the party to which they belong returns to power, the rewards of office have gone to those entrenched in safe seats. The small size of the Parliament has meant that there is little real flexibility of choice of ministers, especially given the informal requirement that they have served a minimum of three years in Parliament. Additionally, the small size of the New Zealand House has restricted the development of a defined apprenticeship system within the institution that might test aspirants to executive office, although some degree of knowledge

Table 3.2: Availability for Selection to Cabinet, 1935–1990

Winning party and election year	No. MPs in govt party	New MPs	MPs in cabinet	All office-holding MPs[1]
Labour 1935	55	28	13	18
National 1949	46	8	16	20
Labour 1957	41	7	16	20
National 1960	46	10	16	24
Labour 1972	55	16	20	28
National 1975	55	25	20	28
Labour 1984	56	17	20	30
National 1990	67	32	20	30

1. This figure includes the Speaker, Deputy-Speaker, the whips, ministers outside cabinet, and under-secretaries.

will probably have been acquired by the habit of concentration upon some policy areas—also a consequence of the small numbers available to call upon in policy formulation and in parliamentary debate. Apart from this expertise, the primary criterion for selection to cabinet is parliamentary experience in terms of the number of years spent in the institution. Seniority is the single most powerful predictor of who is chosen minister. Seniority, too, is the criterion by which ministers are ranked in cabinet. Where people know each other well and it is essential that they work together, and where those who are unsuccessful in gaining promotion are small in number and therefore conspicuous in their failure, then parliamentary seniority is the least controversial basis on which to select and reject.

The other characteristic of Parliament that has had an impact upon the nature of cabinet government has been the high degree of conformity to party policy. Strong norms of loyalty to party have regulated and defined expectations about what is desirable behaviour. Since the early 1980s, however, intra-party dissent has increased slightly as back-benchers responded to cabinets' disregard of party policy. MPs left (or were excluded from) their party caucuses in the last years of the National Government under Muldoon, under Labour, and again after National's return to power in 1990. Given the extent of strain within the governing parties, it is perhaps surprising that dissent was not more widespread than it was. Since 1993 this tendency has been exacerbated by the imminence of MMP. The last decade or so, however, confirms rather than disproves the strength of conformity as a binding norm of parliamentary behaviour. When cabinets have decided on a particular course of action, they have been hardly ever thwarted by their caucuses.

Why have parties remained so united, even through a period of radical change, when cabinets have persisted with patently unpopular agendas? First, the belief in the value of party loyalty is a feature of any political party, especially ones with established apprenticeship and recruitment systems. But in New Zealand the norm of loyalty is reinforced by the strong bonds that develop between politicians in the small parliamentary parties. Second, one feature of New Zealand politics both produces and reinforces the norms of loyalty resulting from partisan political socialization inside and outside the chamber: the habit of majoritarian decision-making within the party caucuses. Participation in caucus and caucus committees has been long established in the New Zealand parliamentary parties.[30] This kind of involvement, valuable as it is in using back-bench as well as front-bench talents, also commits the participants to the actions of the group. When in opposition, caucus prepares itself to govern again through policy development. When in government, caucus committees, as will be shown later, form close links with ministers, helping both to advise them and provide them with an extra source of policy feedback. Governing-party committee chairs, moreover, have normally also chaired the relevant parliamentary select committees. Active participation, conformity with the decisions of the majority, and the belief in the value of loyalty to the party, all become inextricably entangled with one another. Chapter Four on leadership and cabinet selection demonstrates the force of this tradition. In this way the shape of the political structure—the smallness of the House—has worked with the party variable to influence the nature of the political process.

The third explanation for the historic ties between individuals in the parliamentary parties is that it is rational political behaviour to conform simply because the small Parliament restricts the real choice of ministers. Thus the eligible and unsuccessful are relatively few in number, making 'failure' obvious, and discounting institutionalized, respected, alternative opportunities for political advancement within the institution for the ambitious (say chairing select committees).[31]

New Zealand cabinet ministers are politically trained men and women. They have had extensive political experience before they enter Parliament. They have taken part in the variety of activities that make up the work of the New Zealand MP, and they have developed some knowledge about particular policy areas. They may or may not be able to use this knowledge in a ministerial post. On the whole, ministers have not been expert in the areas they administer, and neither are they expected to be. Ministers, like MPs, are, however, expected to be loyal to party and to respect collective cabinet solidarity, to be able to communicate their views to others, and to behave in ways that are compatible with their colleagues. They have not been expected to diverge more than slightly from the views of their cabinet colleagues or, indeed, to demonstrate an individuality in any way that might be construed as implying criticism of their parties. Any such divergent behaviour has been viewed as disruptive to party goals. The next chapter relates how the cabinets have been chosen, emphasizing the party and institutional behavioural norms that have evolved as part of that process, and the relationships between leaders and MPs.

4

LEADERSHIP AND
CABINET SELECTION

Cabinet Selection in New Zealand: Introduction

The primary function of political parties is to recruit political leaders, a process that reaches back to the bases of grassroots support of parties and the selection of candidates to contest elections. In systems of cabinet government such as New Zealand's, the political executive is then drawn from amongst the victorious contestants. The process of recruitment is regulated by formal rules and informal norms about what constitutes effective party representatives and leaders. The latter are generally taken for granted; by definition norms are accepted modes of behaviour only challenged in times of leadership crisis or when groups (for example Maori, women, or unionists) are excluded from access to political power. The formal rules of political recruitment, in contrast, are regularly challenged, revised, refined, and debated, as the history of candidate selection in New Zealand has demonstrated. A superficial glance at the rules developed by the National and Labour parties for selecting cabinets in New Zealand would appear to suggest that there has been relative stability in this aspect of leadership selection. In reality the story of cabinet selection is a great deal more complex than first might appear.

The Labour and National parties provide an excellent study of contrasting methods of cabinet selection: caucus election and prime ministerial selection. On the one hand there are the two major political parties with their different formal rules of promotion. On the other hand there are the constraints provided by the political structure, particularly the cabinet which must be drawn from Parliament, unicameralism, and the small size of the legislature compared with other similar states. Thus institutional forces and organizational rules interact with one another. Especially interesting are the consequences for cabinet selection and the relationships between cabinet and caucus when the formal rules are broken or bent.

Before we examine what has happened in the two parties, it is instructive to look back, for history demonstrates that the very un-British idea of electing cabinets was not unique to the rising socialist party that provided the impetus for the creation of National.[1]

The Idea of Elective Ministries

In the early period of New Zealand's development it was

> emphatically the House which made and unmade cabinets. Such elections as were held either confirmed the existing ministry without change or led to a few substitutions in personnel. The House was supreme over the ministry, not the ministry over the House. . . After 1876 ministries still continued to be servants of the House, but slowly they are forging the weapons to dominate it.[2]

With the development of cohesive political parties, beginning with the hegemony of the Liberals in the 1890s, demands for participation by the MPs in the selection of cabinets began. There were attempts to replace the traditional, Westminster selection system with elected ministries in both New Zealand and Australia. This movement reached its peak at the turn of the century. It was not the sole prerogative of the emerging Labour parties. David Syme, especially, influenced Australian political thinking.[3] He believed that an MP was originally a delegate, that Parliament must again be made responsive to the demands of the individual constituency in order to make government representative, and, to achieve these aims, constituencies must be able to recall their MPs and ministers must be made responsible to Parliament as a whole, not to their colleagues only.[4]

In New Zealand the demands for an elective ministry went much further than in Australia. In 1891 a parliamentary committee reported in favour of change, although no action followed, but the demand in New Zealand continued to be raised.[5] In Australia, however, the demand had already begun to subside by the time the First World War began, because of the amalgamation of the non-Labour groups in 1909–10. In New Zealand the demand for elected ministries was being made a decade later in a situation where the party system was still entangled.[6] In 1920, responding to MPs who wanted an elected ministry, the Prime Minister, William Massey, said, 'There are two alternatives: either that the members of the dominant party will elect the members of the Cabinet, or, failing that—I am not sure whether I am putting it correctly—that the system of the elective Executive will be brought into operation.'[7] His reply to the demand that had evidently been made within his party was 'no'. The Prime Minister 'is "the" Minister, and the other Ministers are his assistants. I am not attempting to magnify my office when I say that. I simply state the constitutional position. Now, the theory has been this, by implication at all events: that in the case of Ministers, I had the right of appointing to the positions they occupy today.' Massey also pointedly mentioned his habit of discussing appointments with his colleagues.[8]

A Labour MP, E. J. Howard, agreed with Massey's analysis that an Executive elected by the House would in effect be elected by the dominant party, although for somewhat different reason:

> Any man who is a student of politics must know that even if you had an elective Executive in this House the members of that Executive must be elected from the other side of the House, because only today it registered forty-five votes. What say would we on this side of the House have in the election of such an Executive? It seems to me that it is merely a matter of policy with the dominant party. If we of the Labour party came into power we would elect our Executive.[9]

Elective ministries in a parliamentary system where cabinet is chosen from the majority party would indeed be or become caucus elective ministries. Howard, though, saw no constitutional problem in a cabinet being elected by the governing party caucus; Massey, on the other side, somewhat vaguely, cites constitutional practice. As the written parts of New Zealand's constitution have never stated how a cabinet is to be chosen, Massey was arguing from what was the established practice both in New Zealand and in Great Britain. No doubt his appreciation of the benefits of retaining patronage and, moreover, his realization of the need for strong leadership also contributed to his desire to retain his position as cabinet selector.

Selection and Election in the Labour Party

The habit of majoritarianism was established in the Parliamentary Labour Party (PLP) during the long years of opposition from 1916 until 1935. With this convention went a deliberate dispersion of power among the members. Harry Holland, leader from 1919 until his death in 1933, encouraged these practices and the beliefs about the rightful distribution of power in a labour movement upon which the processes were based. Holland accepted participation in policy-making by the small number of Labour MPs and did not dispute the constitutional right of the Labour Party conference to make overall policy. His attitude to being leader was, however, ambiguous. Although holding strong beliefs about making decisions democratically, he also saw the need for a leader to educate the mass of the workers and to attract electoral attention. Thus, from earliest days, leadership has posed a dilemma within the Labour movement.

As the number of Labour MPs grew during the 1920s, some disciplinary controls were needed to maintain party unity. Regulations were invented on such matters as leaving the House, following the majority opinion of the caucus (a majority decision being binding upon all), and the order of precedence in parliamentary debates (to be determined by ballot instead of being dominated by the senior members). Until 1964 there were three-yearly leadership elections, held at the start of the parliamentary session of an election year. (The 1957 *Caucus Rules*, however, made no mention of this timing.) In 1964 the *Rules* were altered so that the three-yearly elections were held 'as nearly as practicable to the beginning of December in the year prior to the General Election', giving new leaders more time to become established before a general election. The leader at the time, Arnold Nordmeyer, who favoured the change, was ousted by Norman Kirk in the following year. Ironically, Kirk's challenge was probably helped by the change. Since then this rule has not always been followed. Although Wallace Rowling resigned at the scheduled time in 1983 in recognition of the caucus criticisms of his leadership, David Lange resigned as leader (and Prime Minister) before December 1989, Geoffrey Palmer resigned after only thirteen months in favour of Mike Moore taking over just before the 1990 general election, and Helen Clark successfully challenged Mike Moore for the leadership soon after the 1993 general election. The 1990 *Caucus Rules* nevertheless continues to institutionalize the practice of triennial elections. The rules about the selection of cabinets have not been so clear.

The First Labour Government
By 1935, then, a firm tradition of following majority opinion had been established in the determination of policy, in the settling of policy disputes, and in the election of parliamentary party officers, including the leader. Elections were held by exhaustive ballot according to party constitutional practice.[10] In accordance with the established way of doing things and with the belief in the Labour Party that the cabinet must be responsive to the caucus, it was held that a Labour cabinet would be elected by the caucus. It does not appear, however, that this had become a written part of the caucus rules. Although evidently there were caucus rules in existence from the earliest days of the Labour caucus, neither the 1957 nor the 1964 versions dealt with the election or selection of cabinet ministers.

In power there were countervailing forces to established habits and beliefs. Party unity, discipline, and effective public relations all demanded a degree of assertive leadership. When the pull of an attractive, strong, and successful leader was added to these other tendencies towards leadership control, tension developed between the leadership and the expressed values about democratic control, a marked feature of socialist, social democratic, and labour parties.[11] But the story of the selection and election of the New Zealand

Labour cabinets is a particularly effective demonstration of how this tension manifested itself and its consequences.

After the initial jubilance and speech-making at the first meeting of the Labour caucus after the 1935 election,[12] Rex Mason, MP, moved that the leader, Joseph Savage, be asked to select the members of the cabinet and to report back to the caucus at an adjourned meeting. The motion was carried unanimously.[13] As had happened after the election of the first (short-lived) federal Labor Government of Australia, the leader had been given a free hand in the formation of his government. In the 1908 Australian case, though, the motion was carried that future Labor ministers would be recommended by caucus, and by 1910 the word 'recommended' had been changed to 'elected'. By 1920 the elective method was firmly established in the Federal Labor Party, and in the Labor parties of the six states.[14] In contrast, the New Zealand Labour Party seemed to have very quickly discarded the habits and traditions of the long period spent in opposition, and it took many years for caucus to reassert its control over cabinet election and, moreover, to develop clear procedures.

From reports of those present, and from contemporary press comments, caucus was appreciative of the role played by Savage in the electoral victory.[15] A retrospective view, from Rex Mason, denied that he put forward his motion at the instigation of Savage; rather, so many of the new members were 'strangers to one another. How would they make any useful contribution to the selection?' And cabinet representation of the different parts of the country was necessary but a ballot might not achieve this result. Mason emphasized, 'I want it to be clear that the caucus had no idea that the power of appointment was anything but their power and it was being exercised by their wish. Consequently there's no question about whose power it was to make an appointment on a subsequent occasion.'[16]

The elective principle had been cast aside, raising doubts about the legitimacy of the leader's new powers in the eyes of some, especially when Savage continued to insist upon selection rather than election. Individual discontents, born of a disappointment that could be justified in the minds of the disappointed in terms of principle, became expanded into group disapproval of Savage personally and meshed into policy disagreements, especially about financial management. The central ambivalence about the leadership role, always much more pronounced than in the National Party, became voiced discontent in the PLP of the 1930s. Tensions between cautious ministers and vocal, active caucus members grew, and the attempted sharing of the responsibilities (and salaries) of the ministers between ministers and back-benchers failed.[17] In mid-1936, a young MP voiced the doubts felt by many in the caucus when he moved that 'while recognising that special circumstances prevailed when the first Labour Cabinet was appointed, this Caucus realises that such conditions obtain no longer and expresses its allegiance to the Constitution of the Labour Party in that all future appointments to Cabinet shall be elected by Caucus'.[18] The PM responded that the resolution was 'out of order because it is the present system'.[19]

The remainder of Savage's prime ministership was punctuated by battles between him and some members of caucus over democratic control. At one stage, after Savage had lost a vote on cabinet election, the matter was referred to the annual conference of the Labour Party.[20] The National Executive then acted, 'and in accord with the Party's constitution proposed that a special meeting of the caucus and the Executive be held to resolve the situation'.[21] In February 1939 a combined committee of the two bodies met, chaired by the Deputy PM, Peter Fraser. A compromise suggestion was put forward by the executive:

> That the Caucus shall during the session of Parliament preceding the General Election select the Prime Minister and he shall be asked to select the members of the Cabinet, but the selection of Cabinet shall be subject to agreement by the majority of Caucus and failing such agreement the appointment of any one or more Cabinet Ministers shall be referred back to the PM until agreement is reached.[22]

This tedious procedure was accepted by caucus and was supposed to be implemented after the next election, 1941, but the election was delayed because of the war until 1943. Instead of the matter resting there, however, it came up at the 1939 Conference as part of the response to the 'Lee Letter'.[23] Savage mentioned this compromise agreement in his report to Conference. There was a motion to endorse the agreement, adding the proviso that, when there was a deadlock in the caucus, the leader, after consultation with the National Executive and Conference, 'if such consultation with Conference be practicable, shall decide the matter in dispute after giving full weight and consideration to the opinions expressed at such consultations'.[24] Two MPs unsuccessfully tried to confine the motion to the question of cabinet selections, fearing interference with caucus supremacy over policy matters even when a majority of caucus disagreed with the Prime Minister.[25] This compromise never appeared in any version of the *Caucus Rules* that I could discover. Shortly before his death, Savage resisted an attempt to enlarge cabinet, but the Prime Minister, who by this time was dying, insisted that the MPs only vote for or against his candidate (for one vacancy), and the candidate was then narrowly elected. Moreover, Savage would only accept his own choice of under-secretaries.[26]

It is difficult to know to what extent the arguments in the Labour caucus between 1935 and 1940 were disagreements about the method of cabinet selection, to what extent they were policy differences (especially over general financial policy and the details of the social security legislation), or whether these were the differences between a left and a right wing. Or were they merely the consequences of a disgruntled group who felt they had been illegitimately excluded from cabinet? At the time, policy questions— especially over the extent to which the cabinet was prepared to use social credit methods of financial management—became firmly knitted into the problem of the right way to select the cabinet.

Whatever the basic causes for the dissension, these years illustrate certain aspects of leadership. The Prime Minister's continued use of the power of patronage handed him by caucus in 1935 did provide a firm basis of support for his views from amongst those he favoured. Nevertheless, given the degree of resentment that built up he could not maintain his domination over caucus and needed the support given him by the extra-parliamentary organization. Once this support had been granted, and in the face of the adulation felt by so many of New Zealand's population towards Savage, caucus was powerless to impose its wishes upon him. Moreover, the Prime Minister's extended use of the power to appoint cabinet was a mistake: eventually it was seen as a refusal to acknowledge that what caucus had granted as a privilege, caucus could thereafter withdraw. As Savage denied the traditional function of caucus to make decisions using the vote, so he diminished his own authority as chosen leader of that caucus. Furthermore, for five years there were very few changes made to the cabinet or within it, despite the uneven quality of its membership.

Caucus discontent continued with the election of the next leader (despite the 1940 expulsion from the Labour Party of a prime dissident, John A. Lee). Peter Fraser was opposed by two other MPs who together gained nearly one-third of the votes.[27] A motion was proposed that a majority decision be binding on every member of caucus. Fraser ruled this out of order and the caucus backed his ruling.[28] Neither would Fraser allow the election to be by secret ballot. Fraser was to some extent conciliatory for, although he put forward a motion that caucus confirm in office the present ministry, he stated that in a month he would consult with caucus again and suggest additions to cabinet and/or alteration to portfolios. He thought the whole issue of cabinet personnel should be reviewed before the 1941 session of Parliament. This did not satisfy everyone and an amendment to Fraser's motion was proposed: that caucus nominate the ministers. After discussion this amendment was withdrawn and Fraser's motion passed.[29]

Despite Fraser's early affirmation of his authority, he shortly after conceded to caucus by allowing an election by secret ballot, using preferential voting, to fill the vacancy caused by Savage's death. Walter Nash was unanimously elected deputy leader.[30] Two more vacancies were created at the end of 1940 by retirements for health reasons. Fraser successfully moved the remaining ministers as a block. Because Fraser had decided there should be a Maori in cabinet, P. K. Paikea was then elected. On 29 November 1940 Fraser was unanimously elected leader for the next three years.[31] There is little doubt that Fraser's concessions to caucus greatly relieved the tension between him and the back-benchers. Fraser continued to fill vacancies and add ministers through election, although in 1942 he did bring, with the support of caucus, the president of the Federation of Labour, Angus McLagan, into the Executive Council and the War Cabinet by appointing him to the Legislative Council.[32] After the 1943 election there was the problem of whether or not there would be a complete re-election of cabinet. At the February meeting an amendment was carried that the PM nominate the sitting members of cabinet and that the members of caucus vote in favour or against each member, those with a majority of votes being the ones elected. (The motion that every MP be submitted to ballot was lost.) Unsurprisingly, the ministers were all re-elected.

After the 1946 election, Fraser nominated the ten sitting ministers and others nominated new names for ministerial posts. Tirikatene, apparently in a separate election, was elected unopposed to represent Maori. However, one minister (Rex Mason) received fewer votes than did either of two other contenders. Fraser asked that no statement be made about Mason in the meantime and then extended the total number of cabinet ministers, adding the two new members while retaining Mason. Two months later Fraser suggested in caucus that Mason be appointed to the Supreme Court but moved that, for the moment, Mason remain a minister and that the matter be reviewed prior to the session. Obviously Fraser wished to avoid any appearance of party disunity after the narrow 1946 election victory by four seats. In May 1947, when a vacancy occurred, caucus re-elected Mason to cabinet and elected a new minister, Mabel Howard, the first woman minister.[33] The last of Fraser's ministers to be appointed went into cabinet in October 1947 when ten contenders stood to fill a further vacancy.

Painfully, and at the expense of party cohesion, the basic issue of cabinet election had in practice been resolved by the time Labour completed its first term of office in 1949. Vacancies were filled by nomination from caucus and then by a secret, exhaustive ballot, but still unresolved was the situation following the party's return to office after a general election. Fraser had not conceded the propriety of caucus's action in not re-electing a minister. Moreover, he retained both the power to state how many ministers he wanted in cabinet and also the power to appoint under-secretaries.

The Second Labour Government

When Labour regained office in 1957 there was no doubt that cabinet would be elected by the PLP. Between 1949 and 1957, however, leadership selection had been a problem. Walter Nash and C. F. Skinner became leader and deputy respectively in January 1951 after Fraser's death, but Nash's position had not gone unchallenged. After a wrangle about when a vote should occur, Nash defeated Arnold Nordmeyer on 23 June 1954. The opposition to Nash had been over-estimated.[34] Under Nash, the Labour Party improved its position in the 1954 election and won in 1957.

The PLP was discreet about the election of the 1957 cabinet and no press reports escaped. The following account is, therefore, based upon the series of interviews with the MPs (nineteen) of the time and on the Sinclair summary of the caucus minutes. Nash prepared the procedure for the election of the cabinet and the other officers before the caucus and the process was approved by caucus.[35] Nash's careful preparation was obviously designed to prevent the criticism and dissension that had characterized the cabinet appointment process of the previous Labour government.

First, the Speaker was elected, then the cabinet, consisting of the PM and fifteen others, all by exhaustive ballot. To be elected, a member had to have the votes of more than half those present, and, if caucus did not get the full cabinet complement on the first ballot, only the members that had received a majority of votes were approved. Second and subsequent ballots were held until the necessary number of members had been approved. For the subsequent ballots the names of those already approved, together with the names of those who received the lowest number of votes, were deleted. The first ballot paper contained all the names of the members of caucus and, if members wished not to be considered, they removed themselves from the list. The six newly elected members, and Nash's name, were struck off. The reports given in the interviews stated that a newly elected MP stood up and removed himself from the ballot on the grounds that there was no chance that he would be elected, and then the other new members dropped out. Three Maori members withdrew, evidently because they wished to give Eruera Tirikatene (Southern Maori) a greater chance of becoming a minister. He was the leader of the group and there was at that time general acquiescence within the caucus that at least one Maori ought to be in a Labour government. There seems to have been no suggestion that the Maori minister be elected separately. Thirteen were elected on the first ballot and one on the next. After some discussion, the names of those who had received the lowest number of votes (five) were dropped, and the last minister was declared elected.

Opposition Years and Rule Formalization

In 1963 caucus discussed the rules of cabinet election and a sub-committee, chaired by Nordmeyer, was set up. Although it was decided to continue with the caucus election of cabinets, no rule to this effect was drawn up. The resulting changes did, however, include the leadership election alteration already mentioned, and Rule 27 of the 1964 *Rules* stated that: 'At the first caucus after each general election there shall be an election for Senior whip, Junior whip and Secretary of the Party.' Rule 28 on the conduct of elections by exhaustive ballot was added.

The next reported instance of the issue being discussed in caucus evidently occurred in 1971. A full discussion took place, precipitated by a motion that cabinet be appointed by the leader.[36] Because wide disagreement was revealed, a small committee was set up to consider the issue. Four different situations were evidently considered. The first was when Labour wins an election after a period of opposition. Balloting for ministerial positions was recommended. Second, when Labour wins again after a term in office, then a complete re-election should occur. Third, if a minister dies or resigns then it should be left to the leader to fill the position, approval for this to be sought from caucus. Fourth, when there is a change of leader when the party is in office, the new leader could if he or she wished put a resolution to caucus 'that Cabinet other than the Leader and Deputy-Leader should now be re-elected'. If the new leader preferred to retain the established members, naturally he or she continued to have the right to re-allocate portfolios. The report was received but no actual change was made to the rules, although it was unanimously accepted before the 1972 election that the cabinet would be elected by exhaustive ballot and that the leader would then allocate the portfolios.[37]

The interviews conducted in the early 1970s showed widespread acceptance of the basic principles although not all the potentially contentious details were settled, as the subsequent story of Labour's cabinets has demonstrated. Twenty members were asked how, in the Labour method of electing cabinets, ministers could be dismissed when their performance was unsatisfactory. Nine replied either that there was no machinery for the dismissal of ministers or that they did not know how a minister could be dismissed or who would do the dismissing. Another four MPs believed that, once appointed, ministers remained in their posts until death or retirement. Three thought that ministers could be voted out of their posts by caucus, and three that the leader could dismiss a minister and then go to caucus and ask for the election of a replacement. One believed that the PM could warn a minister and then go to caucus for confirmation of a recommendation that the minister be replaced. An illuminating comment was: 'I don't really know how a minister would be removed. It is not an easy task, particularly in our set-up. It would be a pretty tough thing if someone was stubborn—it would be over to the leader to get him in and tell him to resign.'

MPs in interview were also asked whether or not there would be an automatic re-election of the entire cabinet after a successful general election following a term in power. Of the seventeen MPs who discussed this, twelve believed that there would be a complete re-election, two believed that there would be none, and three did not know what would happen. Nearly sixty years after the creation of the Labour Party, the rules governing the selection and dismissal of ministers were not yet clear to the participants. The evidence of the interviews also was that, although most on balance favoured the elective method, their attitudes were very often mixed, with suggestions that PMs might find it easier to work with ministers when they could choose their team, and that MPs could be tempted to court popularity. Nevertheless, the general verdict was that those who were elected knew that they had the confidence of the PLP, and that 'it gives everybody a chance to express an opinion'. It was said that 'collective judgement is better than the judgement of one man' and that the system encourages 'tolerance' and 'working together'.

The Third Labour Government, 1972–75
When Labour won in 1972, Norman Kirk had been leader since 1965. That he had had time to consider the complexities of cabinet election showed in my long interview with him in 1971. Kirk declared himself to be fully in favour of the elective method, describing the caucus as 'weighing up personality, character and commonsense'. The lessons from party history had been learned, judging from his comment that traditionally in Labour there had been 'a quite strong opposition to the idea that one man has the right to rule over others'. He said, 'The election must not leave behind any hard feelings or sense of injustice.'

The first caucus after the 1972 election began with the usual congratulatory speeches and then quickly settled into serious business. The following report of what happened is based upon interviews, although much of this meeting was reported in the press. Kirk gave the order of the ballots with ministers first to 'give every person a chance to stand for minister, not like last time'. Because there were new portfolios planned in the manifesto, he intended to increase the number of ministers by two to a total of twenty. The increase was agreed to by caucus. Balloting would be exhaustive. Voters could vote for any number of candidates up to the total required and 29 votes were necessary to become a minister. From the reports received, Kirk described every aspect carefully, allowing members to think about his proposals and question them.

The leader made four points to guide the voting. First, voters should 'select according to ability to do the job'. Second, 'cabinet must reflect the fact we have Maoris and should reflect the fact we have women'. Third, there should be a geographical balance, and he stressed that there should be adequate South Island representation. Fourth, 'any procedure we have today has to be fair and simple'. Then, to hasten the business of voting, Kirk moved that in the first two ballots those who scored five votes or fewer would be cut out. Thereafter, the bottom two would be cut out. Caucus assented. Before balloting began a member asked if there would be under-secretaries appointed. Kirk said not, but he would be guided by caucus as to whether he appointed them or caucus did, as there was no provision in the caucus rules about their selection. One member moved that under-secretaries be appointed and that Kirk choose them. This was approved.

Eight people removed themselves from the contest (five new members and three others). Kirk then produced the major surprise; the ballot paper listing the MPs' names had been arranged geographically, with the members from the electorates within each zone listed appropriately. The zones were: northern North Island, western and inland North Island, central North Island, Wellington, northern South Island, central South Island and southern South Island. (There was, it seems, a ballot paper that had been sighted a day or so earlier, one that listed the members in alphabetical order, but Kirk seems to have changed his mind.) Fifteen members were elected on the first ballot, but it took six further ballots to elect the eighteen ministers. The other positions were then elected. The major surprise was the election of Roger Douglas and the omission of his father, Norman, a spokesperson on labour issues and a member of the Party Policy Committee. No Aucklanders were elected after the nine who came through in the first ballot, so it seems that geography was a factor in the minds of the voters.

By 1974 the problems of the economy and the ineffectiveness of some cabinet ministers had given rise to much criticism from the media and from within caucus. After discussion with some MPs, Kirk moved a notice of motion at the end of the 11 July caucus meeting to the effect that the rules for electing cabinet be clarified so that, if vacancies or a vacancy occurred between elections because of retirement, resignation, death or dismissal, then the leader could go to caucus with a name or names which the caucus could then reject or endorse. Evidently some MPs favoured instead a complete re-election of the cabinet, feeling that, if the motion were passed, then the election of a full cabinet after a successful election in 1975 would be endangered. Others felt that even some change in cabinet would be better than none and Kirk's motion would be acceptable if put to a secret ballot and, likewise, if ministerial replacements under this rule were rejected or agreed to by secret ballot.

In the caucus the following week, Kirk said he felt he needed some extension of the power to allocate portfolios during the time between elections. He then moved his motion, clarifying that the name or names proposed by the PM must be endorsed by secret ballot by a majority of all the members of caucus. If a minister refused to accept Kirk's advice to resign, that minister could go to caucus where he or she would have the right to appeal, such appeal to be determined by secret ballot. Kirk added that he realized that the motion constituted an extension of his powers. The final vote was heavily in favour of the motion (44 to 6).[38] Norman Kirk did not have the opportunity to utilize this new rule. He died one month later.

Before the new leader and the composition of cabinet were decided, there were two procedural issues to be settled. First, would the change immediately to be effected take the place of the three-yearly election of the leader and the deputy? Second, would the vacancy caused by Kirk's death be filled by an election for that vacancy alone or would there be a complete re-election of cabinet? On 2 September three notices of motion for the Friday caucus were introduced. Hugh Watt, deputy, moved first that Caucus Rule 26, concerning the three-yearly election of the leader and deputy, be set aside to enable both posts to be filled immediately, and second that the cabinet vacancy be filled by election. (This may have harmed Watt's chances for the leadership.) Joe Walding moved a third motion, that all ministerial posts be recontested after the election of the leader and the deputy. It was decided that the third motion should be put second.

During the week between Kirk's death and the leadership election the weight of support within caucus, particularly amongst the younger members, moved from Watt to Wallace (Bill) Rowling, Minister of Finance and fourth in cabinet ranking. (Watt was not helped by votes of appreciation from both the Party National Executive and the Federation of Labour.) There was some division within caucus although it would be overly simple to see the disagreement as traditionalists and unionists versus intellectuals and technocrats.[39]

All fifty-four members were present to elect cabinet, as were the party president, Charles Bennett and the party secretary, John Wybrow.[40] Rule Number 26 was set aside and Rowling was elected in the one ballot. Watt offered his congratulations and announced that he would not seek the deputy position, but he would put his name forward for cabinet. An exhaustive ballot made Robert Tizard the new deputy. Caucus resumed in the afternoon and first had to deal with the two further motions. Before the discussion began,

Rowling suggested that Watt be included in the cabinet without having to win a ballot and this was approved, leaving seventeen positions open. Rowling said also that, although he believed that cabinet as a whole should be recontested, he hoped that, since there had already been some changes, there would not be too many more.[41] Walding's motion took precedence over Watt's and was carried on a show of hands. Rowling did not vote. The other motion lapsed. Ballot papers were then distributed with the names set out geographically as before. Twelve members withdrew before the first ballot, which elected sixteen to cabinet, including one newcomer (Ron Bailey). After a further five ballots, Phil Amos, who had been in cabinet, was very narrowly re-elected. Later it was announced that the under-secretaries were to remain the same but with different responsibilities.

Despite the discontent with the performance of some of the 1972 ministers, the caucus had made as little change as possible, simply electing one replacement member and giving Phil Amos a fright. According to reports, Rowling was disappointed at the extremely limited nature of the changes, which he himself may well have encouraged by his warning before the balloting. But Rowling's warning cannot have been the only deterrent to more radical change. Perhaps there were aspiring ministers in the caucus who, knowing that they were unlikely to gain promotion, took care not to insert new members who might stay on after a successful general election, thus blocking their own chances. Perhaps, too, cabinet solidarity gave the ministers a solid block of basic support. Or perhaps loyalty bound the voters to spare the poor ministers from the ignominy of publicized failure. Moreover, the maintenance of party unity after the death of Norman Kirk was undoubtedly seen by many as an overriding need, indeed more necessary than the invigoration of the cabinet for the next election.[42] By 1974 most of the major issues about cabinet appointment in the Labour Party had been resolved, right to the details of voting procedure. But in 1974 the final effect was conservative.

In Opposition Again, 1975–84

Although the complete re-election of cabinet after Kirk's death could have been regarded as a precedent to be followed in the future when one PM was replaced by another in mid-term, interestingly it did not find its way into the additions to the rules accepted in 1976. In 1975, a caucus committee revised the *Caucus Rules*, suggesting amendments and new rules. The 1974 inclusion of the motion proposed by Kirk and adopted by caucus that caucus agreement to replacements must be done by secret ballot was not, however, mentioned in the revised rules of 1976. It was proposed and accepted that, when in government, 'the caucus shall elect the members of the Cabinet, the size of the Cabinet to be determined by the Leader (Prime Minister)', that the leader would allocate the portfolios in cabinet, and that when in opposition the spokespersons would be appointed by the leader.

The discussions in caucus have to be placed in the context of what had been happening in the extra-parliamentary party. After the 1975 defeat, the party president, Sir Charles Bennett, said the party might be concerned about the way the cabinet was chosen. This hint was taken up and a remit at the 1976 Conference proposed that the PM and Deputy select cabinet. The constitutional committee of conference recommended against the remit. The convener, Ted Keating (an MP during the second Labour Government), said that 'One of the greatest battles of the caucus of the first Labour Government had been to win caucus selection of Cabinet. And he believed the current Labour caucus strongly favoured the system of caucus selection.'[43] The motion was heavily defeated.

By 1976 the Labour caucus had decided to retain the elective method with all its faults. Besides, it is doubtful whether the PLP would have publicly conceded that they were anything but happy with the existing method, for to indicate otherwise might have risked a Conference vote for change and so imposed a ruling upon the caucus which, since the 1930s, had been free to make up its own mind on this matter.

Wallace (Bill) Rowling had not done well in the public opinion polls; there had been constant criticisms of Rowling's apparent inability to oppose Muldoon in the combative style to which New Zealanders had become accustomed. After much tension within caucus, and after surviving attempts to replace him at the end of 1980, and again in 1981, by appealing to the grass roots membership, Rowling resigned in February 1983 and was replaced by David Lange. Interestingly, given the argument here concerning the significance and impact of participatory norms, this leadership change gave rise to discussion in the extra-parliamentary party about involving ordinary party members in the choice of leader. A remit had been passed at the 1982 conference proposing that all MPs must consult their Labour Electorate Committees before proposed changes of the parliamentary leadership. It was noted that the actual degree of member/party consultation during the leadership change had varied, and that there was no way of guaranteeing that MPs considered members' views when they voted.[44] In the event no changes were made.

Under Rowling's leadership there had been an attempt to create a shadow cabinet. This was not trouble-free; Roger Douglas was sacked as shadow spokesperson for transport when he made public an alternative economic policy without first obtaining party backing. When David Lange became leader, he moved back to allocating policy areas to all MPs, although this system included senior spokespersons with co-ordinating responsibilities. The return to apparently egalitarian norms did not solve Labour's internal tensions, which were already manifest when it won the July 1984 general election. In April 1984 a battle had been reported on economic policy between Jim Anderton, then the party president, and Roger Douglas, 'the first public breach of the peace pact' that had been drawn up at the previous year's annual conference.[45] In May, Lange was publicly saying that Labour was back together again, a peace that proved to be only temporary.[46]

The Fourth Labour Government, 1984–90

On Tuesday 17 July, in the midst of the post-election crisis over the exhaustion of the country's reserves, Robert Muldoon's recalcitrance, and the devaluation of the currency, the caucus met to elect its cabinet. There were eighteen posts available since David Lange, and his Deputy, Geoffrey Palmer, were automatically ministers. Lange also appointed six under-secretaries. After the 1987 election there were four cabinet vacancies due to retirements and Kerry Burke's shift from cabinet to become Speaker. All the positions (except for leader and deputy) were, however, up for re-election, confirming the practice of the complete post-election 'spill'. David Lange expanded the executive by being permitted to appoint four ministers outside cabinet, plus four (non-Executive Council) under-secretaries. This expansion of the leader's patronage hardly represented a concession on caucus's part; it is highly unlikely that caucus would refuse such a request given the wider opportunities it offered ambitious politicians. The large 1987 team gave Lange the opportunity to reward those MPs who had done well, but also:

> Unstated was a form of damage control by quelling the vociferous protests from some who had narrowly missed original Cabinet selection, the need to dilute back-bench opposition to the government's often contentious economic policies, the conciliation of contrasting interests in the wider party, and the necessity for strengthening administrative competence by easing pressure on some heavily burdened senior Ministers.[47]

Lange also sought to contain the economic drive of the Minister of Finance, Roger Douglas, by making two new ministers, Michael Cullen and David Butcher, the Associate Ministers of Finance, replacing Richard Prebble and David Caygill, who shifted to other positions.[48]

Despite, or perhaps because of, the expansion of the executive, it proved to be no cohesive team. The PM himself took a portfolio, Education, partly to signal a switch away from the economic priorities of Labour's first term and towards social issues.[49] The acrimony and policy tensions that were never far from the surface between 1984 and 1987 developed to dominate the party's second term. Just over a year after the 1987 election, Richard Prebble, Minister of State-Owned Enterprises, was sacked (5 November 1988). He had first been removed from his portfolio because of his radical policies on asset sales, but was quickly removed from cabinet altogether when he vigorously criticized Lange personally. Then, only a month later, the Minister of Finance, Roger Douglas, wrote to the Prime Minister saying that he (Douglas) could 'no longer work as Finance Minister in a Cabinet led by you'. Lange was quick to accept this as a letter of resignation, citing the letter, received that morning, at a press conference on 14 December 1988.[50] There had been major differences over economic policy, particularly Douglas's proposals to continue the changes to the taxation system, beginning with the imposition of GST, by shifting further from the progressive tax system.[51] Again, policy disagreements were combined with attacks on Lange. Trevor de Cleene, a minister outside cabinet, friend and ally of Douglas, resigned from his position on 14 November 1988.

Besides losing de Cleene, and in effect sacking the Minister of Finance who had given his name to the changes driven through by the Government, David Lange also had become the first Labour PM to dismiss a minister (Prebble). It is ironic that it was the exercise of this authority, clearly given him by the caucus rules evolved over decades, that marked the effective end of Lange's leadership. Like Muldoon, when he dismissed Quigley, the Prime Minister's actions rebounded upon himself, reducing his own authority. On 21 December 1988, and again on 29 June 1989, Lange had to fight challenges to his leadership.[52] But Muldoon, unlike Lange, could choose his own replacements for cabinet posts. Indeed, the Labour Party *Caucus Rules* stated that extraordinary vacancies 'no matter how caused' were to be filled by the PM 'selecting a person or persons and nominating that person or persons to Caucus for approval'.

In the event, Lange permitted caucus to elect two new ministers and, on 3 August, Douglas was re-elected to cabinet with a new minister, Annette King, who only very narrowly defeated Lange's other major problem, Prebble. The restoration of Douglas to cabinet rank had happened despite Lange's attempts to prevent it. After a caucus meeting on 4 May, when Lange was pressed to restore Douglas to the cabinet, the PM, in a televised speech, told the delegates at the Wellington Regional Conference of the party 'that as far back as April, 1987, Douglas had been proposing to "build growth on the rubble of social services"'.[53] According to a former senior minister there was evidently strong feeling in caucus that Douglas's ability could not be ignored. Also Geoffrey Palmer, Deputy PM, appears to have attempted 'to bring both Roger Douglas and Richard Prebble back into the fold'.[54] Such a collective expression of lack of faith in the PM's judgement inevitably was interpreted by Lange and the mass media as signifying an erosion of his authority and, perhaps, the destruction of his will to exert that authority. On 7 August 1989 David Lange resigned the prime ministership, becoming Attorney-General and a minister outside cabinet.

Lange was succeeded by Palmer, and Helen Clark was elected to be Deputy PM, the first woman in New Zealand to achieve such a high post. When Palmer first took over he inherited the Lange cabinet, although he made some portfolio reallocations. (Douglas became Minister of Police.) Six ministers, it was announced late that year, were planning to retire from Parliament at the 1990 general election (Stan Rodger, Michael Bassett, Roger Douglas, Robert Tizard, Russell Marshall and Colin Moyle). Palmer seized the opportunity to create a 'new look' cabinet and asked them all to resign their positions. In February 1990, seven new ministers (including Prebble) were elected to cabinet, and four ministers outside cabinet were appointed. There was a complete re-election of cabinet. Extraordinarily, given Palmer's past criticisms of Prebble as Minister of State-Owned Enterprises, he was restored to that post when the Prime Minister allocated the portfolios.[55]

Palmer, in turn, resigned on 4 September 1990, having lost the majority of the ministers' support (although believing that he had sufficient caucus votes to survive a ballot),[56] and in response to the very low support he and the party were receiving in the polls. The new leader, Mike Moore, took over Palmer's cabinet for the very short period before the 1990 election. Palmer became Minister of the Environment, outside cabinet.

Selection in the National Party

The way in which the National Party selects its cabinet reflects its origins and, moreover, its readiness to adapt traditional habits and beliefs to the peculiarities of the New Zealand social culture and political structure. In National, the elected leader, the Prime Minister, chooses the ministers whom he or she wishes to have in cabinet but, as a response to the small, tight-knit parliamentary party, National prime ministers have generally consulted extensively amongst their colleagues. Thus the outward form of the Westminster model is retained and much of its spirit. The Prime Minister alone takes responsibility for the choice. But what happens in practice in the New Zealand National Party is distinctly different from what happens in the Conservative or Labour parties in the House of Commons. Modification has occurred in the form of informal consultative practices which in turn have affected relationships between ministers and Prime Minister and between Prime Minister and caucus.

The National Party, 1936–1949

At the time the National Party was formed in 1936 out of the remnants of the Reform and Liberal (United) parties there seems to have been no claim for an elective ministry. Adam Hamilton became leader. Hamilton, 'the unspectacular caretaker',[57] was then replaced by the belligerent Sidney Holland in 1940. Under Holland's leadership, caucus began to meet regularly and specialized caucus committees were introduced, thus enabling National to attack the Government more effectively.[58]

The youthful party had been given some decision-making rights. Would it demand more, including perhaps the right to select cabinet, when it reached maturity and political office? On the contrary, the caucus did not develop the democratic argument to the point of asking for cabinet election as had Labour from its earliest days. An element of deference to the National leader has remained from 1936 until the present, at least so long as that leader is winning elections. Undoubtedly also the need to bind tightly together the ingredients of the former Coalition against the victorious Labour Party meant a strong leader was necessary. Massey's view that the leader should choose the ministers was adopted.

Sidney Holland and the First National Government

The 'straw poll', an informal, advisory poll of MPs where the results were known only to the pollster, had its first use in Sidney Holland's period as Prime Minister, but not for the purpose of cabinet selection. Before 1947 there was no official deputy leader in the National Party. Holland ensured that his own favourite for the position, Keith Holyoake, was chosen by asking all caucus members to state their preferences in writing to the leader. This achieved its purpose of defeating William Sullivan for the post. It was not until 1957, when the deputy leadership again had to be settled, that the party 'permitted itself the luxury of a ballot'.[59]

Little is documented about Sidney Holland's methods of, or criteria for, appointment to cabinet. The MPs and ministers who were in Parliament while Holland was Prime Minister mainly revealed in the interviews conducted during the early 1970s that political memories are short. There was no mention by those interviewed of Holland having consulted the parliamentary party when he formed his first cabinet in 1949. Nevertheless some consultation about the process of selection for cabinet posts seems to have occurred. A newspaper reported in 1949 that many of the senior members had been given interviews by Holland.[60] On the whole, however, as a former minister said,

> When Sid Holland went into Parliament in 1935 there were only about nineteen members so what tended to happen a little bit there, I suppose, was that the strong men of the party were those with the longest service. . . The cabinet pretty well chose itself.

The almost indistinguishable claims of old loyalties and long service would have settled most of the places.

In 1954, with a diminished majority in the House and a number of ministers having retired from cabinet, it was necessary for Holland to select some new ministers. Those interviewed disagreed about whether Holland did or did not consult.[61]

Keith Holyoake, John Marshall, and the Second National Government, 1960–1972

Very late in the day, two months before the 1957 general election which the National cabinet (correctly) feared it would lose, an ill Sid Holland was persuaded to resign the leadership.[62] He was succeeded by Keith Holyoake, who then spent the next three years as Leader of the Opposition. John Marshall defeated Jack Watts for the deputy position. Holyoake brought in a new minister in 1957 but otherwise inherited Holland's team for the rump of the National administration.

It was Keith Holyoake, the arch-representative of consensus politics in New Zealand, who really developed the practice of the 'straw poll'.[63] Although it is not known whether or not he took a poll for his 1960 cabinet,[64] there were press comments about a poll taken in 1966 saying that one had also occurred in 1963. Holyoake was quoted: 'I usually consult members of the caucus on this sort of thing. There is a clear understanding in our party that the leader picks his Cabinet, but there is also a clear understanding that we try to follow democratic processes.'[65]

The 1966 selection was not without its difficulties for, as one report said, only three names were called for to fill the vacant positions left by retiring ministers.[66] This caused some disgruntlement among senior back-benchers who saw their chances for cabinet receding. The new ministers were announced and the Prime Minister sent a telegram to the National MPs that said 'the trio chosen represented the consensus of the caucus poll 10 days ago on potential Ministers'.[67] The danger was, of course, that it was too easy for the caucus to check amongst themselves and discover what the caucus consensus had been when only a few names were called for. It was not a method that Holyoake tried again for occasional vacancies. In 1969 Holyoake again asked for written suggestions from caucus members. He had a series of private consultations with individual ministers and some, evidently, wrote him personal letters suggesting cabinet changes. Also there were consultations with senior back-benchers.[68]

The consultative process, on the face of it, was kept inside the caucus room although there were several hints of outside advice. Holyoake once mentioned that he had sometimes asked editors and reporters of newspapers.[69] In my interview with him, however, Holyoake denied this. Probably the truth was that he had had informal conversations with newspaper editors. When discussing the appointment of Ralph Hanan as Minister of Maori Affairs with me, Holyoake said, 'I did consult a little on that one and, very rarely, on that one I consulted outside.' Presumably Maori were consulted. Possibly Holyoake also consulted the Federation of Labour over Peter Gordon's suitability for the post of Minister of Labour.[70] Certainly, groups make their feelings known to the Prime Ministers of both parties when they have definite views about a potential minister for their area of interest.

Almost half of those National MPs who were interviewed in the last years of the Holyoake Government offered some comment on the 'straw polls' (21 out of the total 46). It was found that it was this informal aspect of the selection process that was the subject of criticism in the party, not the formal method, the principle of the Prime Minister choosing his ministers. From the evidence of the interviews it seemed that about one-quarter of the MPs had reservations about the polls, feeling that the PM should either pick the ministers on his own or with his deputy. The polling was referred to by one person as 'the silly nonsense, the charade you go through'. Another comment was,

> My personal view is that it is more of a sop. It helps [Holyoake] perhaps to get a consensus about what the party wants. There is a lot of danger in this. If you ignore this, people feel they are being ignored. It's a waste of time. We talk about it ourselves and, when someone goes in that no one has wanted in, the feeling is that the MPs' requests are being ignored.

None of the 'dissidents', however, wanted caucus to elect the cabinet. The majority of MPs felt that the polling of MPs' opinions was either harmless enough or actually a help to the Prime Minister: 'There's no harm in a straw poll as an indication of the way caucus was feeling. . . . I'd hate to see it as election by caucus.' Moreover, 'It gives an indication of how the boys are thinking.' (Presumably the opinions of Esme Tombleson and Rona Stevenson did not count. Neither was promoted into cabinet by Holyoake.) There were no unreal expectations about the effects of the poll upon the Prime Minister's choice, and there was no evidence that MPs disagreed with Holyoake's own view that no MP 'can see the whole jigsaw puzzle of setting a whole cabinet together as one right from the centre can, but the opinions were very useful'.[71]

The interviews on this aspect of the parliamentary career revealed another illuminating facet of leadership control over the selection process. Partly in solicited responses, partly in the course of general conversation, and sometimes in answer to other questions, there emerged a pronounced emphasis on the importance of loyalty to the leader. With the exception of a handful of MPs, National members generally were reluctant to say that loyalty was over-emphasized to the point where it became disadvantageous to be critical of the leadership. This, of course, is a more particular aspect and consequence of the general norms of loyalty and conformity so frequently observed as a characteristic of the New Zealand Parliament.

After Holyoake's resignation from the leadership in February 1972 his successor, John Marshall, also conducted a straw poll on cabinet composition.[72] It was suggested in 1972 that Marshall involved his deputy, Robert Muldoon, more in the cabinet-making process than Holyoake had involved Marshall. Certainly both the new PM and his Deputy in February 1972 jointly interviewed many of the 'former, continuing and new ministers before the team was finally decided'.[73] Also, it was noticed that Muldoon supporters were given important jobs in cabinet. This, however, could have been a placatory gesture by the victor, Marshall.

Robert Muldoon and the Third National Government, 1975–1984

Robert Muldoon defeated Marshall in the bitter leadership battle which culminated in Marshall's resignation in July 1974.[74]

Muldoon in December 1975 continued the practice of taking a straw poll.[75] Undoubtedly some discussion over portfolio allocation usually took place, although Muldoon's authoritarian leadership style would have precluded real opposition to his arrangements.[76] Muldoon's own story of the 1978 cabinet has no mention of caucus consultation on the composition of his executive but neither, also, does he refer to his dismissal of a minister.[77] Between 1978 and 1981 his own position was threatened. Unhappiness within cabinet and caucus during the 1978–1981 period over 'Muldoon's combative style and interventionist economic policies',[78] and uneasiness because of the loss of the East Coast Bays by-election in September 1980 occasioned by Frank Gill's appointment as Ambassador to Washington, led to the abortive 'colonels' coup' in late 1980. Headed by three junior ministers, Derek Quigley, Jim McLay, and Jim Bolger, and encouraged also by some support within the party organization, the Deputy, Brian Talboys, was persuaded to challenge Muldoon for the leadership. Muldoon counter-attacked, organizing ministerial, party, and public support. The coup collapsed: the numbers were uncertain; Talboys was overseas and, in the circumstances, unwilling to continue with the challenge either from abroad or when he returned home.[79]

The 1981 cabinet was the product of a limited choice of ministerial talent, for the party had suffered a steady erosion of votes and seats after its sweeping 1975 victory, a process of attrition of votes well under way by 1978 when the Government had had a respectable but reduced majority of ten seats over Labour and Social Credit (which had won one). In 1981 that majority had been cut down to two—just one after selecting the Speaker. Apart from Gill's shift to the world of diplomacy, three ministers had retired, however, and one was defeated, thus allowing a trickle of new blood into the 1981 cabinet. But cabinet between 1981 and 1984 was an unhappy institution. There were continued problems of party and cabinet management under Muldoon; two MPs, Marilyn Waring and Mike Minogue, publicly dissented from the PM's decisions and voted against the Government on occasion; and others rebelled against the whips. Within caucus Muldoon was faced by Quigley's public criticisms of the Government's economic strategy, which led to his sacking from cabinet (see Chapter Nine). The July 1984 snap general election saw the defeat of Muldoon's Government; and November of that same year saw the end of Muldoon's leadership when he was defeated by his Deputy, Jim McLay. Under Muldoon's long leadership then, consultation seems to have been informal, except for the 'straw poll' in 1975.

Jim Bolger and the Fourth National Government, 1990–
Muldoon was not content to rest peacefully on the back benches in opposition. Instead he conducted a campaign against the man who had defeated him. A measure of the bitterness of the debate was when, having been demoted to 38th ranking by McLay, Muldoon said it was 'Just the latest action by a panic-stricken leader who has reached the stage where it is not a question of whether he goes but when.'[80] McLay did poorly in the opinion polls, the caucus was divided, and the balance of support swung towards Jim Bolger, the Deputy, who then won the leadership in March 1986.

National lost the 1987 election but bounced back with a huge majority in 1990. There were few survivors from the Muldoon administrations. The caucus contained thirty-two MPs who were new to the job, and, including the Prime Minister himself, only four MPs who had held ministerial office. The cabinet was evidently constructed by Bolger himself, working with his Deputy, Don McKinnon. An indication that there was some discussion over the allocation of portfolios was given by one member of the cabinet, in interview. The minister commented:

> I think the Prime Minister did a fairly good job actually of trying to match personalities and abilities to portfolios. . . . Some people got some portfolios

they didn't like, but normally everyone got portfolios they were capable of undertaking. I guess that was because while you indicated a preference [on] what you would like, you also indicated a preference [on] what you would hate.

As other ministers indicated, however, for some their portfolios were complete surprises. Keith Holyoake, it was rumoured, had required all ministers to write signed but undated letters of resignation as a condition of their initial appointment. In answer to a question in Parliament, Jim Bolger denied that he had sought such letters from his ministers.[81]

Bolger took at least one gamble with his team when he appointed as Minister of Maori Affairs, Winston Peters, a high polling MP, known for his outspoken criticisms of some leadership decisions. But Peters was the only Maori in caucus with parliamentary experience. (His brother, Ian, had won a seat in 1990.) Peters attacked his Government's economic policy and paid scant regard for established policy processes when he promoted his Ministry's report on Maori development, *Ka Awatea*.[82] After eleven months in office, Peters was sacked, primarily for his disloyalty to the Prime Minister (see Chapter Nine).

After the 1993 general election, when National lost a range of marginal seats and only narrowly clung on to office, there was back-bench pressure for the cabinet to present a new face to the public. It seems that party and caucus opinion favoured removing Ruth Richardson, Minister of Finance, and replacing her with someone less associated with neo-liberal economic policies. Indeed, one report said that the president, John Collinge, together with the five divisional chairpersons, met with Bolger to argue for Richardson's replacement and also for the replacement of several urban with rural ministers. The same report says that Bolger asked all the National MPs for their opinions on the composition of government.[83]

Thus the consultative practice reasserted itself in a time of perceived crisis for the party. Richardson was indeed removed from the Finance portfolio and then resigned from cabinet because she would accept none of the portfolios offered her by the Prime Minister; Richardson was the sacrificial lamb on the altar of the Government's macro-economic strategy. (In 1993 Richardson also resigned from Parliament.) The almost equally controversial Minister of Social Welfare, Jenny Shipley, became Minister of Health. Another minister, Rob Storey, also lost his cabinet position; and Maurice McTigue lost his seat. Two new ministers were appointed to cabinet posts, bypassing the three ministers outside cabinet who retained those positions. The fourth, Graeme Lee, was removed. Jim Bolger enlarged his executive phalanx by creating three parliamentary under-secretaryships.

Conclusion

Although the Labour Party's *Caucus Rules* have been clarified over the years, and the main principles of the elective cabinet are set down, there are still grey areas now covered by convention rather than written rule. These conventions are as follows. First, there will be a re-election of the entire cabinet after a general election whether that election elects a new Labour government or re-elects one (1957, 1972, 1984, 1987). Second, a change of leader, for whatever reason, is followed usually by a cabinet 'spill' (Rowling in 1974 and Palmer in 1990). Mike Moore's ministry did not follow this pattern, but there was no time for a new cabinet to be elected and establish itself. Third, the PM has the power to choose ministers outside cabinet and under-secretaries. The problem of dismissal remains acute, as David Lange's experiences demonstrated, for not only does a dismissal rebound upon a Prime Minister by indicating the limits of authority as much as the extent of it, but also it raises the question of who should appoint the replacements: caucus or Prime Minister. The democratic, participatory convention suggests the former, and prime ministerial authority and cabinet solidarity suggests the latter.

There is a lesson to be drawn from the New Zealand Labour Party's experience of elective cabinets. That is, that when a Parliament is small and the party is also small and, moreover, cohesive and participatory, then leaders can only challenge collective, majoritarian decision-making successfully for a limited time. Much more than in the National Party, the position of a Labour Prime Minister is imperilled when he or she neglects the party's participatory history. Thus the story of Labour's selection and election of cabinets tells us a great deal about why Labour Governments which last more than a few years have disintegrated into factional battles. The authority of the Labour Prime Minister is always conditional, always circumscribed, and Labour cabinets have to be understood in the context of this complex relationship between leader, cabinet, and caucus.

But National leaders also must respect the participatory norms of the New Zealand Parliament, although ideologically the party has more sympathy for leadership powers. The National Party evolved its own leadership selection methods and leadership style. National from the beginning firmly grasped the significance of strong leadership in New Zealand politics. This precept was accepted both by the parliamentary party and its extra-parliamentary organization, and has led over the years to some degree of ruthlessness about leadership replacement. Every National leader has been replaced when the party—outside as well as inside Parliament—felt it could not win the next election.[84] Most were persuaded to retire for the good of the party (Hamilton, Holland, Holyoake, and Marshall). Muldoon and McLay were defeated in ballots of the caucus members.

Belief in strong leadership in National is backed by a practical willingness to give the leaders strength through the power of patronage. A National Prime Minister, then, chooses cabinet. The party, however, is a creature of its beginnings as well as an organization sufficiently able and flexible to deal with changing circumstances. The claims of those who asked for elective ministries have their reflection in the National caucus of today which similarly demands the right to participate in policy-making. The party has not been unaffected by what Duverger has called 'the legitimacy of democracy . . . the dominant doctrine of the contemporary age, that which determines the legitimacy of power'.[85]

The participatory instinct should be seen in the context of National's early establishment of a decentralized and democratic method of candidate selection, focused on the electorates, which strengthened its claim to represent legitimately the anti-Labour forces. It is interesting that some National leaders sought to legitimize their positions and power within the parliamentary party through the practice of conducting 'straw polls' amongst caucus colleagues to test out opinion as to who should go into cabinet. The consultative middle way of cabinet election evolved by Holyoake may also in part have been due to the desire to reconcile the disparate elements of which National is made up—Reform and United formerly and, since then, town and country—but not to go so far as to attempt this by having an elected executive that would represent the factions.

With individual consultation there are some elements of democratic decision-making and the various points of view are voiced and considered. But the leader retains the power of patronage and the overt demarcation of group conflict demonstrated by voting, particularly dangerous in a small party, is avoided. The pattern that evolved was the product of a small parliamentary party where the loyalty and conformity of behaviour typical of small and medium-sized groups set up expectations of consultation in return for the authority granted to the elected leader. Robert Muldoon's period of prime ministership, despite his occasional consultation on cabinet composition, was contrary to this tradition. His style was to retain as much power as possible in his own hands, as demonstrated by his retention of the Finance portfolio; relationships between him and his caucus were certainly not peaceful. Muldoon therefore marked a radical shift in the style of National prime ministers. The next leader to become Prime Minister, Jim Bolger, set out to heal the divisions within party and caucus. But between 1990 and 1993, although the intent was there and the mechanisms were in place, cabinet-led, radical policy change continued to confirm the move away from the close interactions between cabinet and caucus of the Holyoake years. Jim Bolger's government was caught between two forces: the institutional and historical pressures towards consensus and consultation, and the imperative towards the priorities of ideologically driven executive government.

It has often been said that, because Parliament and hence the parliamentary parties are so small, the two methods of cabinet selection and election make little difference in practice to which MPs become ministers. Seniority, above all else, counts. Nevertheless each of the two methods, themselves products of party ideology and institutional behavioural norms, have different impacts upon the nature of cabinet government and prime ministerial authority. Furthermore, in neither of the parties examined here has there been a history of Prime Ministers regularly sacking their ministers—another illustration of the constraints of choice and flexibility in a small institution.

5

MAKING DECISIONS: GOVERNMENT BY COMMITTEE

Cabinet government could not operate in New Zealand or anywhere else without a substantial basis of agreement among ministers on larger issues together with a willingness to compromise on details and on tactics.[1]

Introduction

A persistent metaphor in political science has been the 'system', conceptualizing the workings of a polity as either a biological or a mechanical (especially cybernetic) entity. Parties, the government bureaucracies, and interest groups are depicted as providing inputs into the central arenas of the political system. The outputs are the policies which, in turn, feed back into the system. Thus we have a self-regulating mechanism or organism. One of the many problems of the metaphor is that it tells us nothing about the operations of the 'black box' at the centre, the group or organization that converts inputs into outputs. To some extent this is not, however, misleading, for at the heart of every political system there is an élite group which conducts most of its business in secret. The New Zealand cabinet is no exception; the convention of collective cabinet responsibility by its very logic entails privacy and confidentiality.

Despite the secrecy of the decision-making processes, over the years some insights have been garnered into how New Zealand cabinets conduct their business. This is partly due to the relative openness and accessibility of New Zealand ministers and parliamentarians, and partly due, also, to the operations of the Official Information Act 1982. This chapter attempts to analyse the decision-making process of cabinet by putting together information from published sources and from interview data.

There are two main topics in this chapter: the process of government by committee, and the power relationships involved. Before the decision-making processes of full cabinet and the cabinet committees are discussed, however, I briefly discuss some contextual, structural aspects—for structures are important in their own right since they are about the boundaries and limits of power and authority.

78

Cabinet Structure

Three factors have shaped the structures of cabinets: the overall shape of the public service (historically labyrinthine and containing many agencies even after the shrinking of the state in the 1980s), the practice of retaining a relatively large cabinet with few or no ministers outside it, and prime ministers' perceptions of how power should be allocated, divided, and shared.

Despite the goals of both Labour and National after 1984 to shrink and rationalize the New Zealand state, the political executive remained large. There were twenty in cabinet in both governments, and between three and five ministers outside cabinet. Indeed, Jonathan Boston makes the point that the stated objectives of the public sector reforms made

> no mention of the relationship between the machinery of government and the organization of the cabinet, the number and allocation of portfolios, or the capacity of individual Ministers to cope with the range of issues that might fall within the province of a particular department (i.e. span of control problems). Yet such concerns have been at the heart of machinery of government deliberations in most other countries.[2]

Most ministers have several portfolios, and some ministers have a mixed selection of their main ministries and part-shares of others. (See Table 5.1.)

Thus policy co-ordination should be straightforward, since all or most ministers represent their departments and ministries in cabinet. In another sense co-ordination is complicated simply by the numbers involved, both in terms of ministers with interests in an issue and the range of public agencies involved. Competitiveness—bureaucratic and ministerial—through the representation of interests thus contends against co-ordination in policy maintenance and formulation. This can be seen as an admirable example of pluralistic democracy, or, alternatively, as thwarting directed policy formulation and coherence. It can be regarded as providing 'contestability' of policy ideas or as an inefficient waste of time and human resources. I shall return to these issues later.

The three-fold impact of public service structure, the large cabinet, and the views of the individual prime minister, can be demonstrated through two examples, one recent and the other from the third Labour Government. A 1992 article pointed out that six ministers were at that time overseeing the Ministry of Commerce: the ministers of Commerce, Energy, Tourism, Communications, Consumer Affairs, and Business Development. Each also had other responsibilities. The Ministry of Commerce at the time contained separate operating divisions: the Ministry of Consumer Affairs, reporting directly to the Minister of Consumer Affairs; the Ministry of Tourism, 'tucked somewhere within the business policy and programmes division' but acting

Table 5.1: The National Ministry, November 1990[1]

Ministers	Portfolios Held	Associate Positions Held
Ministers in Cabinet		
J. B. Bolger	Prime Minister	
D. McKinnon	Deputy Prime Minister External Relations & Trade Foreign Affairs	
W. F. Birch	Labour Immigration State Services Pacific Island Affairs	
R. Richardson	Finance	
P. East	Attorney-General	
J. Falloon	Agriculture Forestry Racing	
D. Kidd	State-owned Enterprises Fisheries Railways Works & Development	Finance
P. Burdon	Commerce Trade Negotiations Industry	External Relations & Trade
S. Upton	Health Environment Research, Science & Technology	
J. Banks	Police Tourism Recreation & Sport	
J. Shipley	Social Welfare Women's Affairs	
W. Cooper	Defence Local Government	
D. Graham	Justice Disarmament & Arms Control Arts & Culture	
L. Smith	Education	

M. McTigue	Employment	Finance
R. Storey	Transport Statistics Lands Survey & Land Information	
W. Peters	Maori Affairs	
D. Marshall	Conservation Science (DSIR)	Agriculture
J. Luxton	Housing Energy	Education
W. Creech	Revenue Customs Government Superannuation Fund	

Ministers not in Cabinet

K. O'Regan	Consumer Affairs	Women's Affairs Health
R. McClay	Youth Affairs	Education Social Welfare Pacific Island Affairs
G. Lee	Internal Affairs Senior Citizens Civil Defence	
R. Maxwell	Regional Development	Employment Immigration
M. Williamson	Communications Broadcasting	Health Research, Science & Technology

1. The minor responsibilities have been omitted (e.g. 'Minister in Charge of the New Zealand Security Intelligence Service' (the PM), and 'Minister Responsible for the Serious Fraud Office' (P. East).

Source: G. A. Wood (ed.), *Supplement to Ministers and Members in the New Zealand Parliament* (Dunedin, Tarwode Press, 1992), pp. 11–12

as a specialized policy unit advising the Minister; and energy and resources. This six-headed department had extensive regulatory and development powers. As the author commented: 'Think again if you reckon the cabinet has a much easier job nowadays after cutting the Public Service down to size and kicking the state bit by bit out of business.'[3] I should add that, according to the evidence of the interviews, the twenty-one business development boards that the ministry was overseeing reported directly to the Minister of Business Development. Such are the complexities of cabinet portfolio allocations and arrangements in New Zealand.

The other example comes from transport, where historically departments were incrementally added in response to technological changes and in the absence of alternative sources of finance and bases of administration.[4] In 1961 there were three departments (Transport, Railways, and Marine), the Civil Aviation Division, two corporations (National Airways and the Tasman Empire Airways), and a National Roads Board. In 1964 a separate Department of Civil Aviation was created. By 1972 a (new) Transport Commission had been set up to examine freight movement associated with seaports, a permanent heads-of-department committee had been established to advise on rapid transport, a committee of inquiry had been set up to investigate urban passenger transport, and as well there was a cabinet committee on shipping. In 1968, the establishment of a Ministry of Transport with expanded functions was approved by cabinet but Railways, Marine, and the corporations remained outside. In 1972 Marine was divided, with Fisheries going to Agriculture and the rest to the Ministry of Transport in the form of a Marine Division.

So how did Norman Kirk arrange his cabinet to deal with Transport? The 1962 Royal Commission of Inquiry had reported that 'At Cabinet level co-ordination will be easier if one Minister holds all the transport portfolios'. A Cabinet Committee on Transport would also continue to be necessary.[5] This had been the structure when Labour became the government. Kirk, however, gave Transport, Railways, and Civil Aviation to three different ministers, each with other, non-cognate, portfolio responsibilities. This splitting of responsibility for a general area was typical of Kirk's portfolio allocation. It was believed that Kirk was endeavouring to break up the administrative power of the public service in order to put the power of decision-making back into the cabinet room.[6]

Kirk's notion of cabinet decision-making leant toward competition and independence at both the cabinet and administrative levels. The whole structure of his cabinet illustrates how he saw the role and tasks of party government, revealing his emphasis upon cabinet direction and control over policy. The experiment was not altogether successful, however. When

Muldoon became Prime Minister in 1975 he followed the co-ordinating rather than the competitive model and gave all the transport portfolios to one minister. As a footnote, Jim Bolger in 1990, having inherited the new, slimmed-down public service where major transport areas had been devolved to territorial authorities, corporatized or privatized, had two ministers with responsibility for areas of transport.

Transport has been, then, a classic example of the problems of co-ordination being pushed up to cabinet level because its separate structures make co-ordination lower down difficult. It would appear that the most practical cabinet solution would have been to have put at least the major portfolios in the hands of one minister. This did not always happen.

Some ministers are laden with several weighty departments and cannot possibly give their full attention to all. Generally, ministers have too many minor portfolios, reflecting the multi-unit system of New Zealand government. The overall structure of New Zealand government requires complex mechanisms of co-ordination to overcome these difficulties. It is supposed that the collective wisdom of cabinet will provide inter-minister and inter-agency co-ordination. Thus structure interacts with behaviour: the cabinet's collective coherence has been necessary for it to impose its will on the administrative fragmentation beneath it. The characteristics of the cabinet structure may also have helped the personalization of politics in New Zealand, and prime ministerial power.

The idea of the two-tier cabinet as a solution to the structural problems has been around for a long time; it is periodically revived as a solution to cabinet's inefficiencies. Kirk, for example, proposed such a structure, and it was revived by Mike Moore when Leader of the Labour Party. Norman Kirk explained in interview in 1971 that a two-tiered cabinet would enable some people to delegate and to have more time to spend on policy-making rather than administration. The second-tier minister could devote time to the detailed examination of policy. This proposal was opposed by Keith Holyoake who felt that it would lead to inefficiency, prevent departments from being able fully to express their views, and lead to the loss of touch with departments because the inner circle would not have regular contact with them. He said: 'Either a Minister is responsible for his Department or he is not . . . there is no half-way house. The cabinet committee system was sufficient, especially the Economic Committee.[7] Holyoake's argument rests on committees uniting ministers personally representing each department, and on an idea of ministerial responsibility that is more myth than practice in New Zealand government. It is of interest that Kirk's successor, David Lange, took the first step towards a two-tier ministry by appointing ministers outside cabinet, a move continued by Jim Bolger.

Spreading the Workload

In 1935 arrangements were made for non-cabinet members to help the ministers and share the emoluments, although the ministers were to remain responsible for their portfolios. This broke down because of 'inescapable personal friction' between members who wanted responsibility and ministers who did not want to lose any.[8] Since then several arrangements have been employed: the use of under-secretaries, associate and/or assistant ministers, as well as ministers outside cabinet.

Although under-secretaries can take much of the load from their ministers, their roles are strictly circumscribed. It is the ministers who must answer to their colleagues in cabinet, in caucus, and to the Opposition in the House. The work of an under-secretary tends to be confined, therefore, to limited administrative matters (Muldoon as Under-Secretary to the Minister of Finance handled the decimalization of the currency) and to assuming part of the burden of meeting delegations and speaking to groups. Important policy matters must still be dealt with by the minister. Sometimes, if given a delegated task specifically by the minister, under-secretaries have attended cabinet meetings, especially if they have been given the responsibility of looking after a particular portfolio area. On the whole, though, as one National under-secretary explained in interview in the early 1970s, the position 'involves decisions but not decisions of policy—decisions within established policy—that is, at administrative level'. And since the demarcation between policy and administrative matters can be notoriously difficult to define, and since the instinct of the under-secretary is therefore to proceed cautiously, the workload of the minister may not be appreciably diminished. It can, in fact, produce yet another problem of co-ordination.

Associate and assistant ministers may or may not attend cabinet, depending on their status. The difference between an associate and an assistant minister is somewhat indistinct and is probably primarily a hierarchical distinction. An assistant or associate can usefully serve as a 'stand-in' for an absent or overseas minister and for committee work. Sometimes these ministers additionally have portfolios in their own right which may lessen the usefulness of their assistance to the minister to whom they are attached. Jim Bolger, perhaps because he had ministers outside cabinet (and under-secretaries, also, after the 1993 election), used only the 'associate' label. Ministers outside cabinet in the Bolger Government had regular meetings with the Prime Minister in lieu of the full cabinet meetings. These occurred 'not as often as we would like, or he would like, I guess, but those are very good'.

An example from the 1990–93 period of how responsibilities can be shared out was education, which has always been demanding because of its volume of correspondence and numerous requests for speeches and meetings. Even if a government is not initiating change, education requires considerable systems maintenance. If a government is also planning reforms, as the 1990–93 National Government was, then it is a particularly work-intensive and politically salient portfolio. Three ministers were involved, two in cabinet and one outside, each minister with 'clearly defined roles'. The main Minister, Lockwood Smith, kept responsibility for policy right across the educational sector whilst the operational areas were devolved: Smith kept tertiary operations himself, and gave primary and secondary schools to Roger McClay (a former teacher), and early childhood to John Luxton, also responsible for buildings. Evidently, 'the whole thing was split two ways to ensure that no one could hive off down a track on their own. Once a week we meet formally, to discuss and plan ahead and co-ordinate strategies . . . the problem is the need to be careful never to enable the media to try and claim [a] difference of opinion.' And, 'So whatever issue arises for us, we will usually need to consult at least one of the others . . . and then if any one of us is away, others cover.' The minister outside cabinet handled much of the correspondence, the 'ministerials', and the meetings with groups.

Sometimes associate ministers are responsible for the drudgery of legislation preparation but, of course, only the responsible minister may present a bill to Parliament.

Co-ordination amongst ministers with associating responsibilities was not usually seen as a problem, according to the evidence of the 1990s interviews—although the ministers might well have chosen not to discuss the difficulties. Most groups had regular arrangements for meetings outside the formal cabinet committee structure. Finance, for example, used to 'meet every Monday at the beginning of the week and prior to cabinet, to go through any issues that will arise at cabinet level. And then we meet quite regularly during the week and probably two or three times during the week to look at issues that come up that are causing concern to [the Minister].' The issues were then processed through the Expenditure Control Committee.

However collaborative the process of policy-making, ministers outside cabinet may feel excluded. This is particularly likely when those in the centre of power far outnumber those excluded from it. Thus it is surprising that New Zealand ministers have not chosen a more British structure for their administrations, with a small cabinet and a large ministry outside cabinet. Defining the boundaries of collective responsibility can also pose difficulties: ministers outside cabinet 'have to sing the same tune as everybody else and yet . . . don't have any influence on the debate'. When asked whether this was a difficulty in caucus, the minister responded, 'But I don't have too much difficulty, you know, c'est la vie, this is the position I'm in, and come the time when I may be round the big table I can have an input, but in the meantime, I'll just continue to do the job that I've got.' In sum, for another of the ministers outside cabinet, 'it's not easy because you don't have the same access to knowledge of some decision-making, [you] don't have access to the Prime Minister in the same direct way that others have, and at the same time you have cabinet responsibility, to comply with the decisions, and abide by them without demur.' Nevertheless, opinions varied. Another non-cabinet minister said,

> I have no complaints personally, because I have access to the cabinet if I want to go on a departmental matter. . . . I probably would feel disappointed if one day I didn't have an opportunity to sit in the cabinet, but I'm a great believer in the value of experience in this place, and I think we undervalue experience, particularly in ministers. And I'm pretty happy to learn to walk before I get asked to run.

The Cabinet

The Role of Cabinet

If we mean by 'cabinet' the full complement of ministers meeting together to make decisions, then cabinet does not make all or even most of the decisions. Perhaps ninety per cent of all decisions are made by cabinet committees, according to a minister from the fourth Labour Government. The evidence from the National ministers did not contradict this generalization. Thus it is more accurate to conceive cabinet itself as heading a system of committees, all theoretically working to common purpose, than it is to see it as a single encompassing organism, or a solitary 'black box'. Nevertheless, the collective body of cabinet, that is, all ministers meeting together, is the authoritative body for the taking of decisions. The *Cabinet Office Manual* states that:

> Cabinet Committees have various powers delegated from Cabinet. These should be exercised in a way which avoids overwhelming Cabinet with minor matters. ALL Cabinet Committee decisions are reported to Cabinet for confirmation either as recommendations contained in a separate Cabinet agenda item; or as part of the 'weekly report', which refers to Cabinet all other Committee decisions made during the previous week.

And, 'Cabinet must retain the ultimate power of decision. MINISTERS AND DEPARTMENTS MUST NOT ACTION CABINET COMMITTEE DECISIONS UNTIL THEY HAVE BEEN CONFIRMED (OR AMENDED) AT THE FOLLOWING WEEK'S CABINET MEETING. . . .'

Cabinet meets on Mondays for anything from a few hours to all day, depending upon the agenda and the personal style of the PM who, as chair, can influence the order and composition of the agenda, the informal rules of the meeting, and the pace of discussion. Indeed, one of the key prime ministerial powers is control over the official agenda. Apart from the PM's general influence over the policy programme, 'There are three resources open to prime ministers in cabinet; they can keep items off the agenda; they can flood it with items; or they can list them in an order most convenient to themselves.'[10] An example of the first tactic was when, according to members of his then cabinet, Robert Muldoon, Prime Minister and also Minister of Finance, was the only minister who knew the details and had seen the papers relating to the dollar crisis of mid-July 1984.[11] But generally in New Zealand the order of the agenda is left to the Cabinet Office, thus leaving timing and pace in the hands of the chair. Also the unusually long agendas for cabinet characteristic of New Zealand and Australia tend to give 'a distinct advantage to dominant prime ministers like Fraser and Muldoon'.[12] In the six months ending 31 December 1991, cabinet had met 28 times and considered an average of 29.5 agenda items.[13] Evidently the Muldoon Government usually considered about 35 items, seemingly a rather greater number.[14] These raw figures, however, tell us little, since they do not discriminate between major and minor agenda items and issues.

Except for the Secretary to Cabinet (or assistants), no public servants attend cabinet. Ministers outside cabinet attend only when particularly required to do so. Cabinet meetings, and the meetings of cabinet committees, aim to be consensual, are confidential, and only the formal decisions are recorded, not the discussions that precede them. These characteristics reinforce and protect the consensual nature of the decision-making process. The *Manual* warns that ministers and officials 'should not disclose either proposals likely to be considered at forthcoming meetings, or the nature or content of the discussions and the views of individual Ministers expressed at the meeting itself.'[15]

Submissions to cabinet must be received by the Cabinet Office (CO) by 9.00 on the Thursday morning before the Monday meeting of cabinet to allow time for the CO to prepare a summary of the submission, to gather any other necessary material, and to copy and distribute the submission to all ministers. There are stringent requirements laid down in the *Manual* for the submission of late papers.[16] The unstated purpose of requiring papers to be submitted on time is to protect the collective decision-making authority of cabinet, for ministers can hardly be expected to contribute usefully to discussion if they have had insufficient time to read the papers. One of Roger Douglas's tactics whilst Minister of Finance in the fourth Labour Government was to submit papers too late for ministers to assemble arguments against his proposals. Another Douglas tactic was to argue out major economic policy initiatives with his Finance cabinet colleagues and then take them directly to Cabinet 'once they were confident that they could command a majority in support of their agreed policy recommendations'.[17]

Votes are very seldom taken at cabinet meetings. Keith Holyoake once said, 'it would be a minor tragedy if you had to take votes in Cabinet. Immediately there would be the danger of little caves [sic] establishing, or little groupings that might become permanent groupings, and in a team that works as closely together as Cabinet has to over the years, that would be thought a very great danger.'[18] Holyoake's attitude is not an uncommon one: 'Where the solidarity of the group is highly valued, a formal vote with its revelations of division in the group will not be considered a democratic means of decision-making.'[19] Indeed, Holyoake said to me that it was 'years since I just went round the Cabinet' getting their opinion on a subject. Once a decision has been reached it must be supported collectively by all the ministers.

What does cabinet do? The *Manual* states that the areas on which cabinet takes decisions include:

—major policy issues;
—important spending proposals and financial commitments;
—proposals involving new legislation or regulations;
—matters which concern the interests of a number of government
    departments;
—controversial matters;
—ratification of international treaties and agreements.[20]

Cabinets also discuss other important business such as political strategy; and there is a weekly report which sets out all the decisions made by all the cabinet committees which met during the previous week. The issues, and the decisions made on those issues by full cabinet, are contained in the cabinet minutes. Also, for example, with political patronage appointments (on advisory boards and so forth) and bills to be introduced to the House, cabinet might decide to take the issues to caucus, perhaps then to be referred back to a cabinet committee or full cabinet at a later stage.

The New Zealand cabinet has notoriously been concerned with the minutiae of policy decisions. There were hints in the interviews that cabinet still deals with issues that would be better dealt with at other levels. 'Cabinet can easily become bogged down by relatively trivial matters that could either be dealt with at ministerial level or be dealt with at departmental level, rather than clogging up the machinery of government.' Nevertheless, it has been reported that cabinet no longer deals with the details it once did, particularly on expenditure items, such as whether or not 'the Forest Service should purchase a tractor for use on the West Coast'.[21]

Cabinet as a collectivity certainly plays a strategic role in terms of political strategy, but it has been too big, too cumbersome, and too loaded with poor ministers at the tail end, to act as a policy strategy body. An observer noted that cabinets have not taken on the policy strategy role 'with any alacrity but have preferred to operate principally as a forum for collective decision-making on individual issues thrown up by the range of portfolios. (All the big issues *end up* in Cabinet of course.)'[22] On individual issues, and on the big issues, cabinet acts as a forum within which conflict can be expressed and resolved.

The Politics of Internal Disagreement

Cabinet must be publicly united to survive. Yet, at the same time, it contains ministers with frequently divergent political viewpoints and, naturally, ambitious, competitive, even combative personalities. Even with a PM as dominating as Robert Muldoon, there was conflict within cabinet, including objections against the Leader's views. A minister who had served under Muldoon said in interview, 'I fought the battles I thought I could win with him. And I did win quite a few. General principle things, like freezing industry deregulation, transport delicensing—a number of those battles, in which I wasn't the only person of course.' The minister added that, after cabinet has disagreed, 'it's obviously very important that a consensus then develops'. Jim Bolger, it was reported, had been 'actually particularly good at that', allowing discussion to continue for far longer than did Muldoon. This has meant that now 'there's far more opportunity to influence the debate'.

Most of what is known about disagreements within cabinet tends to be the dramatic and controversial policy and personality splits, rather than the everyday process of argument and dispute. Therefore I asked the ministers of the Bolger Government about the sorts of things that ministers differed upon. One minister, when asked about internal differences within the Bolger Government, commented:

> It depends on the issue. If you are looking at, say, divisions over social issues, divisions normally break along lines of consideration of the humanities [sic] and consideration of the financial consequences, and there's always a tension between the two. And there is always insufficient financial resources to do all the things that you would like to in the area of the humanities, so then it's a matter of how you make the decisions, about where you will cut the particular cloth, where you will cut the particular policy proposal.

When asked whose opposition within cabinet should be feared, the minister responded that it was rather a matter of 'being able to get a balance between what are emotional drivers and what are practical drivers—everybody finds it difficult to do things that they know are going to impact in a detrimental way on people'. Similar sentiments were expressed by another minister who said that 'I suppose I feel happy with people [who] are interested in running the nation as a business, rather than away on some sort of welfare binge. We haven't got many on a welfare binge in cabinet.'

The differences that emerged in the interviews were mainly about the pace of the changes to the welfare system being instituted by the National Government, not about overall economic and social goals. In part, though, pace of change was associated by some ministers with perceived ideological position: the 'dry' right wishing to act more swiftly than their colleagues. This was also interwoven with personality differences: 'you feel far closer to those whom you are ideologically more in tune with.' A distinction emerged between the pragmatic and the ideas-driven ministers. The same minister just quoted was wary of opposition from 'anyone on the far right', partly because they were backed by Treasury. Ideology, the minister added, had become much more important than it had been in the 1970s, 'when you had a very homogeneous ideology, and a very practical, more innocent day and age. Now you're very conscious that you're dealing [at] an ideological level with a lot of debate.'

Overall, the emphasis throughout the interviews was upon active divergence and lobbying before decisions were made, and conformity and unity afterwards; hence the lack of cabinet support for Winston Peters who challenged both the regular policy process and prime ministerial authority. The differences within the Government were not, however, to do with the basic agenda of politics, for all were agreed that they were in office to make individuals more responsible for their affairs, and to reduce the scope of the state, thereby, they believed, also improving the economy and the fiscal position of government.[23] The differences concerned the pace of change, the extent to which ideas should drive the political agenda, and personality—'sometimes we have some crazy notion that we're going to lose face unless we revisit the decision we've made and get it right.' The other sort of issue that caused internal dissension was reportedly 'moral' issues.

A minister agreed that there was some log-rolling in cabinet but hastily denied adopting such a tactic:

> I don't doubt that some do. I don't roar round the backbench trying to get support. Perhaps it's not quite so necessary in some of the things that I do, but if there's something which is particularly important I might ring one or two of

the cabinet guys and say, 'Look, this is coming up, I think it's important'. But more than that I don't do; I leave it to their judgement.

Seniority counted, according to one minister. 'Generally speaking, senior ministers, and that doesn't imply cabinet ranking, simply use their seniority to demand a resolution in their favour or whatever they think is appropriate. And that can be a disappointment, because that's one of the things a junior minister has to accept, that's just the way the cookie crumbles.' The senior ministers, it was said, have access to the Prime Minister. A colleague commented:

> There are some power-broking ministers in the key decision ministries—the state service sector and finance ministries, and obviously the Prime Minister and that grouping. What they think will have substantial influence, but I think essentially it depends what issues are running. You tend to get groups of people in cabinet who have expertise in a range of issues.

But another minister disagreed: 'It's the merits of the case that really prevail. It's not whether someone's driving the policy from the top or not, [who] happens to be number one or number two or number three.'

The behavioural norm was strongly consensual because 'If you make competitive decisions, then under the convention of collective responsibility you place just too much pressure on ministers to continue to keep that very important concept of collective responsibility, so decisions as far as is humanly possible must be made on the basis of consensus'. The cabinet would 'spend the time to talk through it and to get to the point where even those who disagree can feel comfortable that they can support the decision'. This last point reinforces the importance of the New Zealand cabinet as a collective decision-making body. Indeed, Patrick Weller has argued that cabinets here and in Australia 'probably make more collective decisions and certainly consider many more items than their counterparts in Britain and Canada. They have a solidifying and supportive role.'[24] The first is certainly true of the 1990s; the second is probably now a less valid judgement. The continued theme of New Zealand cabinet government has been that it is government by cabinet rather than by Prime Minister. Thus the exigencies of party ideology and political structure work together and keep on reasserting themselves over and above the prime ministerial personalities who come and go.

The commonality of long-term policy aim strengthened the position of the Bolger cabinet against the criticisms of many in caucus between 1990 and 1993, especially after the departure of Winston Peters. This was a key difference between the National Government and its Labour predecessor, which was riven by ideological as well as interpersonal dissension. Ironically, however, failing to listen to caucus criticisms put the Bolger government in a similar circumstance to Labour, for in the 1993 general election National lost seventeen seats.[25] Thus ideological unity can unite a cabinet and at the same time help it lose, or come close to losing, an election.

Which ministers were the most effective in cabinet discussion and debate? These were the ministers who demonstrated 'distinctive argument, consistency of opinion, personality, [and] determination'. Those who were practical, logical, and consistent were all rated as adding to personal effect-iveness. Careful preparation was frequently mentioned by the ministers: 'I think effectiveness in Cabinet relates in many ways to how well one does one's homework. If you study the issues very carefully and do your reading on the background papers, I think you can make a much better contribution.' Turning the question round the other way, when do ministers get worried in cabinet? 'The answer is, if you find yourself in a small minority, that's the time to get worried. That's because we operate a majoritarian system, even in cabinet, at the end of the day.'

The Cabinet Committees

> Cabinet committees are meant to exercise fully the authority delegated to them by Cabinet; otherwise the point of establishing them will be lost, the proper business of the Committees will be impeded and the Agenda of Cabinet itself will be unnecessarily cluttered.[26]

Or, as the more recent version of the *Cabinet Office Manual* has it, 'Cabinet Committees have various powers delegated from Cabinet. These should be exercised in a way which avoids overwhelming Cabinet with minor matters.'[27]

The cabinet committees give detailed attention to policy decisions and proposed legislation, consult with the civil servants involved, and report their recommendations to cabinet. In this way much detailed work is avoided by full cabinet. Brian Talboys, a former minister and Deputy PM, once said that the committees are not primarily decision-making bodies, for the full cabinet makes the decision, but instead committees are 'policy-forming'.[28] This comment distinguishes between cabinet as the authoritative body in the decision-making process—as demonstrated by the quotation above from the *Manual*—and cabinet committees as normally the sources of the 'real' decisions, paralleling Bagehot's distinction between the dignified and efficient parts of the constitution. Interestingly, when Geoffrey Palmer when PM was asked in Parliament whether it was 'correct that Cabinet only "rubber stamps" decisions made elsewhere, as reportedly stated by the Minister of Tourism', he replied, 'Detailed discussion of policy proposals takes place at Cabinet Committees and all Ministers concerned take a full part in these discussions. As stated in the Cabinet Office Manual, Cabinet retains the ultimate power of decision, and may direct a Committee to review or further discuss a recommendation made to Cabinet.'[29] Marie Shroff, Secretary of Cabinet, from her vantage point as the only regular observer, says that 'Cabinet can and often does amend the decisions of its committees'.[30]

Although various *ad hoc* committees were set up earlier, the committee system in institutionalized form dates from the early 1950s. Keith Jackson argued that one of the reasons for the relatively early development of cabinet committees in New Zealand was the fact that ministers are more distant from their departments and closer to their ministerial colleagues than are their British counterparts. This is partly a consequence of spatial relationships; ministers' offices in New Zealand are not housed with their bureaucrats but in Parliament Buildings.[31] Indeed, ministers have a building all to themselves (the 'Beehive', designed by Sir Basil Spence). Of course the causal relationship might be the other way around; ministers have been housed together in the precincts of Parliament precisely because their primary relationships are with one another rather than with their senior public servants. Whatever the direction of historical causality, ministers look primarily inwards towards their colleagues and, increasingly, the advisers in their private offices, rather than outwards to the bureaucrats. The cabinet committees play an important role not only in making decisions but in consolidating political relationships and co-ordinating bureaucratic ones.

There has been no research that traces the development of the cabinet committees, and this now would be difficult since names and memberships were until the 1960s seldom made public. (In Britain, it was not until the 1980s that the names and membership of the committees were permitted to become public knowledge.) Austin Mitchell, however, reported that, when Keith Holyoake was Prime Minister, there were nine committees: Defence, Economic and Financial Questions, Government Administration, Works, Transport, Overseas Travel, Legislative and Parliamentary Questions, Social Questions, and Tasman Pulp and Paper. Each of these had about half-a-dozen members and all were served by the Cabinet Secretariat. Mitchell said that Works, Economic and Financial, Government Administration, and Legislative were the most important. Also there were many *ad hoc* cabinet committees at the time, making a total of forty or fifty.[32] This overloading of government by committee pales into insignificance compared with Margaret Thatcher's approximate 160 groups in 1985–86.[33] One of the trends in New Zealand cabinet government has been the way that its processes and structures have become bureaucratized, and the cabinet committee system is no exception. Prime ministers have over the years gradually reduced the number of committees, especially *ad hoc* ones, and standardized the way in which they conduct their business.

Brian Talboys said that in 1970 he was a member of fifteen cabinet committees and that this meant spending ten to twelve hours each week at meetings of cabinet or cabinet committees.[34] He saw the Works Committee as one of the most powerful, but also influential were the Economic Committee, Overseas Trade, Legislative and Parliamentary Questions, and State Services.[35] In 1972, after John Marshall had become prime minister, it was reported that there were eleven permanent committees: Economic, State Services, Social Affairs, Environment, Works, Foreign Affairs, Defence, Legislative, Civil Defence, Honours, and Parliamentary Buildings.[36] This represented a reduction in the number of cabinet committees.

Norman Kirk's Labour administration had nine cabinet committees: Civil Defence, Economic, Honours and Appointments, Legislative and Parliamentary Questions, Parliamentary Buildings, Policy and Priorities (an innovation), Social Affairs, State Services, and Works, with Economic and Policy and Priorities probably the most important. They varied in size of membership from five to eight. There were also subcommittees on transport co-ordination and on efficiency in the State Services. Most ministers were on three or four committees while Wallace Rowling and Kirk were each on five. There was no Foreign Affairs and Defence Committee: Kirk himself held the relevant portfolio.[37] When Robert Muldoon was PM there were about thirteen standing committees.[38]

The composition of the major committees and their chairs are recognition of and have consequences for the inner and informal allocation of power within cabinet—an aspect that is difficult to analyse properly because of the sketchy nature of the information available. Just sometimes, though, fragments reach the public about the inner struggle and how the committees are involved in this. For example, in 1958, the Cabinet Economic Committee was the centre of activity where the Minister of Finance, Arnold Nordmeyer, and the Minister of Commerce, Phil Holloway, were the most active.[39] Another example comes from 1970 when it was announced that Robert Muldoon was to head the Economic Committee. There were thirty-three committees at this time and Economic was of top importance. This chair put Muldoon in a powerful position although, according to one report, his power was curbed by the presence of both Holyoake and Marshall on the committee also.[40]

It is not surprising that the cabinet committee on economic policy, whatever its name, has usually been a key decision-making group. The

Table 5.2: Cabinet Committees: 1990 and 1993

Committee Type	Post-1990 Election	Post-1993 Election
Strategic	Strategy	——[1]
		Implementation of Social Assistance Reforms[2]
Control	Expenditure Control	——
	State Sector	——
Sectoral	Education, Science & Technology	
	Enterprise, Growth & Employment	
	Environment	
		Education, Training & Employment
		Enterprise, Industry & Environment
	External Relations, Defence & Trade	
	Social & Family Policy	——
	Treaty of Waitangi Issues	——
Procedural	Honours & Appointments	——
	Legislation	——

1. —— signifies that the committee continued to exist.
2. This was an *ad hoc* committee until after the 1993 election.

Table 5.3: Members of the Cabinet Strategy Committee and their other Cabinet Committee Positions, October 1991[1]

Strategy Committee	EST	CEG	ENV	ECC	ERD	SAR	LEG	SOC	STA	TOW
Bolger[2]		*2		*	*2	*				
McKinnon					*			*2		
Birch		*				*2			*2	
Richardson		*	*	*		*				
East					*	*	*2			*
Kidd		*		*						*
Burdon	*	*				*				
Upton	*		*			*		*		
Smith	*2					*			*	
Full committee size	10	13	8	8	8	11	7	9	9	8

1. The committee names were as follows: Strategy (CSC); Education, Science and Technology (EST); Enterprise, Growth and Employment (CEG); Environment (ENV); Expenditure Control (ECC); External Relations, Defence and Security (ERD); Implementation of Social Assistance Reforms (SAR); Legislation (LEG); Social and Family Policy (SOC); State Sector (STA); Treaty of Waitangi (TOW). Appointments and Honours has been omitted.

2. Committee chairperson.

* Indicates membership of the committee.

incoming National Government in 1975 set up an Economic Committee to study the economy and review all aspects of it. This committee was the central committee for co-ordination in the Muldoon Government, made powerful because it was supported by an officials' committee that was Treasury-based.[41] There was also at this time a Cabinet Committee on Expenditure, 'set up to scrutinize expenditure with the immediate object of seeing what could be eliminated or deferred'. It consisted of: the Deputy Minister of Finance, the Minister of Justice, the Minister of State, 'and each cabinet minister in turn as his department came under review'.[42] It is a striking difference between National and Labour that the latter party attempted to elevate some sort of overall planning committee over all others (Kirk's Policy and Priorities Committee, containing the five top-ranked ministers; Lange's Policy Committee). In the case of the fourth Labour Government the establishment of the Policy Committee corresponded with the Treasury's similar recommendation for such a group to be formed.[43] The National

Government under Bolger was an exception to its party tradition with its Policy Strategy Committee, perhaps reflecting its reforming purpose.

Changing policy priorities and ideological doctrines have also affected the range and ranking of cabinet committees. Works is a case in point, a major portfolio until the fourth Labour Government diminished and devolved the New Zealand state, transforming the functions of the Ministry of Works and Development, which it abolished, by corporatizing that body's commercial functions and demolishing its policy and regulatory roles. Before 1984, however, the Cabinet Works Committee was responsible for approving the annual works programme for all government departments as well as some semi-autonomous bodies such as Air New Zealand (now privatized) and the Broadcasting Corporation (completely changed), under the various vote categories. Another important committee under Muldoon was the State Services Committee, a further example of how the changed nature of the state has altered the core functions of the committees.

When Jim Bolger became Prime Minister, he altered the system established under Labour,[44] and then, after the 1993 general election, he reduced the total number of committees (see Table 5.2). The cabinet committee system between 1990 and 1993 was expressly conceived to lead and co-ordinate the welfare and fiscal reforms of the state. A key figure said in interview, 'We were confronted with making a number of very wide-ranging changes. To have co-ordinated those would require an immense amount of work, and the only way you can do that is not in cabinet but in cabinet committees, [and in] caucus committee work as well. And that's working well.' Bolger initially chaired nearly all the important committees himself, and then transferred the responsibility of the Committee implementing the social policy changes to Bill Birch. In interview Jim Bolger cited a public speech where he said that he was shifting his emphasis to that of leadership, 'to plan and talk through the next step'. Key government initiatives were worked out in the Policy Strategy Committee on which sat most of the most important ministers. These ministers also, according to their interests and strengths, were placed on other committees, thus providing coherence through their memberships (see Table 5.3). The PM said that the Strategy Committees would be the 'driving force' for implementing the Government's policies, and would also be where 'my senior colleagues and I stand back from the daily round and look ahead to determine how the Government should be approaching the challenges and opportunities New Zealand will encounter in the medium to long term'.[45]

Another central committee was the Expenditure Control Committee, a key player in the budgetary process.[46] Doug Kidd, the first chairperson, said when appointed that there would be a 'fundamental' examination of all spending areas, and no departments would be exempt from scrutiny.[47] The Expenditure Control Committee involved

> pretty detailed work that requires a lot of negotiation with Ministers and Ministries, over where their expenditure's going, whether they want to divert funds inside their existing votes, or applications for existing money, and there's quite a lot of negotiation that goes on in trying to finally set what the Crown will accept as additional funding pressures, or what it will allow to be diverted from where originally it intended it to be in the Budget when it brought down the Appropriation Bill.

The Bolger Government followed the recent trend of using the annual Budget—cabinet's spending and income programme which must be approved by Parliament—as its prime exercise in implementing its overall economic and social strategy. The 1991 Budget was particularly ambitious in the range of topics it covered and the reforms it proposed. The process of preparing the Estimates 1991–92 in 1991 was as follows. After cabinet had agreed to the guide-lines for the preparation of departmental budgets, both the Cabinet Expenditure Control Committee and the Strategy Committee then considered the budget round and the overall fiscal strategy. The Expenditure Control Committee directed its standing officials' committee to work with the chief executives to work out where savings could be made. The reports then went back to Expenditure Control Committee to determine the expenditure level for each Vote in accordance with the cabinet guide-lines, and to decide where the savings should be made. Expenditure Control Committee then made recommendations to Strategy Committee, and from there they went to full cabinet.[48]

At the same time as all this was going on, a review of social policy was being conducted by the Prime Ministerial Committee on Reform of Social Assistance which, between 30 April and 30 July, met twenty-three times.[49]

The significance of the cabinet committees in the making of the annual budget is obvious, a contrast to the Labour Government, when economic and financial policy was made bilaterally between the Minister of Finance and the relevant minister. (In March 1989, however, under Geoffrey Palmer an *ad hoc* committee on expenditure was reconstituted as the Expenditure Review Committee.) One of the ministers interviewed compared the Muldoon years, when even cabinet ministers did not see the Budget papers, to the Bolger Government where 'there's been a much greater level of co-operation and understanding and general discussion on all the issues'. Nevertheless, 'If there's a failure in the system it is the fact that you have a Budget. You should actually have a series of decisions that do not involve a one-off Budget. The Budget's become far too dominant as a decision-making process, and consequently it fails.'

A senior minister in interview observed that, since 1990, the Government had been 'dominated by social policy issues'. One very important committee (initially *ad hoc*, later made a standing committee) was the Cabinet Committee on the Implementation of Social Assistance Reform,[50] designed to put in place the health, social welfare, education, housing, and superannuation changes. A group of top officials (including senior managers from Treasury, the State Services Commission, and the Prime Minister's Department) was appointed to 'manage the business of that Committee. . . . And they have power to actually manage the process of materials coming up, and if it's not a good standard they get the officials to manage it. We don't want to worry about trivia and detail, arguing about fact. I mean if it's fact we want to know what the facts are.'

Another important committee has been the Legislation Committee, which plays a vital role in the passage of legislation by scrutinizing drafts, looks at technical aspects (for example, powers to make regulations in bills), and also determines the order of priority of the drafting of bills. Geoffrey Palmer reported that, in the Labour Government, the senior government whip was a member of this committee, because the whip held responsibility for the passage of a bill through the House.[51]

Since the fourth Labour Government all ministers have been permitted to attend all committees, a safe enough concession given that ministerial work-loads preclude wide attendance. The CO ensures that ministers are aware when issues pertaining to their own areas are being discussed, and, according to the ministers, they then ensure that they attend: 'I don't want to be spending all my time running round all the committees, but where there's a specific matter of discussion, I make it a point to ensure everyone knows that I want to be there during that time, and so there's a bit of flexibility.' When asked whether the views of non-committee members would count as much as the ones who were formally on those committees, a minister who had cited an example of an area discussed by Strategy Committee replied: 'I think everyone's point of view is accepted. . . . I never felt any disadvantage by not being a formal member of the Committee.'

The frequency of the meetings of the cabinet committees varies. External Relations and Defence, reportedly primarily a reactive committee, for example, met only when there was some matter to be discussed. The others met weekly. After the 1993 general election Bolger abolished the External Relations and Defence Committee, and recognized the differential workloads of the committees by stating publicly that the six most important (contained in Table 5.2) met weekly whilst the rest were to meet fortnightly. The numbers attending the committees also varied. There might be 'seven or eight ministers at some of the state sector ones, whereas . . . we'd have four or five normally at the Treaty of Waitangi issues because it's a rather specialized area. But the principle works the same, you get the officials in, you ask them questions if anybody wants to, and then you get on with what you're going to recommend to cabinet.'

Under Labour between 1984 and 1990 departmental officers played a lesser role than previously; the system of officials' committees that previously shadowed the ministerial ones was largely abolished.[52] Members of the Bolger team emphasized in interview that they had revived the officials' committees and, moreover, ensured that top officials were on them. The *Manual* spells out the requirements, saying that each department must have no more than two officials present for any one agenda item; and that they must be waiting outside the committee room before the start of the meeting since agenda items were not always taken in order. Officials are to be 'chosen for their grasp of the subject matter under consideration'. When called into the committee room officials 'should confine their contribution to answering questions posed by Ministers and should leave the meeting room as soon as Ministers indicate that questions to officials are completed.'[53] Submissions cannot be made by officials, only by ministers.

Obviously, ministers and staff will usually go to a cabinet committee with their minds pretty well made up about the decisions they want, having discussed the issues themselves. But committee approval is not always forthcoming:

> They don't get the rubber stamp, because most of the other ministers want to know why and how, and often public servants are given the run-around if they haven't given a suitable reply, or a full enough reply. I notice Doug Kidd—he's always interesting to watch—and he just says, 'Don't hand me that crap.' And the Prime Minister will say, 'Look, come off it, you know, that's just ridiculous.' . . . And so they really are put on a hot spot as officials, and they are expected to perform, and they can get roasted if they don't. But they're paid well for what they have between their ears, and they are expected to perform. Ministers can't [keep] track of everything, and it always amazes me to see the number of people that come in. I sit there sometimes and there's two rows of officials advising! I think aren't there some generalists in all of this? But everybody has . . . their [own] sort of specific responsibility, rather than a more generalist approach.

Reports of the reception of some of the early drafts from working parties on the social reform programme being designed in the first part of 1991 confirm that those involved were frequently questioned as indicated by the last speaker.

The cabinet committee system plays an important part in making decisions and co-ordinating public policy. But it also has an important place in the leadership contest within cabinet. It may be that, with the large cabinet of twenty ministers now in existence, the most important committee of the time will be, *de facto*, an inner cabinet—a small group of ministers who can effectively determine the major lines of policy and carry the decisions in full cabinet along with them. Since Muldoon's time, and of course he himself was Minister of Finance, the finance ministers have taken the initiative in establishing policy initiatives and parameters: ministers outside the finance portfolios have to some extent become primarily reactive to the macro-economic goals and the policy initiatives of finance ministers.

To summarize, what are the roles of the cabinet committees? First, they operate as mechanisms for relieving the workload of the full cabinet. As such, although they do not take the formal decisions, they certainly make most of them. Second, they are participatory bodies which attempt to bring together policy inputs from experts on one hand and ministers on the other, in a forum designed to encourage the exchange of views. Third, the cabinet committees exist to solve policy tensions, contradictions, and inter-agency and inter-ministerial differences at a manageable level. Fierce arguments are much more politically risky at the level of full cabinet, for then they threaten its collective identity and purpose, as happened during the Lange years. Fourth, the cabinet committees structure cabinet power relationships, a task achieved by effective Prime Ministers in ways that both consolidate their own positions and facilitate the goals of government. Key ministers can be placed on key committees. Fifth, like all committees, the cabinet committees exist to help co-ordinate policy formulation and implementation. This brings us to the topic of the next section.

Policy Co-ordination

The ability to co-ordinate policy across the various policies and decisional arenas is one of the primary, if often unarticulated, strengths of the Westminster variant of responsible party government. The doctrine of collective cabinet responsibility does not of course itself assure the effective co-ordination of policy direction and implementation, but it can facilitate it. Despite the apparent relative ease of policy co-ordination in a cabinet comprised of the members of a single party which commands the majority of the votes in the legislature, in recent years there have been many signs that New Zealand cabinet government has not displayed effective programme coherence or achieved coherent policy implementation. This was a particularly worrying characteristic of the Lange Government, when collective cabinet responsibility was itself at a low ebb, especially between economic and social policy, but also within other policy areas; hence the interest in prime minister's departments and other mechanisms to improve the processes of co-ordination. (See Chapter Seven.) An astute observer of the fourth Labour Government has written that, when that Government assumed power, there was a change of attitude, by senior ministers especially, on 'the balance between their own collegial responsibility and their individual authority in their own portfolios'. The latter became more important than the former.[54]

There is no doubt that the more sweeping the policy change planned by governments, the more difficult it is to co-ordinate those changes. Thus, ironically, it may be that the more ideologically committed and united the cabinet, the more likely it is that co-ordinating and coalescing decisions and policies are difficult tasks, simply because ideological cabinets by definition are devoted to change. Even if we put to one side the task of political survival (an artificial intellectual ploy since collective loyalty, policy co-ordination, and political acceptability form an integral trio), the achievement of radical change directed from the centre is a problematic goal. Preserving more or less the *status quo*, or concentrating upon incremental changes, is much safer, as the literature on policy formulation and implementation informs us.

Not only has the New Zealand policy system had to adjust to ideological government and rapid economic and political change, but also the public sector reforms have almost destroyed the idea and practices of a unified public service. In his autobiography, a former Secretary of Justice, J. L. Robson, reflecting on his experience on the Public Service Commission, wrote: 'Inevitably, personal relationships were formed with other senior officers right across the frontiers of public administration and this was a distinct help later.'[55] This world had all but disappeared by the early 1990s.

Not long after Jim Bolger became Prime Minister he complained to the senior members of the public service that it was time

> to break down the 'little islands' culture that's developed in the public service since the State Sector and Public Finance Acts make the chief executives solely responsible to their own Ministers. Individual agencies cannot operate in splendid isolation from each other. There must be prior consultation between Ministers and between Chief Executives where there are proposals in individual corporate plans with implications for other agencies of the State. Many of our policies require a high degree of integration, collaboration, and cooperation between Ministries and departments to achieve best results.[56]

And Bolger went on to say that that was why he had decided to establish an Enterprise Unit as part of a restructured Prime Minister's Department and Office, restructured the cabinet committee system, and re-established the Officials' Committees.[57]

Thus, having taken some relatively minor initiatives at the political level of the executive, the Prime Minister put the blame squarely upon the public sector changes of the mid-1980s. Moreover, as a public servant said to the same Senior Management Conference: 'In broad summary the Government appears not to want political management by its public service, but political agenda management—the agenda being set clearly by itself'—for Bolger also criticized in his speech ideological assertions or value judgements tarted up as serious analysis.[58]

The theme of the Conference was 'What are the Government's collective interests?' Discussion groups had been critical of the set of expectations—fundamental to the Prime Minister's speech—'that Ministers can and will produce some sort of coherent, consistent, mutually reinforcing objectives and outcomes, *and are competent to do*'.[59] So we have a fascinating difference in perspective on the relative roles of cabinet and public service in defining the 'collective interest' of government. It appears, however, that from the additional evidence of interviews with ministers and public servants, there was shared agreement that there was now 'a need for a renewed focus on collective Government and public interests and on providing a quality of policy advice which serves those interests'.[60] Structures and systems were needed to integrate the outputs from the various government agencies. Consultation, part of the integrating purpose, was necessary but it should not be excessive in the way that it had been prior to the government sector reforms. The problems of integration and co-ordination were again referred to by the Minister of State Services, Bill Birch, in his closing speech to the same conference: first, the process of making the structure more collectively responsible would change; and secondly, 'it is the core of our constitution that Cabinet operates on the principle of collective responsibility. We are not going to have fiefdoms operating on their own, doing their own thing, developing within the Government. Chief Executives are therefore charged with implementing Government's policies and not those of individual Ministers.'[61] One wonders to what extent chief executives ought to be expected to act as minders to the barons on behalf of the Crown.

In June 1991 Bill Birch announced the terms of reference for an evaluation of the state sector reforms, especially the workings of the State Sector and Public Finance Acts, and they included looking at the role of individual departments in terms of the overall requirements of Government. The review was led by Basil Logan, a prominent businessman. The review team included officials from the State Services Commission, the Treasury, and the Department of the Prime Minister and Cabinet; and a cabinet sub-committee also was involved. The tenor of the recommendations, too many to discuss here, was that the formal consultative practices between ministers and chief executives, and between governmental agencies, should be extended and clarified.[62]

What, then, were the views of the members of the Bolger Government about co-ordinating policy? Almost uniformly ministers saw co-ordination of policy as a problem for their government. Their explanations for the situation, however, varied. (Interestingly some of the responses had very little to do with co-ordination. I have used their views where appropriate elsewhere.)

First, the problems of government were linked with the problems of the contemporary age:

> I suspect that government today is much more complex than it used to be, even thirty years ago, when the country puddled along pretty much of its own accord, and all the government did was to sort of divide up the spoils! Now it's much more sophisticated, we're very much more part of the international community, the world's spinning a bit faster, you have to get up a bit earlier. We still pass far too many laws about nothing, but when you think back to the days when Parliament sat for six months of the year, now we're sitting ten, and still not enough.

This minister felt that it was not so much the state sector changes that had produced problems, given that the chief executive is still responsible to the minister. What counted was 'the political will of the time, and if a government is cracking at the seams and people hate each other, then they tend to retreat into their corner and nothing gets done at all. So that when we took office, we found a rather unhappy circumstance prevailing.'

Second, therefore, political ineptitude was blamed:

> You've seen the situations where someone says 'this is a bright idea', and suddenly you're implementing it, and you're administering it, and three months later the whole thing falls apart on you. . . You've got to make sure you take people with you, and bring them all along together, and have a good understanding of it. So sometimes some issues get out of the blocks too quickly, and they're halfway down the track before you realize they shouldn't have got out of the blocks.

Nor were all ministers coping well with the requirements of the public sector changes, especially 'getting the hang of the idea that you can write a performance agreement'. In contrast to the ministers who criticized the legislation, this speaker saw it 'as improving enormously (a) the culture, that's critical, and (b) the opportunity, because properly co-ordinated, you can write a set of performance agreements that do reflect the government's priorities.' This particular minister felt that the Government now had better collective co-ordination and integration of social policy, especially through the evolution of key cabinet committees such as Social Assistance Reform, Expenditure Control, and Strategy. Priorities had been set through the budget control exercise. This opinion was shared by a colleague who said:

> I don't actually think you can blame the legislation. I think that there is a territorial argument that has always been there between major departments of government, and it's more often based on prejudice than on the whole issue of outcomes and outputs and how we get there. It is also a political problem that . . . the politicians will sometimes lose sight of the fact that delivering public policy has got to start from the interests of the individuals you're seeking to service.

Third, bureaucratic intransigence or ineptitude was the problem:

> The State Sector Act . . . had advantages in terms of how wages were negotiated, [how] conditions of employment were negotiated; it gave greater responsibility and accountability to the chief executive. But . . . you didn't have the common interest or the collective interest of the firm or the Crown if you like. And so we really had to pull that together. I think it's pretty obvious when you think about it that for any corporate body to operate cohesively then the policy-making must be at the centre. But the administration should be devolved to the managers.

A further comment was that there did not seem to be 'professional relationships across departmental lines; they don't see themselves as colleagues. The common interest of the government doesn't seem to be a part of their environment.' Another colleague expressed it this way: 'The machinery of the public service is not issue oriented, it's very much system oriented. And people don't consult over the most important matters.'

The impact upon cabinet of poor co-ordination at the administrative level was made clear: 'From time to time [we] get departments that are going down a particular course, unaware of the fact that they are cutting across the planning, the prospects, or the developments that are going on in another body. And then it gets to ministerial level and you have to try and unscramble that.' Several times in interview the management of Crown property was given as an example of lack of co-ordinated policy: 'We're saying "Look, it's not on for departments to desert property owned by the Crown and go out and lease or buy high-rise buildings somewhere else just because they think it's better", they've got to take into account the overall collective interests of the Crown.' A further example provided was the charging between departments for information, driven by the fact that they are funded for certain outcomes, and supplying information to another department is not one of those outcomes. 'That's but a small example of the breaking down of the old collegiate system to a more independently structured system.'

A rather more specific diagnosis (which saw ministers as also part of the problem) was that:

> There is a serious imbalance of intellectual capital between the key policy agencies. The Treasury is hopelessly over-endowed with skills and there really needs to be a quite concerted effort to erect the same policy capability in health and welfare at least, and probably in environment. . . . Education'policy capability is abysmal, in terms of the key things governments have to do like spend money and run things. . . . It really raises questions about the structure of the key policy agencies, whether one shouldn't really do something very radical there.

When asked for an example, the speaker cited the splitting off of Treasury's budget management function, and added, 'In terms of policy advice, there is no integrated basis and it just seems to me that just reflects the fact that there's a tribalism out there amongst those key agencies which then gets reflected at the Cabinet table: ministers are proxies for departments who've been fighting battles.'

The various remedies to cure problems of co-ordination were also cited, some involving meetings of the officials' committees: 'We're requiring the officials to work together, to work out their combined thinking before bothering to put it to us.' One client-oriented ministry, for example, has such a committee which was then meeting every six to eight weeks, and which brought together people from a whole range of departments, mainly second- and third-tier public servants. One of its goals was to prevent duplication and, hence, unnecessary public expenditure. The minister concerned commented, 'It is hard though, because all the departments are so busy, following the directions of their own minister. Other solutions were sought by key ministers ensuring that they were absolutely co-ordinated with the Prime Minister every single step of the way.' For the finance area, there was a forum of four that met frequently. It comprised the Prime Minister, the Minister of Finance, the Reserve Bank Governor, and the Secretary of Treasury. Also Treasury advisers were almost automatically put on every review committee during the period of change from the budgetary cuts of welfare benefits in December 1990 through to the wide-ranging changes of the 1991 budget.

So the ministers largely blamed others rather than themselves for the difficulties of co-ordinating policy formulation and implementation, although a few were rather more self-critical. It is, of course, difficult to tell after the events of the last two governments whether their problems were the result of factors endemic to cabinet government or, alternatively, were substantially of their own making.

The Prime Minister, Cabinet, and Policy Co-ordination

What the discussions of co-ordination failed to illuminate, however, was the significance of the Prime Minister as the pivotal source of authority and power and thus responsible for providing direction and coherence to public policy. It has been in response to this role—a response enhanced by the ambitions of governments in office to institute radical policy agendas—that prime ministers have created their own department and office. The failure of the Prime Minister to provide programme coherence, create the right sort of balance between the healthy, pluralistic competitiveness of cabinet and its adherence to united purpose, can destroy that person and the government, as evidenced by the career of David Lange. Yet this task, in a television, opinion-polling age, is an unenviable one.

The second point is that the near-absence of constitutional constraints upon cabinet power, the unwieldy size and structure of cabinet, and the wide range of ministerial abilities, can permit prime ministerial domination, as evidenced by Muldoon's career. But also there are equally compelling competing forces, collegiality in particular. Moreover, there is also the considerable autonomy possessed by individual ministers.

6

MAKING DECISIONS:
THE ROLE OF THE MINISTER

Introduction

Despite the fact that in every system of cabinet government most decisions are made unilaterally, there is little known, here or elsewhere, about the decision-making roles played by individual ministers.[1] Here I wish briefly to set out the scope and parameters of the roles of the individual ministers, including their perceptions of their overall roles—whether they see themselves as primarily policy formulators or managers.

What does the *Cabinet Office Manual* say about individual ministerial autonomy, especially the areas on which ministers have discretion, and those matters which must go to cabinet? Except for the important statutory powers possessed by ministers, the areas over which they have discretion are defined negatively rather than positively, that is, ministers have authority to act on the matters which do not have to go to cabinet or cabinet committee. The *Manual*, outlining the levels of responsibility, says that, 'As a general rule, Ministers should put before their colleagues the sort of issues on which they themselves would wish to be consulted. Where there is uncertainty about the level and type of consideration needed, departments should seek advice from the office of the portfolio Minister, or from the Cabinet Office.'[2] Thus discretionary action depends upon ministers' apprehension of risks and their appreciation of customary actions as much or more than it does upon procedural guide-lines. As a 1972 document said:

> There will be times when a Minister chooses to bring to Cabinet a matter he [sic] could properly decide himself. He may do this because he anticipates that the decision will have repercussions that will be felt by the Government as a whole, or he may do it because he knows that one of his colleagues has strong views on the matter. Cabinet will be grateful to a Minister who demonstrates his concern for collective responsibility in this way.[3]

Given the absence of written guidance, what is the role of the minister? This chapter will assemble the available evidence from the written and verbal sources, and then discuss how ministers perceive their roles.

Ministers, Cabinet, and Cabinet Committees

The individual minister serves as both conduit and initiator in the decision-making structure. In the first category, ministers, using their policy advisers, have to facilitate government policy that is established collectively through the cabinet and the cabinet committee process. The key mechanism by which this purpose is achieved is the cabinet and cabinet committee submission. As has already been shown, almost all submissions go to cabinet committee before they are presented for the scrutiny and formal decision of full cabinet.

The *Cabinet Office Manual* lays down that all submissions must contain:

—the proposal;
—background information;
—comment on the reasons for the proposal;
—an account of the consultation undertaken;
—recommendations.

Also, where necessary, the submissions should include:

—financial implications;
—legislative implications;
—publicity.[4]

Ministers and public servants are enjoined to be brief, although they are also expected to summarize the arguments for and against the proposals, giving reasons for the recommendations of the submission. Even when the various departments with interests in an issue agree on the substance of the recommendation, alternative courses of action have to be set out in the submission. A precise recommendation must be made. A submission must generally recommend one of the following alternatives: invite (a minister to act in a certain way); direct (a department to act); agree (to a proposal or course of action); approve, authorize, defer or decline (a recommendation); note (an action taken or to be taken); or confirm (important when a minister is notifying colleagues of actions taken under statutory or delegated authority).[5]

It is primarily the task of the department concerned to see that the correct consultative procedures have been undertaken, although, of course, the minister carries out a monitoring role in this regard. The participants are given clear guidance in the *Cabinet Office Manual* as to the relevance of the various departments for the various policy areas.[6] And departments are advised that cabinet prefers different views to be part of the submission, even if opposing it, rather than comprising separate reports. As indicated above, any submission with financial implications must be passed to Treasury for comment; Cabinet Office is empowered to reject proposals which do not fulfil this requirement. Full financial details must be contained, including the Parliamentary Vote against which expenditure is to be made.

Ministers also, however, act as ultimate decision takers on issues that do not go to the arenas of collective decision makers. From the public service, from caucus committees, and from groups outside the governmental system, come policy proposals, disputes to be settled, and a host of minor decisions to be taken. Several portfolios generate a great deal of work that is almost always unilateral: Immigration, for example, and the position of Attorney-General. Each of these has, by virtue of its office, legally defined areas of discretionary decision-making. The Minister of Immigration has statutory powers to decide upon the very many immigration appeals. Geoffrey Palmer, as Minister of Justice, was responsible for either 'making or recommending appointments to about 400 positions on about 150 various statutory and allied bodies'. He also was responsible for recommending judicial appointments which, he added, involved 'substantial consultation with interested parties such as the Law Society or other professional groups'. Recommendations of appointments normally have to be approved by the Cabinet Honours and Appointments Committee, cabinet, and caucus.[7]

Ministers also either enter office with specific goals they wish to pursue within their portfolio responsibilities or else develop initiatives whilst in office. One minister in discussion with me during the 1990s explained how a complaints process in one particular area was being established. This was one of the issues 'that concern me'. In another area the minister was promoting work on publicity material to be distributed through the schools. A further example was a minister who had initiated a review of all the programmes in a particular portfolio area. Ministers and Associate Ministers of Finance have particularly onerous roles in the year-long budgetary process. Much of that work was reportedly 'detailed, consistent work'. The two key tasks in Finance are to work through the budgetary process to set the expenditure targets, and then, 'having made the decisions about our budget, how we now live inside the constraints of that budget'.

The devolution of the state promulgated by the fourth Labour Government removed from ministers many tasks carried out by their predecessors. Now, the state-owned enterprises, for example, are

> driven very much by the plans of the enterprises themselves. We have to go through the processes of approval of their business plans, approval of their statements of corporate intent, and then deal with the specific issues as they arise. So, that is really driven by some very clear and concise matters that you know are going to occur twice a year, and that's dealing with the corporate

plans and those sorts of things, and then driven really by the organizations themselves, in that if there are problems you have to deal with those as they arise.

The minister added an illuminating comment about the National Government's future plans for SOEs. A further component to this portfolio responsibility was 'when we decide that we are going to market one of those particular businesses and move them from public ownership into private ownership'. This required

> quite a high level of intensive activity, normally for a relatively short period of time until you get the process underway, but a sales process generally takes about six to eight months, so there's quite an extensive period of activity surrounding that business as you go through that process.

The public sector reforms were an attempt to shift ministers' attention to focusing upon the strategic policy agenda, leaving their public servants to deal with detail and the implementation process. But judging by the response of one minister, further devolution was necessary, for there was still the tendency not to spend sufficient time on major issues, 'spending quite a significant period of time on issues that are of a minor nature, trying to make decisions on some 10, 20 or 100 thousand dollar issue when there's something that costs 100 million dollars in waiting'.

Ministers are also key communicators, establishing links between the Government and the various parts of New Zealand society. One of Bolger's ministers commented, 'Bear in mind in my area you had an adversarial, almost emotional suspicion by business of government that we had to change. And we have had to re-establish a dialogue, a consultative process. . . .'

Time, Tasks, and the Minister

Given the various tasks and roles to be performed by ministers, it is to be expected that managing their time efficiently can be a major problem. Indeed, Palmer, reflecting on his own executive experience, wrote that 'The life of a Minister is a life of constant even frenetic activity.' His view was that the 'key role of Ministers is to make decisions—big decisions which decide the course of the country'.[8] Since there is, again, very little known about this, ministers were asked in the 1990s interviews about how they coped with their bundles of portfolios.

Personality is obviously an important factor: 'Some ministers have confidence in allowing more of the decision making to take place at departmental level, and other ministers want to make certain that they know everything that's going on.' Unsurprisingly the traditional 'big' portfolios grab the most attention of those ministers who have to grapple with the fostering of a bundle of portfolios. But personal style, the political salience of the portfolio area, and the particular interests of the minister concerned, all appeared as factors in determining how ministers allocated their time. The interviews also showed that time allocation was one of the most difficult tasks faced by the ministers simply because it involved deciding upon the order of priorities as well as achieving efficient outcomes.

Chairing the major cabinet committees is a particularly large commitment for the few ministers who are in this role since, evidently, it can take as much as forty per cent of a person's time. But the evidence of the interviews was that all ministers spend a substantial proportion of their time upon the activities of the collectivity: 'The amount of time you have to spend on cabinet papers, which have nothing to do with your own portfolio, would cost you probably twenty-to-thirty per cent of your whole week. It's the time you require to think about it, and discuss it.' A colleague commented, 'Then you have got your cabinet committees, and they have a bad habit of dropping papers on you, normally the night before the meeting, and you really have to make some decisions about how hard you're going to work through those, relative to the other things you're doing.'

These sorts of comments suggest that 'cabinet' government rather than 'ministerial' government has a high degree of priority and legitimacy, for ministers intent upon their own worlds of policy and ministry would not accord the activities of the collectivity such high priority. Furthermore, the tone of the interviews also suggested that real debate exists round the cabinet table, at least under the chairing of Jim Bolger.

Ministers ride (or are driven by) a weekly cycle, primarily dictated by the cabinet meeting on Monday and the requirement that all submissions to cabinet and cabinet committee must be into the Cabinet Office at least two working days before the meeting concerned (that is, by early Thursday for cabinet itself). The general pattern is for ministers to have a regular meeting with the Chief Executive of the ministry or department of the major portfolio area immediately before the Monday meeting. This allows the minister to be briefed both on areas concerning submissions that are directly relevant to the meeting of that day and also where the department has an interest in an area. Then usually there are also other set times for weekly meetings when the rest of a minister's portfolio responsibilities are discussed with chief executives.

'Ministerials', letters to ministers, are time-consuming although again this depends upon the portfolio concerned and the degree of conscientiousness of the minister, who generally has merely to sign the letters. One minister who had dealt with about 1450 since taking office (this was the minister's estimate) said, 'I normally do try to skim them and if it seems it's something I don't know about, I normally will go back and read the original letter too, so I pick up a bit of knowledge in case I meet the person. [I] can't always do that.' Also there is the minister's own correspondence, perhaps between 30 and 35 letters a week to dictate. Between his appointment at the end of 1990 and early March 1993, the Minister of Police, John Banks, reportedly answered 14,542 letters concerning Police matters, and personally wrote 64 articles. In the previous financial year he had signed 5,817 letters and issued 62 press statements.[9]

Several ministers reserved parts of their portfolio load to the evenings. Or else the weekends were the times for the overload aspects of the job. A minister with three areas of responsibility used to spend two days a week on the major portfolio and one on each of the two minor ones. Then 'I just worked all weekend reading the longer things that I couldn't get to read during the week.'

The role of 'good management' by the ministers' personal staff members was emphasized by the ministers interviewed. A senior minister, praising the senior private secretary, said, 'He and I decide what our priorities are: we do a lot of critical path programming and we actually plan just about every hour of every day.' Despite their private office staffs, several ministers appeared to have little organization in their lives. When one was asked how time was allocated, the response was, 'I don't. If there's something on my desk that needs to be done, it's just done.' A fairly frequent complaint was that 'there's an awful lot of reacting'. 'I've really just got to make almost constant, if not multiple times of the day, judgements as to where the urgencies and priorities are now being identified, the knowledge of what my government wants to do, where the policy development must be emphasized.' Again, the view was:

> I think [the order of business] is somewhat too reactive. And it tends to be in response to, I guess, the workload that is generated, either by groups within the sector, demands for discussion as I've just had, meeting at conferences, or by officials and the papers that they're presenting for decisions . . . yes it tends to be reactive.

This minister said that, when travel was involved, an effort was made to combine jobs relating to the various portfolios needed to be done in a particular locality.

When asked how time was allocated, a minister new to executive office gave the honest reply:

> Probably not well. . . . Last year I divided my time badly and was in many ways not in control of my own time. Now I'm dividing my time up into some

time being available to meet with people. I've got some time available to meet with my key officials. Not too regularly, because they could take up all your time if you allowed them. I keep that quite disciplined. Then I have the interest groups that I meet with regularly . . . though not too regularly again, because again they could take all your time. . . . Then you've got time which I'm now budgeting each day for my own thinking and work. Last year I did not put enough time into my own work . . . reading key material, thinking further, you know, thinking. I don't mean sitting there and staring into space, I mean reading and analysing and that kind of thinking, and planning. And then a fourth area of time is time with my office officials, my office staff. Because that's critically important.

For obvious reasons, issue salience, as well as portfolio size, helps dictate the order of priorities for ministers: 'It depends on the issues of the day. . . . Now at the moment there's one or two things happening that are requiring quite a bit of time, so that that takes a lot of time one week and maybe absolutely none or very little the next week.' Some portfolios, too, are wide-ranging in their scopes, such as Internal Affairs, Justice, and Education. Each is rather like, as one minister said, 'a centipede'.

For one interviewee, 'the big killer in my area is actually reading reports'. A colleague announced a sweepingly negative judgement on the paper work generated by policy initiatives:

All the restructuring . . . getting rid of the quangos, the opening up of the select committees, have amounted to nothing. If you look at the cabinet, the papers already this year would be well above last year. And the reason for that, of course, is that we had an intense round through the Expenditure Control Committee which I'm a member of. Maybe it's going to subside a little bit; so far it doesn't look like it. We're changing things too often, we have to do better what we are doing rather than just change it simply because they think it should be changed. . . . We're carrying on as the worst example in the civilized world of an over-regulated and over-legislated country.

The extent of travel undertaken by ministers throughout the country can also be time-consuming (and exhausting). Its extent partly depends upon the demands of the portfolio but also upon personal preference:

The other factor that intrudes on your time is also speeches and thus far in my portfolio I've given seventy-five speeches outside the House, and by the time I get to the full year I will probably have done ninety anyway. So, that normally means unless the speech is in Wellington that you've lost half a day. . . . So if you actually try to evaluate your time you can say that it's forty-five days disappeared. You were talking to people, you were listening to people, you were sitting on an aeroplane, you were reading papers on an aeroplane and sleeping on it. But it's not as productive as being in your office.

Not all ministers actually have that workload, some of them, by comparison Simon Upton, prefer actually to stay in Wellington; he does not give many speeches, not too many press releases. But he loves getting stuck into the depths of policy. Whereas I do not love getting stuck into the depths of policy. Basically I will look at the resolution of policy rather than at the creation of it, so his skills are in that area, mine are not.

Palmer, who was also Deputy PM as well as Minister of Justice and Attorney-General, reported that in 1986 he gave eighty-five formal speeches and probably the same number of informal ones. He also made ninety-one speeches in Parliament.[10]

The Bolger Government evidently had a roster system for ministers attending Parliament:

Ministers are guaranteed they'll be in the House three hours a week anyway, plus question time, plus any time that you have a particular responsibility. And if I have work that I can do in the House and I've caught up on dictation and phone things, well I will go down and provide some backup, because it's important that there is a presence, ministers who are listening to what is being said by back-benchers.'

Ministers also have to answer questions in Parliament, an important aspect of the public performing role of the minister, and, moreover, a vital ingredient in the accountability process. Ministers answer questions (oral and written) only within the areas of their own responsibility. Although ministers are supplied with the 'answers' by their public servants, they still need to be prepared to respond to supplementary questions. The questions range from the 'patsy' ones from their own back-benchers, designed to broadcast the achievements of their government, to the more searching and politically dangerous ones from the Opposition. In the financial year 1 July 1991 until 30 June 1992, when Parliament met on 80 days, ministers answered 1,597 oral questions, and provided 11,119 written answers.[11]

Ministers also must fit into their weeks other tasks: 'And then of course the most important part of the job from the point of view of one's survival is looking after one's electorate.' New Zealand ministers usually return home at the weekends, and spend part of that time (often Saturday mornings) holding their electorate 'surgeries'. They also attend local functions. These duties can be difficult to cope with:

The frustration I have is in finding the time to put into the constituency work and I would rather have more time to put into preparation of speeches and meetings with groups and organizations. It would be good if there were more time but there is no more time, and I find that most of my constituency work from this end is done late at night. The end of the day is the only time left to finally address the constituents' correspondence.

Attention, too, must be devoted to the parliamentary party, especially meetings of caucus which occur weekly when Parliament is in session, and either attending caucus committee meetings or at least meeting with the committee chairperson. This last ministerial task, about which little is known, forms the subject of the next section.

Ministers and the Caucus Committees

One of the distinctive characteristics of New Zealand's version of cabinet government is the role played by caucus committees. Ministers play the roles of advocates and defenders of government policy in the weekly meetings of full caucus. Their relationships with their back-bench colleagues are, however, much more fully developed within the institutionalized caucus committee system, a feature also of earlier governments. A minister in the Bolger Government recalled being on the social welfare and education caucus committees, saying that 'The two then ministers were excellent in terms of making available to us departmental officials and so on. It was Merv Wellington and Venn Young. They were very good, and they also attended quite regularly, but they also gave us the chance without them there to be with the Director-General of the organization.' This reveals the established interrelationships between back-benchers, ministers, and public servants, and touches upon constitutional relationships significantly different from those of Westminster (see Chapter Two). Because little is known about the nature of these relationships, the ministers of the Bolger Government (and three caucus committee chairpersons) were asked about the use made of these committees. I received a variety of responses, as the following selected extracts illustrate.

A few ministers in the National Government used their caucus committees to help them fight particular battles in cabinet. For example, one committee was employed 'to move outside of a more right wing Cabinet than the inclination of the majority of caucus, to transfer that decision making into the caucus arena in a manner that Government obviously can't ignore'. This particular minister's views were 'anathema to the [Business] Roundtable, probably anathema to Treasury'. Therefore, the minister concerned used the committee to gather evidence on the policy issues concerned, evidence then used to support the minister's own views (and, evidently, caucus committee members' too). But ministers did not always win policy arguments, even with the aid of their caucus committees:

> I don't think I've ever had a situation where at the end of the day I haven't agreed with the caucus committee, privately, I mean. Publicly I've got to take the position supporting the Government. They [the committees] know that they've had their chance of input. . . . I've lost and they've lost and that's all there is to it.

Another example was Winston Peters who, as Minister of Maori Affairs, reportedly took his report on Maori development, *Ka Awatea*, to the caucus committee for approval and used that in his public argument over it with Jim Bolger and other members of cabinet.

Most ministers, however, used the committees for less political purposes, to examine the details of policy, after its initial formulation, and to examine the submissions if in legislative form (a task that might properly be thought that of the relevant select committee). Because of the very close relationship in terms of membership between caucus and select committee chairpersons and members, keeping the caucus committees involved helped facilitate the legislative process. The committees discuss a bill, 'And then you have to have these people that are available [in] the Introduction stage to speak in favour of it, [and] a select committee to hear submissions but keep it on a straight, reasonable path. . . . I can't see how ministers would get legislation through without having a team of people that were going to back it.' The view was colloquially expressed that 'Without your caucus committee you're dead.' Back-benchers were crucial to advocate government policy. Superannuation policy, it was reported, had been discussed by ministers with the caucus committee as well as the caucus itself, because of its political salience. Confidential, pre-budgetary fiscal information had even been released to a caucus committee in order to test its response.

Partly this role was a matter of communication, for, 'particularly in a big caucus like this, the chairman or chairwoman role of caucus committees is quite critical. . . . It's very important to try and avoid an executive/caucus demarcation, and the relationship between the chair and yourself is critical.' The minister continued thus: 'From time to time the cabinet has been caned for not keeping caucus members informed, and equally not keeping Party members informed, and I don't think we have done that task particularly well.' It was easy, when under pressure,

> to get yourself totally wrapped up in that decision-making process, and forget that your caucus colleagues may not know about it, and certainly your Party members won't know about it until they read about it in the newspapers. Which brings me to the point, the immediacy of media reporting, often before we have made an official release, [which] means that it is extremely difficult to actually get material to caucus, never mind to your Party members, who would like to be informed prior to a general release, because obviously they feel they've got a privileged position in terms of what they do within politics.

Ministers varied a great deal in the extent to which they made use of their caucus committees. For example, they might be employed to discuss overall policy themes and directions, rather than to examine details, because:

> Nearly all our back-benchers are brand new. They don't have any background. I know this from my own experience; your first three years is all about learning about the job. Unfortunately now we've got people who want to run the country the day they walk in the door. There's always been that tendency, but it's never been as strong as it is now.

A similar comment was that 'Back-benchers have got a million and one things on, they're all over the place. Very few back-benchers actually get their minds around issues to the point that they can combat the executive.' Nevertheless, despite this sentiment, the minister had a committee chair 'who I really treat as an associate minister. . . . I just say, "Look, you turn up at any meeting, anywhere, any time".' It was the chair's job 'to keep the rest of them informed, I can't run round doing that. But I've got a back-bencher right inside things. I use caucus committees as a time to explain things, but they're not really driving the policy in any sense at all, I don't think that they're as significant as everybody makes out. They are possibly reactively significant.' A measure of policy, even personality, compatibility between minister and committee chair is crucial; in 1991 Mike Laws was removed from his chairperson's position because of his outspoken views on work schemes.

Some committees, too, tend to be more independent than others in the issues they choose to study. A minister who brought issues to the committee's attention said: 'and they bring up some of theirs if they've been travelling around the country and we try and co-ordinate where we're going in the future.' The role of committees in providing feedback to ministers was obviously important: 'I'd go along to the caucus committee and we'd talk over what we're doing, what bills are coming in, and whether they agree or not, what we can do about this.' In a sense these are the minimal roles played by government caucus committees. They are 'sounding boards', because 'If you cannot satisfy your caucus committee by and large you are not going to satisfy caucus.' Caucus committees were important for issues that were 'politically sensitive'. Quoting Robert Muldoon, a minister said that 'it's the job of your officials to give you advice. And it's the job of the parliamentarians to put a human face on that advice. And what you have with your caucus colleagues is people who have a very close involvement with what's happening in communities right round the country, so they give you a balance coming from that perspective, that you won't get from a bureaucracy which tends to be rather isolated here in Wellington.'

Special caucus committees had been created:

> I'm putting together a caucus team to work with the officials, with some
> outside people as well, on analysing how the devil can we actually manage this
> asset better. We have all sorts of expertise in caucus, and we want to harness
> some of that expertise. So both the standard caucus committee and special
> committees are very useful.

Ultimately, though, it is the minister who 'drives the work'.

> He's [sic] got to get the legislation through, and make certain it's acceptable to
> the caucus. . . They have some ideas, and they've been proffering ideas to
> me. And I'm looking at some of those, or mulling them over at the moment.
> But it is ministerially driven, I'm sure of that.

A colleague agreed:

> I believe that a lot of the work has to be done personally. It's interesting in this
> day and age, where people talk about the need to work team skills. I find
> though in my life experience that you've also got to be able to actually get
> stuck in and do detailed work yourself, that relying on everyone just
> contributing a bit to the team often can end up with a very superficial analysis
> of what's going on. So, I found that I did a great deal of research myself.

Someone else estimated that 'About fifty per cent of the time I make
suggestions as to what the committee might put on its agenda.' Nonetheless,
even when the minister controls the agenda goals of a committee, that
committee can have a substantive input into public policy. In 1991, for
example, National caucus subcommittees conducted reviews of the
automobile industry[12] and of the textile and garment industry for the Minister
of Commerce, Philip Burdon. There was also a subcommittee on tariffs which
worked in conjunction with an officials' committee.[13] The back-benchers
went out and discussed policy proposals with a range of industries. The
impact was that the process of tariff reduction was slowed down. Regular
discussions also were held with the Commerce Commission.

Finally, we can gain some idea of the contact between minister and caucus
committee from the following:

> I've got three caucus committees that I have to interface with. I normally
> attend their meetings, whenever I'm in town, and certainly I'm scheduled to
> attend their meetings above all other things [but] that doesn't always quite
> work. And the chairman of the committee normally sees me once a week to
> talk about what he's doing. I allocate certain things that I will do and certain
> things that they will do, and essentially if I have delivered them a number of

tasks out of the things that we want to put into a legislative programme, I expect them to progress it through by talking to officials, meeting with people, and then advising me of what their view is. And obviously if I'm in a meeting from time to time I'll participate as a member of the committee. On the other hand, there are some issues that I will decide that I will deal with, and I will refer them to the committee when they're about at the same stage. Because otherwise, the committee cannot handle all the work, and I can't refer everything through them, and I try to find those areas where really we need to have a consensus view, as opposed to [when] you simply need to make a decision. If there's a decision needed after consideration I'll make that; it's a case of working through issues and getting consensus and a viewpoint that's saleable.

The minister continued:

They certainly play through ideas that they pick up from their own business round the country, and the input may be made directly to them. Some people might think that it's easier to get to them than to get to the minister. They're probably right . . . so there is some advantage in going directly to a caucus member [but] there is a disadvantage that you won't get a direct reply. So they bring up a number of ideas. [One committee] had an initiative they wanted to take up. . . . I thought it was an excellent idea and I said, 'Well, OK, I'll allocate you a little proportion of one of my staff's time to pick the project up and see how you go.'

Defining the Role of the Minister

Overwhelmingly the ministers interviewed in the early 1990s saw themselves as adopting the roles of leaders and policy initiators. For the purposes of the 1970s research on MPs and ministers, and this 1990s study, 'role' can be defined by the structurally and organizationally given demands, by individuals' orientations or conceptions of the parts they and others are to play, as well as the actual political behaviour of those individuals.[14] A few examples of how ministers expressed their views and their activities will illustrate the widely held perceptions of their proper roles.[15]

First, there was the minister who said, 'I'm very much in a leadership role. I'm dragging—maybe that's not the right word to use—I'm trying to take [the department] into the twenty-first century right now.' A second said, 'I think that everybody who becomes a minister is already playing a leadership role, because you head up a very significant business enterprise in terms of the ministry that you lead.' A third, who believed leadership and managerial skills to be necessary, responded that ministers needed to be able to develop and think through a programme, and to

drive it through and not have somebody else dictate their agenda to you, particularly officials. And I think [you need] to have managerial skills. That means that you can manage that programme through to successful implementation. I think probably that the other skill that modern cabinet ministers need, and I don't profess to having all those skills, are really presentational skills . . . increasingly, particularly with television presentation, they're becoming a critical part of being able to get a programme through. So it doesn't matter how well thought through the programme is, or how skilful your usage of the process, if you don't have the presentational skills, then, when push gets to shove you may not be given the benefit of the doubt by the population, and to that extent pressure then goes back on your programme.

'Management', however, was seen as primarily the responsibility of the public servants.

Management is largely their responsibility and they're accountable to me for management. I expect them to manage well, that's given. I don't try and manage them, but I do challenge much of what they're doing, and that's one of the exciting things in politics, you actually are continually challenging the advice that you're given, trying to improve its quality. And if you're not, you're sort of going out to get contestable advice. That really is an exciting part of being a minister.

One of the leadership tasks was 'the most challenging and the least known leadership role . . . to try and support a Department that is constantly being burdened with change and increasing pressure over the last decade'.

In terms of the skills required, one minister said that leadership must be 'visible, authoritative, and competent, and also of such merit that people will be persuaded that you're right, and want to do what you're doing, and want to respond to what you're asking of them'.

Another response was,

My role is to communicate the big, broad, strategic overview. Their [public servants'] role is operational. It's not leadership—that sort of assumes that I'm the top of a long pinnacle, but I'm not, we're quite separated. And the Public Finance Act has really underlined that separation very clearly. I think a good minister is somebody who can get the best and the most out of the people who work around them . . . [somebody who] has an easy manner with the people outside the public service, with whom he or she may deal, somebody who's on top of their subject—they can't be arrogant—somebody who listens to what is being said, even makes the odd mistake and says 'whoops'.

And a further view was that, as much as anything else, a minister needed 'a practical knowledge about how systems work and how people work; a reasonable amount of commonsense . . . an ability to work with intelligent people, working with other people. But, in effect being able to see the big picture.' Communication was very important, a number of ministers pointed out. In 'cabinet committees and caucus and cabinet, it still comes back to the ability to express yourself extemporaneously and to be able to—not rhetorically—argue in a reasonable sense your case'.

A good minister should be 'creative and introduce policies and ideas that are for the betterment of New Zealand'. The minister added that:

> Sadly, today in the modern world, a good minister is one who seems to keep his portfolio out of trouble . . . and the Government out of trouble. A good minister really should be one who has some bright ideas and produces some policies that are going to make everybody better off. The other ability is to think through the commonsense factors in issues . . . understanding the way things are going to work, rather than thinking the theory.

Also mentioned was

> enthusiasm for change, working on the long-term needs of the people [ministers] represent, and working it back to the short-term problems and trying to see beyond those, and to set up the sort of structures and communication systems that allow the needs of that group to be met. Not necessarily the wants. I think a good minister has the power of lateral thinking to assess where the portfolio is at at the time of appointment—areas which need to be attended to, where improvements can be made—and get on with it. Probably the most important thing of all of those is getting on with it.

However, another felt that a good minister

> needs to be able to apply his or her mind to the policy issues; they also really need to be able to assimilate all of the advice that comes to them, and then make sound practical decisions on the basis of that advice. That's much more important in my view than the ability to be able to stimulate and personally develop those policy initiatives.

Politics within and beyond cabinet were significant. Overall, a minister thought, 'is the ability to be able to be seen as still aware of the public's concerns and wishes, and also implement the policies that the majority of your colleagues finally decide you have to implement'. Although primarily a leadership role, part of being a minister was 'representing the interests of that group in the community that you are appointed to represent, and how they interact with the rest of the people. And it's a resources and a people issue.' Ministers do not need 'expert knowledge' but 'you've got to have a knowledge of politics, which can only be learnt on the job. One reads most of the books about politics and has a good laugh, because it's only insiders who really know. But you need . . . the mental, intellectual training . . . these days, to be able to grasp the issues, they're so complex'.

This view was reiterated:

> A minister doesn't have to have a degree at all [but] to have a capacity to
> understand the issues at stake, to synthesize the material that is put before that
> minister, and to be able to argue the case with advisers is quite crucial. And,
> you know, the Prime Minister is one of the best at it, and he doesn't have the
> advantage of having had a university education [and] Koro Wetere in the old
> government—very, very good, very sharp, very quick to analyse issues.

Some ministers regretted their lack of time for reflection and policy
development:

> I would tend to say that I see my role more as a one-man board of directors
> who is co-ordinating the policy within the Department. Unfortunately, I think
> because of the burden of the work . . . the way that it has grown, ministers get
> too involved in the technicalities of administration. Ministers really need to be
> able to spend more time, I believe, being reflective on their job.

And ministers need 'to sit back and think about the responsibility that
they've been given, and ask themselves . . . where they want to end up at the
end of their period in office, and draw up a plan of work according to that. I
think that in the past I've observed lots of ministers who've actually been
there to sign departmental correspondence for a period of time and have
achieved very little else.'

Hence the contemporary ministers saw their roles as ideally policy
initiators, even if they themselves did not provide the core ideas, and even if
they themselves or others were unable to live up to this model. Intellectual
ability was important, but particular expertise and formal training were not
seen as vital for the task. Communications skills, however, were very
important to the ministerial role. How do the self-perceptions of the ministers
of the 1990s compare with those of an earlier era?

The Changing Role of the Cabinet Minister

One of the aims of my research of the early 1970s was to determine, through
interviews, the characteristics seen as desirable for ministers. The New
Zealand MPs of the 1970s placed, comparatively speaking, unusual emphasis
upon personal characteristics, and this was carried through to the ministerial
positions.[16] Both the Labour and National ministers emphasized personal
character attributes: a sense of humour, 'keeping your feet on the ground', a
capacity for hard work, honesty, loyalty and, above all, integrity. These
desired characteristics perhaps resulted from the close proximity and
intimacy of the MPs' working surroundings. The respect paid to personal

morality and what might be loosely labelled civic values reflects the remarkably small amount of corruption in the New Zealand political system. Or it might have constituted recognition of the importance New Zealand society of the 1970s placed upon moral convention. These sorts of characteristics were scarcely mentioned by the 1990s ministers, an indication, perhaps, of a changing political culture.

Conciliatory and communicative skills, on the other hand, were valued highly then as now. The cabinet system of government places a great deal of importance upon the task of explaining and defending policies in Parliament and caucus. There is also the daily interaction with the variety of participants in the policy-making and administrative processes—with public servants, deputations from interested groups and individuals, back-benchers, and other ministers. The situation is different when ministers are not also members of the legislature, as in the Netherlands, for example, or in the USA. Constitutional laws and conventions affect the ministerial role, and keep constant certain desired characteristics. A comment from the early 1970s was, 'You've got to have ability but I wouldn't take a really brilliant soul who was colourless, or who wouldn't mix. Above all he [sic] must be a good mixer, to mix with all groups from the farmer down to the labourer.' Thus the model of the role of the minister projected by the parliamentarians interviewed reflected the realities of the continuity of structure and process. Indeed, the contemporary demands of television have undoubtedly made communication skills even more important than they were.

The role of the New Zealand minister was perceived in both sets of interviews as that of the generalist. Expert knowledge of particular areas of social and economic life was not required. Rather, expertise was to do with demonstrating that a minister can learn about a topic and speak on it; an ability transferable, in theory, to any portfolio. Given the limited choice of ministers available in New Zealand's small House, this is probably a realistic expectation.

In sharp contrast to the 1990s, however, the National ministers of the Holyoake years mentioned administrative ability as a requirement for a minister more often than leadership ability, legislative ability, or the capability to solve problems, make decisions, or arrive at good judgements; indeed, the latter skills were scarcely mentioned. A minister needed to have 'a liking for administration', and must have executive ability: 'I regard myself as an administrator rather than as a legislator. I probably do the least legislation of any of the members. I think that administration is the biggest factor in the retention of the government back-benchers. Governments are judged very much on administration.'

The comments of the 1970s Labour ministers were no different from their opponents in terms of the required attributes. For instance, 'There's got to be a basic ability there to, first of all, be an administrator and, secondly, you've got to be able to get on with people.' The party differences which might have been expected to exist during the 1970s between a reformist party and a party of the *status quo* were revealed in the different priority respectively placed on ideological and intellectual skills by the Labour and National MPs. Labour were more conscious of the policy fulfilment aspects of a minister's work whilst the National members saw the ministerial tasks as more of a brokerage role, emphasizing the conciliatory skills required of ministers.

During the 1970s and early 1980s, cabinet policy-making, according to a former Secretary of Treasury, tended to be an 'inductive process': 'Policy is established by Cabinet over time as the cumulative result of a series of responses to particular circumstances. Only occasionally does policy emerge from a deductive process, as a result of strategic thinking which transcends the preoccupation with particular circumstances. Most such policy occurs in the period just after a General Election.'[17] Policy was made cumulatively in order to allow consensus to develop. This type of decision-making was fundamentally dependent upon a political agenda derived from sources outside cabinet: party manifestos; the public service; and those major pressure groups with 'insider' status.[18] Hence the norms of cabinet behaviour emphasizing the good administrator, not the policy innovator. In the words of Keith Holyoake, a minister was picked 'who you believe has capacity for administration, he [sic] must have a certain popularity with the electorate, he must be a good public speaker, a good debater'.[19] Ministers were not so much 'policy initiators as policy legitimators'.[20] Again, the role of the minister has changed; policy is largely now a deductive process, proceeding from 'first principles'. In part, this is the product of the perceived fiscal crisis of the state and past policy failures. It is also a response to the public sector changes.

Ideological differences within the parties were not displayed in the interviews; and they were not featured, either, as factors in the making of cabinets or in the expectations about the representative roles of ministers and cabinets. The evidence from the 1970s interviews confirmed the views of academic observers of the 'Absence of Political Ideas' among New Zealand politicians.[21] In stark contrast, the National ministers of the 1990s exhibited a marked sense of ideological purpose: to continue the transformation of the New Zealand state begun by the 1984–90 Labour Government.

The difficulty is that the transformation of the ideal role of the New Zealand cabinet minister into a policy initiator not only puts ministers into a position where there seems to be the constant possibility of role conflict but also has the effect of placing added strain upon the limited talent available for top political office.

7

ADVICE AND SUPPORT

Cabinet has a dual function: to provide both political and executive leadership. A. D. Robinson described it thus, borrowing the concept of fusion from Walter Bagehot: 'Cabinet represents the fusion of power in the political system; it is the committee controlling the government departments, and it is a committee of party leaders from the majority party. These elements are mutually reinforcing.'[1] Cabinet's relationship with its political party was the topic of earlier chapters. The purpose of this one is to explain cabinet's position as the 'apex of the administrative system',[2] to show how the system of advice to cabinet, Prime Minister, and ministers has developed, and to demonstrate how, in the process, there have been two, apparently contradictory, tendencies: towards the personalization of political advice through the shift to contractually based power relationships; and towards bureaucratization, especially in terms of the internal functioning and advice system of cabinet. Although the primary focus of this particular chapter is upon the relationship between cabinet and the public service and the development of the Cabinet and Prime Minister's offices, I end by outlining the system of policy advice in its widest sense.

It is insufficient to understand the relationship between cabinet and the public service purely in terms of the contemporary system of advice and support, looking back only to the reforms of the public sector implemented by the fourth Labour Government. We need also to investigate very briefly the growth and shape of the New Zealand state in order to understand the position of cabinet within the context of the development of state power.

The Development of the Public Service and the Structure of Cabinet

A detailed description of the growth and development of the governmental agencies is beyond the scope of this work.[3] Summarized baldly, by 1890, after the birth and death of the provincial system of government, there were 31 government departments. By 1928 there were 43, by 1935 there were 41, and by 1946, a grand total of 49. By 1957 the number had dropped to 41 again because of amalgamation, and there were still 41 when the 1962 Royal Commission reported.[4] By 1973 there were the large departments of the Post

Office and the Railways, there were 33 Public Service Departments, and also 'education boards and teaching staff, hospital boards and medical and nursing staff, the armed services and police, and corporations such as the National Airways Corporation and the Tourist Hotel Corporation'. Added to all this, there were over 300 statutory bodies and committees.[5] On top of this complicated heap of bodies sat the cabinet.

How can the complexity, fragmentation, and interventionist nature of this system of government be explained? A primary feature has been the tendency towards centralization characteristic of New Zealand. The drift towards the centralized state has been both cause and product of the nature of government. The social forces and geographical distinctions in the country were never sufficiently strong to counteract this tendency towards the centre. New Zealand's centralized economic and political structure developed and solidified into habit during the nineteenth century when neither private capital nor the alternative, the will of central government to finance decentralized governing units, was present. So, throughout the country's history, centralization has been opposed not by regionalism but by parochialism, the historically small and weak units of local government.[6]

The roots of centralized administrative growth early established themselves. For example, the Marine Boards, set up to control the harbours, failed, and so the Marine Department was created. Districts could not cope with the public works necessary for development, and so the Department of Public Works was created. And, as Polaschek emphasized, all this happened even before the provinces were abolished in 1875.[7] Between 1860 and 1866 six new agencies were added to central government.[8] A further factor was that the provinces could not cope with the land wars between European and Maori. One of the consequences of this internal warring was that an electric telegraph system became necessary and was established by central government in 1865.[9] Confirmation of the inadequacies of regionalism as represented by the provincial bodies came with the creation of the Education and Justice departments.

Another major factor, as mentioned above, was the absence of private capital in New Zealand, which led to the state assuming, very early, developmental functions that only much later were taken over by the state in countries such as Great Britain. The administration of the railways in New Zealand was one such example. Again, the absence of alternative sources of investment meant that the state had to play the major role in scientific research. In 1926 the Department of Science and Industrial Research was set up (abolished and turned into crown agencies by the fourth Labour and National Governments). It is only since 1984, when the contemporary administrative revolution began, that the state has determinedly shrunk itself and devolved functions that could be either set at arm's length from the core state (corporatized) or sold (privatized).

The country's relationship with the rest of the world also provided excuses for the growth of agencies. Involvement in the two world wars saw the creation of several new agencies, including Munitions and Supplies in the first world war and a National Service Department, an Economic Stabilization Committee, and a Rehabilitation Department in the second. Despite New Zealand's early involvement in wars (men were sent to fight in the Boer War) an External Affairs Department was not set up until 1943. Specifically administrative matters, too, have produced their own little administrative growth industry within the Public Service. In 1926, for instance, the Prime Minister's Department was formed. Sub-agencies have broken away from larger units to form independent agencies: the State Forest Department and the Immigration Department provide 1920s examples. This splintering has on occasion been the product of inefficiency. Leslie Lipson reported that the National Service Department was created because during the Second World War, the national service's natural home, the Labour Department, was too inefficient to cope with the demands of the war. So a separate agency was set up which lasted until 1947 when long-delayed reform was begun.[10]

Finally, the reasons for growth can be explained in terms of the way in which governments have responded to and fuelled the increasing expectations about the role of the state. Only the most recent two governments have sought to reverse this tendency and, with moderate success, to change the political culture of which it has been part. The expectations about the extent and direction of state involvement in social and economic life drew responses from governments of all political persuasions, from New Zealand's early years onwards. Equally importantly for the overall execution of government, they created new organizations rather than using existing ones.[11]

Later, during the more conservative period of Reform Party government in the 1920s, marketing boards were created. The period of social reform of the first Labour Government, by comparison with the earlier period of the Liberal-Labour Government, created few new agencies. Mainly, Labour adjusted the existing ones to carry out its policies. It did, however, abolish the railways and broadcasting boards and turn them into departments, for Labour, before 1984, tended to prefer direct ministerial control over government bodies. The few new agencies that were formed in the 1930s were mostly concerned with marketing activities. The 1960s and 1970s saw governments respond to new issues.[12] Departments and boards were formed to deal with conservation and environmental matters. Also a new series of bodies were developed to deal with individual rights: the Office of Ombudsman 1962; the Race Relations Conciliator 1971; and the Human Rights Commission 1977 (which in 1993 was amalgamated with the Race Relations Office).

The New Zealand governmental structure grew haphazardly in terms of the number of agencies created, and also, as implied by the above and criticized by many, in terms of its haphazard organizational structure.[13] Changes were attempted: both the Royal Commissions of 1912 and 1962 had some effect. In the 1960s and 1970s there was amalgamation in the areas of transport, housing, welfare, and defence. Nonetheless, overall the structure was as it grew; and the direction of growth was towards filling immediate needs by addition rather than towards planning how further government functions could be developed within the existing structure.

Once created as separate entities, organizations die stubbornly. Not only do those who work within them urge their continued life but also the pressure groups outside government which have forged comfortable links with institutions urge their continuation. So, 'The result of the New Zealand system is that far too much co-ordination, both of agencies and functions, is thrown up to the ministerial level which could and should be settled further down the pyramid of authority.'[14] The net effect was that power was determinedly located in the hands of cabinet; but, perversely, cabinet could not always exert its power efficiently and effectively because it was swamped by, in the first place, an administrative muddle of responsibilities and, in the second, an inability to delegate. The latter characteristic was in part due to the administrative system just outlined, but it also resulted from the perception of how political power in New Zealand should be exercised, a cultural predisposition towards putting blame and responsibility in the hands of central government.

As can be seen from the explanations given above, reasons for the expansion of the New Zealand state can easily be given. But they do tend to be functional explanations, and like all such 'answers' they pose more questions than they actually solve. When politicians have decided upon or accepted the interventionist state, why have they constructed the fragmented advice system outlined above?

Agency growth has been explained by public choice theorists who posit that bureaucrats, acting in their own self-interests, are, amongst their other characteristics, concerned to expand their organizations (thus enabling them better to survive, making top positions more powerful, positioning them to cope more effectively with internal and external conflict, and so forth). With all the limitations of public choice theory (especially its disregard for altruistic or public-serving behaviour and its general ignorance of the role played by political institutions and processes), the rational choice school of explanation is much more satisfactory than functionalism for explaining why institutions expand in size. It has severe shortcomings, however, when it comes to explaining why the institutions of state expand in number. It would seem to be against the hypothesized, self-aggrandizing motives of bureaucrats to create a proliferation of minor agencies, although we can see that this sort of strategy does invent a whole range of new top positions, albeit frequently relatively weak ones.

Agency proliferation, as opposed to agency expansion, can perhaps better be explained by the self-seeking behaviour of politicians, rather than of bureaucrats. As public choice theory has also suggested, governing parties in representative democracies have sought to gain and retain power by responding to the expressed preferences of the electors, thus leading to the expansion of the state and, of course, public expenditure. Again, however, although this explanation might go somewhere towards explaining why governments like New Zealand's increased the welfare and economic interventionism of the state, for example, it does not really explain why the shape of the New Zealand state developed as it did. Although it is always neater to use single explanations of human behaviour (and more fashionable in social science, thus explaining the attraction of public choice theory for economics and political science), perhaps the answer lies in the interaction between the incentives of political self-interest and the culture of the political institutions. Crudely put, when governing parties move to satisfy the demands of their own followers (ideology) and the needs of the electors (ideology plus a range of expressed and non-expressed preferences), those parties seek solutions in ways that can be explained as follows.

First, expanding the range of state agencies expands also the powers of the individual ministers who are to be responsible for those agencies. Second, once the pattern of single-function (narrowly defined) agencies was established, it became very difficult to break away from this model. Patterns of institutionalization apparently tend to repeat themselves. In New Zealand there was simply no political incentive to do anything else but follow the pattern of the past. Third, if public choice theories of bureaucratic behaviour are accurate when they say that government officials, ambitious to expand their organizations, additionally act to acquire increased power and to avoid or delay carrying out the instructions of their political leaders, then the creation of a proliferation of agencies rather than fewer large ones might well have enhanced the ability of ministers to control the bodies for which they are responsible. In particular it would have aided them to take the detailed sort of interest in policy implementation that has been a characteristic of New Zealand cabinet government.

Hence the nature of the public service, and its relationship with cabinet, are tied closely to the latter body's central and most powerful position in the political system. There were and are no constitutional obstacles to prevent successive cabinets shaping the state in the way they wish. This lack of constitutional constraint enabled cabinet power to be expanded both in functional and, additionally, in institutional terms. But the very sweep of power that has been so constitutionally straightforward to exercise has had its costs, its inefficiencies. In particular, the problem of policy co-ordination has been endemic in the New Zealand political system. Various mechanisms developed to cope: the cabinet committee system; a plethora of officials' committees; and, rather late, a prime minister's department.

The fourth Labour Government, led by the public choice influenced Treasury agenda so carefully and fully laid out in its post-election briefings of 1984 and 1987, undertook the immense task of changing the scope and nature of the New Zealand state. Nevertheless, by August 1990, the government had actually increased the total number of departments and ministries (from 34 in 1984 to 39). There were 20 new bodies (not counting the state-owned enterprises (SOE) which are not, of course, departments).[15] Many of the bodies created during this period were relatively small, policy-oriented ministries. Indeed, one of the main goals of the reorganization was to separate policy advice from policy implementation. Besides forming the SOEs and shrinking the departments Labour had also embarked upon the sale of those state assets which were primarily seen as trading departments. Thus the size of the state was reduced. The number of state servants, 89,105 in March 1986, had gone down to 60,940 by March 1988.[16] The National Government which took power in 1990 continued to reduce the numbers of public servants.[17] However, as was seen in Table 5.1, complexity and proliferation remain characteristics of the new public service, and policy co-ordination remains a problem for cabinets.

The effects of Labour's changes, besides altering the constitutional relationships between state agencies and ministers, changed quite dramatically the relationship between the cabinet and the New Zealand state. At one and the same time cabinet's links with state agencies were shrunk and personalized. Corporatization and privatization reduced the area of the state within the immediate political control of ministers; and the actual system of political control instituted during the transformation of the state itself became bureaucratized. And, as with most bureaucratic relationships, elements of democratic accountability were lost.

The Treasury, prime initiator of the public and state sector changes, continues to have a key role as a control agency, along with the State Services Commission (SSC). The role of Treasury has expanded (nicely fulfilling the predictions of public choice theory) into a broad policy role.[18] Its financial control and policy monitoring and initiating functions and ambitions have increased whilst those of the SSC have been decreased and altered in character. It kept its responsibility for monitoring the general machinery of government and the effectiveness of the departments; and it plays a role in the appointment of chief executives. But chief executives, not the SSC, employ departmental staff—although the SSC has a part to play in appointments to Senior Executive Service positions. These two bodies, the Treasury and the SSC, with the Department of Prime Minister and Cabinet Office (see below), have significant roles as co-ordinating agencies. Also, in their various ways, they carry out the function of monitoring the mechanics of cabinet government as it exists at present. This particular task will continue to be of importance as New Zealand's cabinet system of government adapts itself to the new system of political representation and cabinet formation under the MMP electoral system.

The 1990–93 National Government: Ministers' Attitudes Towards the Public Service

The National Government elected in 1990 inherited a state structure transformed by its Labour predecessor. Despite the constant criticisms made by the National Party when in opposition, when in government National accepted the principles and most of the structures of the new architecture. Anyway, the foundations of the new edifice had barely had time to settle; further time was required to test out the new system. The new government therefore took power intending only to fix the cracks rather than enter into another new period of fundamental alterations.

This section focuses upon the reactions of the ministers in office between 1990 and 1993 to the public sector changes in particular and the system of public service support and advice in general. The ministers' views were expressed in the interviews with them during 1991. It needs to be remembered, however, that the new government with its new Prime Minister, Jim Bolger, aimed to make sweeping policy changes in the welfare system: in particular, to health, welfare benefits, housing, and accident compensation and, to a lesser extent, superannuation. Housing and health, moreover, involved structural as well as expenditure and funding changes.[19] It is perhaps not surprising that these very controversial policy areas provided the foci for most, but not all, the ministers' criticisms of the policy advice, implementation, and co-ordination provided by the public service. It ought also be noted that new governments, especially those bent upon change, are wont to criticize the public service. In 1972, according to J. F. Robertson, a former Secretary of Justice,

The [Labour] Government had a raft of new policies which had been formed without access to information or knowledge of the problems facing government. About three months after the election the Prime Minister, Mr Norman Kirk, called all permanent heads together and told them they weren't helping Government. He told them they were telling Ministers what the problem was rather than helping Government get its new policies on the road.[20]

Four of the ministers interviewed in 1991 and 1992—Jim Bolger, Bill Birch, Warren Cooper, and John Falloon—had been in cabinet during the Muldoon years and had therefore experienced the public service during its previous structure. There were others in the Government who were new to cabinet in 1990 but who had been back-benchers before 1984 and who could be assumed to have had some knowledge and understanding of the impact of Labour's administrative revolution. These were John Banks and Winston Peters (neither of whom was interviewed),[21] Philip Burdon, Paul East, Doug Kidd, Don McKinnon, Ruth Richardson, and Simon Upton, all in the 1990 cabinet; and, outside cabinet, Roger McClay and Graeme Lee. The remainder of the ministers interviewed were new to ministerial office and to being part of the governing caucus.

The ministers were asked questions designed to elicit responses that demonstrated their attitudes towards the public servants with whom they worked and for whose work they were constitutionally responsible. The questions asked of the ministers concerned: (1) their experiences of the kinds of difficulties that arose when ministers came to departments determined to impose certain objectives, (2) how ministers distinguished free and frank advice from bureaucratic obstruction, and (3) the issues on which ministers expected to be consulted.[22] Also, however, other questions (relating to their own goals and skills) elicited responses relevant to their attitudes towards the public service.

Some Praise, Many Criticisms

The ministers varied widely in their responses. Some were confident and positive about the general support and co-operation they had received from their public servants. For example a minister said, 'I have had no problems; it's a question of how you go about it. I accept and respect their confidence. It's like running a business. You have a chief executive.' Several ministers distinguished between their various portfolios, praising some but not others. One minister only, however, when discussing the relationship between minister and public servants, commented on the workloads of the latter. Public servants, particularly those at the senior levels,

> may be told at a meeting at nine o'clock at night that 'you have to do this again', and we want to say that there's no more money, and we want to cater for this many more people, and we want it done by yesterday. And we'll see you at nine in the morning. And the ministers cheerily go back to their offices—they're working hard too. I often wonder if my colleagues really appreciate that [public servants] are people with families as well.

Public servants were also poorly treated in that 'We keep very senior people waiting hours and hours and hours, to sit in front of a cabinet committee for ten minutes. With a bit better organization, maybe the time could be better used.'[23]

A pragmatic view of the situation from someone else was that:

> I don't think I've struck too much bureaucratic obstruction. I begin on the basis that if you get six or eight people sitting round the table their underlying motives are probably not that much different. Whether they're ministers or secretaries or departmental officials, they've all got mortgages to face every month, they've all got the usual things to worry about, and we may have a bit of a wrangle over something that doesn't really amount to a major sort of thing.

One minister, who in general was favourably impressed, said:

> I have been pleasantly surprised at how free and frank the advice is. I wouldn't really know what the political feeling or bias is of my staff . . . which party they would support . . . and I think that shows that their advice is free and quite often informal, and they all often warn me of the political pitfalls of saying one thing or doing another, or [pursuing] a policy direction. . . . I know some of my colleagues have some concerns about the motives of some of their staff in their departments. I have, [but] not too many . . . if I find somebody's advice is not helpful to the Government, I tell them and then probably use somebody else. And I have had occasion to warn, in one of the departments, that 'Your comments have been reported to me. If they're true they [the comments] are unhelpful to the minister and disloyal to the Government, and it shouldn't continue.'

And a colleague who praised highly the public sector reforms said of the prestigious department for which the minister was responsible, 'I've never experienced bureaucratic obstruction; I wouldn't expect it in my department. The freer and franker the advice, the more valuable the quality of the information.'

Almost all the ministers, including the speaker cited above who sympathized with the long work hours of public servants, had some criticisms to make of them. First, ministers had experienced, in the words of one, 'entrenched opinions'. Nevertheless, the opinion of this minister was that both sides had to bear the blame, for public servants 'may have served the government of a former minister and abrupt changes are fairly hard, particularly if the minister that's going to make the changes hasn't thought them through, and is imposing his or her own idiosyncratic touch or attitude on them'. This minister, however, had found it easy to distinguish free and frank advice from bureaucratic obstruction because 'I can distinguish it instinctively when someone's not trying to be helpful'.

Again, 'entrenched attitudes, and people protecting their status' was the response from a minister who had experienced difficulties with a department when attempting to devolve decision making to a regional level (creating redundancies). A colleague expressed the opinion that:

> I think I'm a reasonably good reader, [and] can usually pick if an argument seems to be running another agenda under the surface. But I mean it's just a matter of judgement, isn't it? You'd find out very rapidly if it wasn't, if you accept it and it goes wrong. I reject a great deal of advice or analysis that comes from [one department]. It's a poor quality department, it's been run down.

But the minister went on to praise another department. The strategy was to 'get people over here and start asking questions of them, that's the best way I suppose'. The problem was, however, that 'You have to spend time going over things. It's a waste of my time and, you know, we're employing a lot of people we shouldn't be.'

One department was depicted by the minister just quoted as 'the relic of a bygone culture that's just completely inappropriate for what's being asked for today'. The minister went on to describe a debate:

> I asked, 'Can you just explain to me why it is that we are providing the particular menu of subsidies and assistance to people that we are? Could [you] draw me up a big chart, a big matrix, and we'll go through it?' They were unable to tell me. . . . So that's what you have to do. If you haven't got the capability in-house you have to say, 'Right, we're going to pull in good people from outside', and then it becomes a matter of knowing people, and I spend my life pulling in people . . . getting the best people in the country, to say, 'Look, will you sign up for a year on a part-time basis, or serve on a committee or whatever?'

Another interviewee expressed the relationship between bureaucrats and ministers as 'an uneasy alliance'. Probably 'there always is a shake-down period . . . because bureaucrats will always look on politicians with jaundiced views'. Nevertheless ministers 'will always come up top, because we decide the fate'. Later in the interview the comment was made that, 'Officials don't always necessarily want to support what you're about. . . . We set out to reduce the state. And the cost of the state was too high. But in so doing we unleashed a can of worms where every matter that was defeated was revisited under another guise.'

When asked how ministers know when bureaucrats are being obstructive, a minister said that:

> Certain instincts are required for that. You can get fooled by people with agendas, and there's plenty of them in departments. Some [are] worse than others. The worst would be Education by ten-fold. I guess there's a certain amount of experience with that. It probably brings you to what is the essential thing for survival in this job, and that is understanding human nature. And figuring out what drives people. But the cure to that in the ministerial sense is to be open to contestable advice. . . . I will not accept [the ministry's] advice on anything without consulting those affected first. They [the public servants] found that quite irritating at first; they've gotten used to it now, so they actually go off and consult.

The minister had found that in one policy area this process had been simplified by the sectoral organization of 'very clear established structures which are very representative, and very accountable'. Advice to ministers had 'traditionally and structurally' come through the chief executive. But 'I only have minimal contact with chief executives; I interface directly with those that do the work. I tend to have lots of people come to see me from the department and in groups, and I make them justify their case and argue it.' Public servants 'go for this "yes minister" stuff. . . . sometimes they just agree with what you say, or they try to guess what the minister wants and go away and deliver it. I have no respect for that at all. I expect people to have the confidence in what they put up, and be prepared to justify it.'

The Public Sector Changes
Did the ministers link the changes to the public sector with their criticisms of it? Reference to the performance contracts between ministers and chief executives was made in a discussion on policy co-ordination. The agreements were seen as 'the avenue to achieve better cohesion'. Thus, 'If I require my chief executive to do some specific things, and so does the Minister of Education and so does the Minister of Women's Affairs, those are working documents as far as I'm concerned, and that's the mechanism by which I'm trying to ensure that what the government wants is achieved.' A similar perspective on the public sector changes was:

> I think the combination of the Public Finance Act and the State Sector Act profoundly alters, constitutionally and in real terms, respective roles and

responsibilities and checks and balances. One of the key tools now available to a minister is the performance agreement with the chief executive, and [when] you combine that with the way now under the Public Finance Act that you differentiate between inputs, outputs and outcomes, you have in the hands of the cabinet a new form of collective power and opportunity, and that is to effectively see all the respective performance agreements being imbued with the government's collective requirements. It puts very substantial power and therefore accountability in the hands of the government department. They are contracted to supply a result, it makes them more accountable, it changes the managerial culture substantially for the better if it's a properly managed process, and it's that cultural change brought about by the State Sector Act and the Public Finance Act that I think has been absolutely crucial. And we saw in the last budget, where just in a straight budgetary control exercise, we extracted 600 million dollars and then got a 'windfall' of another 500 million dollars at the end of the year. This is quite apart from benefit cuts, you know. We were able to reduce payments on behalf of the Crown. This . . . effectively allowed us under the Public Finance Act to get 600 million dollars, and that came from a much better definition of outputs, and therefore more carefully set priorities. We actually knew what we were purchasing; we were able to reprioritize. And in respect of the other 500 million dollars, that came because we broke the habit of this end-of-year spending that went on, because that determined the base budget for the following year.

This same minister also brought up the subject of the Official Information Act 1982 which, 'in my view . . . demystifies decision making'. The minister argued that it has improved accountability because 'bureaucrats are much more visible and accountable for their behaviour'. This had helped ministers because if there is poor quality advice 'it'll pretty soon be exposed'.

A different minister gave an example of the usefulness of the Public Finance Act: 'We couldn't work out what we were purchasing from [the public service] from the outputs that [officials] gave us. . . . So we said, we're not interested in purchasing those, thank you, we're going to do it a different way this year.' Accordingly the public servants, after giving reasons why they could not do what the minister wanted, were instructed to separate out the various outputs. They were told,

> You're doing three things: you're doing policy; you're in the business of writing contracts and administering and monitoring them; and you have a service delivery function, with respect to regulatory issues. Now you've got to fit it into one of those three big broad categories, and then design the outputs in terms of those three output classes. That actually led to a complete restructuring of the department. That would never have been possible before . . . without saying to the chief executive, 'I think you shouldn't have this team here or that team there', which is not one's job.

Further agreement about the success of the public sector reforms came from the minister who said that:

> What the State Sector Act and the Public Finance Act have done is substantially improve the quality in the accounting systems and management systems of government. And while they did develop a language of their own . . . outputs and outcomes, they made those changes to try and differentiate from what is a normal commercial balance [sheet]. I'm not sure they did the right thing doing that, but . . . regardless of that, the whole system of pseudo-commercialization of the accounting has been a major improvement in my view.

This minister also felt that the State Sector Act had created a situation like that existing between the chairperson of a board of directors and the chief executive of a commercial organization. This meant that the chief executives, not the ministers, were responsible for staff below the chief executive level. This was a substantial improvement.

Commenting on how frank advice could be distinguished from bureaucratic obstruction, a minister referred to the new era of chief executives. Basically it was up to the individual minister who 'can weigh these things up'.

> If you are open to information that comes in from other people who are experiencing, if you like, the downside of the policies . . . you'll quickly come to grips with it, and I think that one of the good things about the public service now is that people often are running some of these departments who really haven't had much of an association with [them] before. And that's good, because they've got [the] ability to quickly come to grips with the issues, and what needs to be changed and what's good and what's bad.

The minister added further that the Government needed to 'get the private sector coming into the government/departmental process, or seconding people from there, and having a two-way flow of people both ways'. This minister had been stimulated into making these comments by the 'very graphic descriptions of the personnel who are effectively my advisers' made by those who had attended a recent conference of a major sectoral interest group. The minister felt that the members of the ministry would have similarly negative views of those in the industry, and, 'the problem is that in both cases they don't appreciate the environment in which the other party is working'.

A colleague, in contrast, took a different viewpoint. Criticizing public service advice, the minister linked its shortcomings with a lack of bureaucratic accountability:

> I think it's healthy to have a suspicion about the quality of advice from the department. I'm not a big admirer of the public service in this country. I think that the last government of this country and the current government have both paid heavily politically for the poor quality of advice that they've had. . . .

How many chief executives have we seen fired so far? I mean we get hired and fired every three years, but it's easy enough for the public service just to play the waiting game and see off their political masters. If you look at the quality of decision making in the last budget, on superannuation, very basic calculations were not done. Quite apart from the political management considerations which are shocking (that's the politicians' responsibility) . . . they encouraged politicians to sign up to schemes that wouldn't work. And they should have known they wouldn't work. And . . . the quality of the tax advice from Treasury is miserable. We might as well not have the tax advisers in the Treasury. They cause more trouble than they're worth, and the minister who's been responsible for pursuing those items, following their advice, has inevitably come unstuck. We've ended up having to confront the most appalling situations in the select committee process as a result. . . . We need radical change within the public service.

The minister expanded on this theme:

I believe that we've extensively imposed much more demanding standards and given the responsibility that goes with it to individuals, but have not held people accountable for it. . . . I think that we political masters, if you like, have been very poor negotiators on behalf of the Crown [referring to the ministerial/chief executive performance contracts]. We're mostly not skilled negotiators, we're obviously inexperienced in the operation of those sorts of contracts, and we have no skilled advice available to us. So we make a hash of it. . . . It is clear that the level of control exercised by chief executives in quite important respects is quite miserable in terms of policy implementation and communications management, those sorts of things. . . . Take the social assistance reforms area, where we have now the Cabinet Committee that has co-ordinated a lot. There are about eleven ministers with responsibility in the area of social assistance reform. There are similar principles that drive the reforms in each of these areas; whether it's housing or health or social welfare, or whether it's the child support agency, whatever, the principles are essentially the same. . . . All those players are involved. And yet there's no sort of culture within the public service which gets people working together on a project basis. I know they have interdepartmental committees for other things but [they] lack the sort of robustness that's required for them to drive through policy changes. And yet those same departments were in many cases recommending those changes. . . . We're doing what we can to fix it, but I still have the more radical view than most of my colleagues, that there are still some people in senior positions who aren't able to fulfil their obligations, who haven't been moved on.

The minister asked:

When was the last time a chief executive was fired? . . . Take Treasury as an example. I happen to sit on the relatively dry side of cabinet but if you look at things like the revenue forecasting last year, and the Reserve Bank's actions in relation to money supply, enormous damage was done. You could probably measure in thousands the number of jobs needlessly lost in this country because forecasters got it wrong and acted on the basis of those forecasts. Now, it seems to me that nothing has happened which gives me any greater confidence it's not happening again now. . . .

When asked who would dismiss chief executives who were not performing well, the minister replied that ministers should have 'an absolute right, provided they go through a reasonably straightforward process, to get rid of chief executives'. The minister did not believe (responding to one of my comments) that this would lead to a politicized upper civil service, because 'what I'm suggesting is that the process of accountability requires that ministers must be able to get rid of chief executives. . . . How can I be held responsible for the actions of my department if I haven't got the most elementary authority? To despatch the chief executive if I need to. . . . I'm not suggesting that we should politicize the appointment. We should politicize the dismissal process, though.'

Treasury, the focus for some discontent by the above minister, was singled out for critical comment by others also:

I found in [one area] that the Treasury believed themselves to be the keepers of the dogma. . . . I've threatened them any number of times, if they gave me rubbishy advice like that I'd buy a corner dairy for them and make them run it successfully for six months before they're allowed to advise me on anything else. Because they just didn't understand anything about the real world of business. That won't come as a surprise to many people. But, you know, I simply rejected their advice. And a minister must actually have the courage to do that, and tell them why it's no good.

Later in this same interview the minister returned to the issue of Treasury advice, describing how policy views had been sought from outside consultants:

I got to the point where I was breaking out of the Treasury dominance and advice, and was actually at the point of trying to find ways of taking some of the money off them so I could purchase more, better advice from the market. . . . I have to have real advice from the market about business and investment and whatever, and Treasury is incapable of providing that.

When I observed that there were problems about alternative sources of advice in such a small country, the response was:

Yes, New Zealand's a very small pond, and Wellington's an incestuous little village. And you've got to be aware of that too. But you can hire in people not necessarily as consultants; a lot of the consultancy work is very low quality too, I'm afraid. New Zealand is desperately short of management skills across the whole spectrum. Plenty of graduates in economics and law and any other field you like . . . but very few people have got that leavening that comes from a good practical background, starting with good academic qualifications. That's why I actually think, without being arrogant about it, there's nothing quite like general practice in the self-employed environment to equip you to just about handle anything.

Another opinion on Treasury was that:

> I think that there are problems of delay that I have experienced, largely with Treasury I hasten to say, who take a somewhat more theoretical line than I do. And that has caused inter-departmental delays which are frustrating to me. I don't know that there's any alternative to that. . . . But they seem to want to get involved in everything that moves, whether it's financially relevant to them, or they just want to have a say.

One of the main thrusts of the public sector changes was to remove ministers from the processes of day-to-day decision-making, and policy implementation. This principle underlined the reshaping of the public service where, in many agencies, policy advice was separated from operational activities. Also the distinction between outputs and outcomes was another attempt to separate the public servants' tasks from those of the ministers. Several architects of the reforms wrote that one of the conditions for success for the financial management reforms of 1989 was 'the extent to which ministers are able to adopt a role focusing on the key strategic and tactical decisions'. The new regime should deliver them better information.[24] The ministers were therefore asked on what issues they expected to be consulted. Some examples of their responses follow.

One observation was that if there is something that senior officials need to discuss, 'they'll bring it up. And occasionally you'll come across constituents and other things will flash in your mind [and] you'll think "we must have a look at this or do that".' A minister who expected to be kept in touch in terms of getting up-to-date information about the policies and issues of the portfolio areas, as well as getting advice on those issues, commented, 'I expect them to be involved, to give me advice [on] how to tackle that issue, to be prepared to put resources into dealing with it. . . . And they've responded very well.' A minister who had struck no difficulties with the department in responding to ministerial goals explained:

> I would expect them to, and they do, let me know instantly of something which I ought to know [and the minister gave instances of politically salient problems that could arise]. I expect them to warn me if there's been some

> ghastly mistake made or something like that, from a political point of view.
> And keep me abreast of reform needs.

Another view was that the minister would expect to be consulted 'principally on the policy implications of the operational doings' (as distinct from issues of implementation). 'It's simply impossible to try to pretend that you can do any more than that. We daily do pretend—I keep having meetings about micro minutiae—but it's all a nonsense, it's really based on which wheel squeaks.' In comparison, one minister felt that the reforms had been frustrating in that they had taken the minister 'out of the day-to-day management effectively'. The whole relationship between minister and public servant depended much upon the capabilities and perceived roles of the individuals involved:

> A lot of ministers (without being judgemental about ministers, and this is where I'm not to be quoted by name), a lot of them really struggle. And a lot are only as good as their officials who support them, which means that they're not so much leading, they're in a sort of non-executive role.

Ministerial leadership, commented a colleague, was 'making sure the right people are doing the right things and are rewarded accordingly'. The minister continued:

> I'm conscious of departments where there's been uncertainty about who's in charge, that sort of thing. . . . So you can provide that in a variety of ways—initiating new ideas, putting them on a different course, just having meetings with the sectional heads, talking about what they are doing, asking them why they're doing it. . . . It's very much realizing that you've got a lot of people around you out there. You see, political leadership is not a person having a bright idea and saying 'we're going in that direction'. Political leadership is actually taking people with you.

The criticisms of the public sector structural reforms, as opposed to the actions and attitudes of the public servants, were generally fairly minor: 'I think the reforms that the previous government put in place were probably needed, but we will have to be the government that does some of the fine tuning so that it actually works.' The example given was the elaborate nature of some of the reporting processes. Indeed, the following quotation was the only sweeping condemnation made during the interviews:

> What I would say about all this restructuring is that it's wasted; it might look fine but it's created an awful lot of extra work. The Public Finance Act reporting [requirement] is such that ministers are bogged down in papers and their time is wasted. We've introduced a foreign language . . . outputs and

outcomes, a lot of jargon. We now prioritize and scope things till we're blue in the face. And I think it's very bad, because it's removed ministers—and I still use the old language, and refuse to talk in this jargon—it has removed ministers and particularly their advisers from the sort of everyday life of New Zealand by this sort of cell structure that operates in this way. I don't like it, and I'd like to break it down if I could. . . . We spend too much of our time worrying [about] . . . this sort of rubbish, instead of getting on with policy decisions and making things happen. So my complaint would be that these reforms have set up a structure which is so bureaucratic in its nature that we've lost sight of our objectives and we're too wrapped up in the practice of how things run, rather than the end result. . . . The old system was far simpler to understand, comprehend and be involved in than the new one has been.

This same minister provided some perceptive insights, not only demonstrating a critical view of the public service but also revealing what it had felt like as a new minister who was part of a reforming regime:

When I first became a minister, I seemed to be absolutely covered in paper. And I had the distinct feeling that maybe I was being kept like that deliberately. But I think once the new government came in, they [the public servants] got the message that . . . there are budgetary restraints and they haven't got time to go burying a minister under paper any more. I did say [that] to the policy group when I first became a minister and I was being briefed. I probably used rather farmyard language but I think I got the message across that I didn't want any bullshit. I don't like having the wool pulled over my eyes at all, I want things straight and no nonsense. And I think I've had it, mostly, but in the early days there seemed to be a lot of paper. As a new minister, and not ever having been in government, I found it very difficult at first to understand what one actually does—you don't get a job prescription in this. You're not told how things [work], you're just expected to take everything up where it was left off. And I found that quite difficult at times . . . and it's really taken me up until now to actually learn the process.

Despite the tenor of the remarks just cited, however, the single most striking impression gained from the interviews of the ministers of the 1990–93 National Government was their sympathy with the primary thrust of the public sector reforms. The criticisms were mainly of, interestingly, each other, of the public servants themselves, and of particular departments. It is of course impossible to tell to what extent those criticisms were valid ones. Certainly the areas that had come under strongest attack from members of the general public, especially health and education, were the ones that also attracted critical comment from the ministers. But without examining these policy areas in detail we cannot know whether the public servants were failing in their duty to give good policy advice, or whether ministers were failing to heed the 'free and frank' advice from their officials. As far as the ministers were concerned, however—and it is their perspective that is our focus here—most of the criticisms were framed within the assumptions of the transformed New Zealand state: the new, contractual type of accountability relationships between chief executive and minister; the separation of policy advice from operations; the clarification of agency objectives encapsulated in the Public Finance Act; the devolved and privatized commercial activities; and the emphasis upon policy contestability. The next section focuses upon this last aspect, given its significance in practical and symbolic terms to the taking and giving of advice to cabinet, and the New Zealand policy communities.

The Cabinet, the Public Service, and Policy Contestability

In March of 1993 it was reported that, excluding the advice provided in the Beehive offices of the ministers, there were an average of 52 advisers per minister in the departments and ministries.[25] These individuals, with their chief executives, provide the permanent system of advice available to ministers. Most policy advice is provided to the New Zealand cabinet by this body of bureaucrats. As was shown by many of the ministers' comments quoted above, however, an increasingly important source of advice is from outside the public service, especially from the range of consultants now employed both by ministers and by public servants. Contestability is also sought from some sections of the community who are affected by particular policies:

> It's that process of capture, it's allowing them [the public servants] to filter the information you get, that gets you into trouble with the outside world. So it's very important that you say to your department, 'All right, we're going to go and deal with that one. No, I don't want you to write a report about it, I'm very happy to have your report about it but let's go and talk to them, we'll hear what you say and what they say and then we can sit down and work out something that's going to be acceptable.'

This is an aspect of seeking advice that is dealt with in the next chapter.

The purpose of using paid consultants for policy advice, as was also displayed by the interviews, is two-fold: to provide 'contestability' of information and policy views, in essence challenging the views of the public servants; and supplementing the sorts of expertise provided by the permanent advice system—'the core departments aren't able to give quite the policy advice, they don't have quite the expertise'. For example, a whole range of consultants has been used during the process of corporatizing and privatizing since 1984 (spawning a tribe of consulting firms in Wellington, some doing very well indeed out of their contracts). The change processes since 1990, both structural and policy, have also been influenced by a pot-pourri of consultants' reports.

Under the Labour Government, to take just one instance from that period, the Cabinet Expenditure Review Committee authorized a review of the organizational requirements of the New Zealand Police 'which distils into a single document the results of past reviews, overseas research and an up-to-date evaluation in the light of the principles of State Sector reform'.[26] During late 1990 and early 1991 under National, when housing was under scrutiny, for example, Treasury hired a firm from the USA, ABt Associates, to advise it on accommodation supplements. The firm Buttle Wilson was also employed during the housing changes to conduct a scoping analysis on the various options available for selling Housing Corporation mortgages.[27] Again, in August 1993 a consultative group headed by Jeff Todd (a senior partner at Price Waterhouse) was set up to advise the Minister of Education, Lockwood Smith, on the funding of tertiary education and training. This group employed consultants to advise it. It was reported that, by 14 February 1994, $62,712 had been paid to the consultants (excluding GST).[28]

The way in which this type of advice has developed, the rapidity of its growth, and the range of issues on which reports have been written, are topics beyond the scope of this book. Its effects upon the nature of New Zealand government have, it appears, been profound, both in terms of the direction of advice given—primarily neo-liberal economic doctrine—and in terms of how this policy system has affected relationships between ministers and public servants and, moreover, the way in which ministers perceive their own roles. For, more than in the past, ministers have been made to feel free to seek advice from elsewhere, not the 'unpaid' advice from pressure groups, fashionably perceived to be tainted with self-interest, but paid advice, for some reason seen as 'neutral'. Such freedom of action has had its costs, as was apparent from the interviews, for, by having a wider range of advice in their hands, ministers run the risk of overburdening themselves and the decisional structures.

Moreover, frequent use of consultants can undermine the authority of the advice of public servants. Of course this can perhaps be no bad thing; expert consultants can challenge the tired, historically-based assumptions of public servants. On the other hand, because those public servants have frequently a much greater depth and grasp of policy issues, the advice of the permanent, institutionalized bureaucracy should not be undermined.[29] Consultants, unlike public servants, have no 'duty' whatsoever to the public interest; and neither do they have a continuous, constitutionally sanctioned relationship with cabinet ministers, based upon offices rather than individuals, and lasting through changes of government. The latter characteristic provides a strong incentive for public service advisers to provide neutral advice. Consultants, in contrast, have the sole task to provide expert advice that pleases the paymaster. Thus this aspect of the advice system to cabinet is based upon short-term personal relationships, where continuity of role and neutrality of advice are not emphasized. This can liberate policy advice, for consultants might also produce refreshingly original ideas, but ministers need to assess their contributions against those who have 'duty' rather than 'loyalty' to them. The evidence of the interviews indicated that not all ministers clearly distinguished between the two sources of advice, and their respective faults and virtues.

The notions of duty and loyalty have been recently distinguished and refined by John Martin. He agrees with John Roberts that 'duty' is preferable to 'loyalty' when characterizing the public servant–minister relationship, 'because "loyalty" implies, I believe, a personal relationship which may exist but which is not required. Duty is always attached to the office.'[30] Again in Martin's words, '*within the law* "duty to the government of the day" is the paramount, or presumptive, duty of the public servant'.[31] The idea of 'loyalty', however, has been a developing hallmark of administrative and political behaviour in central government in New Zealand, as evidenced by the ministers in the Bolger Government, in their search for contestable advice. As a normative notion, 'loyalty' competes against the notion of 'duty' as desirable attributes in policy advisory systems.

'Loyalty' has also to an extent become a working criterion of the roles of chief executives, because they are linked contractually through performance agreements with their ministers. This relationship in itself has become personalized through the idea of the contract, the accountability between official and politician, for these agreements are between named individuals and not by virtue of the offices held by them. Furthermore, the temporary nature of the contract, for ministers come and go and chief executives in New Zealand are on fixed-term contracts, also serves to personalize the relationship. Despite the personalization of politics newly implanted at the top of the public service, the basic structures are classic bureaucracies recently modernized by managerial fashions adopted from the private sector. Thus there is some conflict here between competing notions of public service. This was evident in the interviews of the ministers.

It is probably wise to see the relationships between ministers and public servants as characterized by endemic suspicion rather than trust and co-operation. In this sense the contemporary stress upon 'contestability' is a recognition of reality. The very system of cabinet government itself is built on structured opposition, not only between government and opposition but also between the political and the administrative executive. One does not have to live for long in Wellington to discern the politely veiled disdain of the public servant for the politician. The 'veil' provided is the respect required by the constitutional relationship between public servant and minister. And the attitudes shown in the interviews of ministers towards their public servants often displayed discontent, even contempt.

It is not surprising, therefore, that there has also developed a separate system of advice to the Prime Minister, designed both to strengthen the incumbent's policy capacity and to provide policy co-ordination, thus challenging the traditional agencies. Further, individual ministers have strengthened the advice available to them in their private offices. The ways in which these ministerial and prime ministerial advice systems have developed also demonstrate bureaucratization and personalization. As the New Zealand constitution itself changes with the advent of coalition governments, this aspect of cabinet will expand and develop further.

Servicing and Advising Cabinet and the Prime Minister

The offices of cabinet and Prime Minister have had an interesting and complex history which demonstrates the interwoven trends of bureaucratization and personalization. The first of these has been shown by the development of specialized public service agencies, containing increasingly expert staffs, to service the needs of cabinet as a whole, and the Prime Minister in particular. As Max Weber wrote:

> Bureaucratization offers above all the optimum possibility for carrying through the principle of specializing administrative functions according to purely objective considerations. Individual performances are allocated to functionaries who have specialized training and who by constant practice learn more and more. The 'objective' discharge of business primarily means a discharge of business according to *calculable rules* and 'without regard for persons'.[32]

Weber linked the process of bureaucratization with the type of authority based upon 'rational authority', the rule-bound, neutral organization. This was one of three ideal types in Weber's schema, the others being characterized as 'traditional' and 'charismatic' authority. Although, along with bureaucratization, personalization has also developed in New Zealand cabinet government, this latter trend fits tidily into neither the 'traditional' nor the 'charismatic' categories; we are not talking about monarchs or their equivalents or, usually, about charismatic leaders as understood by Weber.

Nevertheless, these latter two models serve to focus attention upon individual leaders, a personalized version of political authority that is quite contrary to the rational/legal form of the modern bureaucracy. And both the personalized and the bureaucratic forms of authority have found their way into the inner reaches of cabinet government. In short, Roberts' and Martin's distinction between the 'duty' of an employee—the public servant—and the loyalty of an employee—based upon a contract between specific persons—is as appropriate and illuminating a dichotomy here as it was in the discussion of the public service and the use of the consultants. How and why this apparently paradoxical situation has occurred within the internal advice systems of cabinet and Prime Minister are the topics of the following sections.

Servicing Cabinet and the Prime Minister: The Early Years
On 29 January 1948 Foss Shanahan became the first Cabinet Secretary to be admitted into a meeting of cabinet. In 1949 he depicted the responsibilities of the Cabinet Office (CO) as: facilitating interdepartmental co-operation; 'reconciling, where necessary, the conflicting interests of Departments'; monitoring the implementation of cabinet decisions; and servicing the standing committees of cabinet or officials.[33] (Since 1988 the CO has also serviced the *ad hoc* cabinet committees.) These functions have very much remained the tasks of the Office, whatever its precise title and administrative situation. Indeed, there had been a felt need during the Second World War for a more adequate body to provide for better co-ordination and, among other things, a system for verifying that action had been taken on cabinet decisions.[34] The Prime Minister in 1949, Sidney Holland, suggested that those matters ought to be the responsibility of the Cabinet Secretary.[35] The New Zealand CO did not, however, assume the task of policy advice to the Prime Minister, as did the British agency of the same name.

Until the restructuring of the Prime Minister's Department in 1975, and the appointment of the Advisory Group created by Muldoon, Prime Ministers had to rely upon their External Relations (later Foreign Affairs) staff and other senior public servants, such as Treasury officers, for advice. As Jonathan Boston has pointed out, Prime Ministers were fortunate enough to have had a series of outstanding public servants in both the CO and in Foreign Affairs; and Prime Ministers usually also took the foreign affairs portfolio, giving them access to public service advice and enhancing their own political authority. Boston has further argued that, because the post-war Prime Ministers were seldom policy initiators, 'they had less need for a large personal staff or a high-powered, multi-disciplinary team of professional advisers'.[36] The tiny group of advisers provided for Prime Ministers had nevertheless been criticized. The 1962 Royal Commission favoured the strengthening of the Cabinet Office, for example, and during the 1960s the CO expanded its functions to cope with the needs of the developing system of cabinet committees. Also, more help was given to the Prime Minister for writing speeches and for publicity purposes.

In order to disentangle their histories, the development of the agencies designed to support cabinet and the Prime Minister is demonstrated chronologically in Table 7.1. The prime focus of this study is, however, the period since 1975.

The Contemporary Cabinet Office

In most respects the role of the CO today is as stated by Foss Shanahan in the late 1940s. The 1989 statement of outputs under the Public Finance Act 1989 for the CO gives a good indication of its functions. Its outputs were: (1) to give 'constitutional, policy and procedural advice on the nature of the Executive Council and Cabinet process' to the Prime Minister, ministers, government departments, and the Governor-General; (2) to provide secretarial services to cabinet, the cabinet committees, the Governor-General, and the Executive Council; (3) to administer the Royal Honours system; and (4) to produce publications such as the *Cabinet Office Manual* and Cabinet Office Circulars. The latter are government management directives which are distributed to all ministers and chief executives.[37] An additional important function of the CO is its role as keeper of cabinet papers of the current and previous administrations. (After 25 years most papers go to National Archives.)

The CO is responsible for an awe-inspiring amount of reading, monitoring, and shifting of pieces of paper. In the first nine months of 1990, for example, it handled 738 cabinet papers (including petitions and regulations). Added to this load were 1100 papers for cabinet committees. And the Cabinet Secretary observed that the length of submissions was increasing.[38] The CO guards its neutrality fiercely, since this is essential to its authority as a neutral, prestigious secretariat, concerned with efficient cabinet government. Over the years, as can be seen from Table 7.1 and the subsequent parts of this chapter, it has had different homes. But it has always had a degree of autonomy.

Advice and Support for the Prime Minister: 1975–90

'I am getting information that no government has ever had before, by way of confidential statistics from various business enterprises, producer boards and other sources. And it doesn't go into departmental files. It comes directly in here.'[39] In many ways Robert Muldoon was the first modern Prime Minister. Like Margaret Thatcher in Britain, he built up his own private system of

Table 7.1: The Development of the Offices of Prime Minister and Cabinet, 1926–93

1926   Establishment of the Prime Minister's Department.

A small secretarial department was formed to service the Prime Minister and the cabinet. The Secretary of Foreign Affairs was also the Head of the PM's Department. A member of the PM's Department acted as Cabinet Secretary; cabinet meetings were irregular; and no minutes were taken of meetings.

1943   Establishment of the External Affairs Department.

The Prime Minister's Department (including a small Prime Minister's Office and, from 1949, the Cabinet Office) was a fairly autonomous unit within External Affairs, linked with that Department through the joint Permanent Head.

1947–9   Development of the Cabinet Office (CO).

Led by Foss Shanahan, Secretary to Cabinet from 1945, the cabinet processes were formalized: there were regular meetings, a cabinet agenda, and minutes. In December 1949 Shanahan became Secretary of the Cabinet.

1975   Establishment of the Prime Minister's Department (PMD), formally separated from the Ministry of Foreign Affairs.

It contained separate elements: the CO; the Prime Minister's Office (PMO); the Press Office; the External Intelligence Bureau, and the newly created Advisory Group. The CO was a separate part of the PMD (total staff about 75); the Cabinet Secretary was administratively subordinate to the Permanent Head.

1987   Bifurcation of the Prime Minister's Department into its autonomous parts.

The two parts were the CO and the PMO. The latter included the Advisory Group, the Press Office, and the Prime Minister's private office staff. (The External Intelligence Bureau became part of the Ministry of Foreign Affairs.)

1988   The State Sector Act was passed.

In April 1988, in accordance with the Act, the CO and the PMO became departments of state headed by two chief executives.

1989   Publication of *Review of the Prime Minister's Office and Cabinet Office*.

The Report proposed: (a) Prime Minister and Cabinet Office (part of the bureaucracy); and (b) the Prime Minister's Office (for political advice).

1989   Establishment of the Department of the Prime Minister and Cabinet (PMC).

The components were: the Advisory Group; the Analytical Group; the CO; and the Domestic and External Secretariat. Also there was the Corporate Services Unit. The Prime Minister's Private Office was established to provide media and secretarial support and political advice.

1990   Expansion of Department of the Prime Minister and Cabinet.

PMC made responsible for services to the Vice-regal Office and for Government House.

1991   Further Expansion of the Department of the Prime Minister and Cabinet

The External Assessments Bureau became part of PMC; the Change Team on Targeting Social Assistance was established; units providing policy advice on health sector changes were established (the National Interim Provider Board, the Health Reforms Directorate, the Coordination Group). The Enterprise Council (an independent forum of business leader) was supported by its own 14-member group within the PMC.

Sources: J. Boston, 'Advising the Prime Minister in New Zealand: The Origins, Functions and Evolution of the Prime Minister's Advisory Group', *Politics*, Vol. 23 (1988), pp. 8–20, and 'The Case for a Department of Prime Minister and Cabinet', *Public Sector*, Vol. 12 (1989), p. 7; D. Hunn and H. Lang, 'Review of the Prime Minister's Office and Cabinet Office' (1989); P. G. Millen (Secretary of the Cabinet), 'Introduction and Historical Note', Cabinet Office, *Cabinet Office Manual* (Wellington, 1979); 'Report of the Department of Prime Minister and Cabinet' (1 June to 30 June 1990), pp. 3–6, and (1 July 1991 to 31 December 1991), pp. 4–6; and J. B. Ringer *An Introduction to New Zealand Government* (Christchurch, Hazard Press, 1991), p. 60.

policy and strategic advice. There had been some dissatisfaction amongst the members of the Labour Government about the quality of advice available to the Prime Minister, and when Robert Muldoon won the 1975 election he immediately set about making changes. Within the reformed Prime Minister's Department (PMD), the Prime Minister established a new Advisory Group, popularly known as the 'Think-tank', headed by Bernard Galvin (deputy secretary of Treasury).

The members of the group were involved in the following sorts of issues: when there were inter-agency disputes; where the policy situation was 'particularly fluid'; where there was 'no clear sponsor' for dealing with an issue; or when there were, as an Advisory Group member was quoted as saying, 'issues that the bureaucracy is ill-structured to deal with and doesn't like'.[40] As we shall see, this last role has been a recurring one, and reappeared in particularly lively form between 1990 and 1993. The primary weapon possessed by the group was persuasion: because it could not itself initiate papers for cabinet, it either had to persuade the departmental officers on the interdepartmental committees (where it had representation) of the group's perspective, or else convince the Prime Minister of its case, and leave it to the Prime Minister, in turn, to convince cabinet.[41] Like all such political organizations lacking in independent decision making and policy implementation powers, the group depended upon the patronage of its sponsor, the Prime Minister, to support it in the bureaucratic underworld of tactics and argument. Of equal importance was the calibre of the leadership of the group itself; it was a wise move to head the group with a respected, senior public servant from the core public service, thus to some extent at least diffusing the inevitable suspicions about the group's possible capture of the ear of the Prime Minister to the detriment of the voices of other ministers and agencies.

When David Lange became Prime Minister in 1984, he continued with the same structure; that is, he had a group of private secretaries and press officers, and the Advisory Group of between eight and ten, drawn from the public and private sectors. In his time, however, the head of the group from 1985 was not a senior public servant but a former academic and Director of the Opposition Research Unit, John Henderson. Each member of the group was in charge of a particular policy area, and each took part in interdepartmental and cabinet working committees. Despite the change of government the character of the Advisory Group remained similar to that which had existed under National. Boston has written that it 'remained small, youthful, largely non-hierarchical, multi-disciplinary, essentially non-partisan, and short-term in its policy focus'.[42] Its primary tasks were: liaison between ministers, interest groups, and departments, including providing the Prime Minister with an 'early-warning system'; and playing a role in the formulation and analysis of policy, particularly contributing an independent viewpoint.[43]

As Jonathan Boston has also noted, however, 'Despite having some talented people, the Advisory Group was no match for the formidable resources available to [Roger] Douglas from the Treasury and his Beehive Office. This imbalance became increasingly obvious as the conflict over economic and social policy deepened.'[44] Lange lacked the resources to cope with Douglas's challenge. And some ministers, including Douglas, criticized the influence of the group (then a mere eight members).[45]

In 1987 the PMD was split into the Prime Minister's Office (PMO) and the Cabinet Office, two separate departments funded with one Vote. The PMO was to provide policy advice, co-ordination, support services, and news media liaison to the Prime Minister. It was headed by the Director, John Henderson. The Prime Minister's Advisory Group continued, comprising eleven advisers and support staff. The 1989 Report of the PMO provides an illuminating list of the committees and working parties on which members of the group had taken part, from chairing working parties on early childhood education through to membership of the two Officials' Committees on Maori Development.[46] Harvey McQueen has observed that, when he was appointed to the PMO in 1988, the Office was understaffed: 'everyone worked under tremendous pressure', and turnover was high. The staff, rather than acting as a 'think tank', tended to react to immediate problems and issues. 'Compared with the services available to other Ministers, the Prime Minister's Office was way behind.'[47] Moreover, there was a real problem about the different functions that the Advisory Group had to perform. John Henderson, for example, when Director, advised the Prime Minister on defence issues and also chaired the weekly meeting of a communications committee which tried to co-ordinate the flow of information from throughout the ministers' offices.[48]

In 1989 changes were made to the Prime Minister's Department, by then led by a new Prime Minister, Geoffrey Palmer. A review had been carried out by Don Hunn and Henry Lang in response to the sorts of criticisms made above of the Lange support system. Policy co-ordination, also, long a problem for New Zealand cabinet government, as we saw in the last two chapters, had been made more difficult by the public sector reforms. The quality of advice from the PMD needed to be improved and the number of expert advisers expanded. Moreover, 'there is a widespread view that the line that should exist between political and bureaucratic advice has become blurred'.[49] The political and administrative advisers should be placed in a separate Private Office. The arrangements should be flexible 'so that each incumbent has the ability to impress his or her own personal stamp on them'.[50] The staff should be employed on contracts which should be linked with the Prime Minister's term of office.

Hunn and Lang advocated bringing together the CO with the advisory side of the PMO in order to combine the advisory and co-ordination functions under a single chief executive, thus improving the policy co-ordinating task of the Prime Minister. It would also provide for better accountability.[51] The CO would be brought back under the umbrella of the Department 'to see that the Prime Minister has proper oversight of the Cabinet machine, which he chairs'. The CO, however, needed some independence because of its constitutional function in serving the Governor-General and the Executive Council, as well as cabinet.[52] In 1989 the Department of Prime Minister and Cabinet (PMC) was created.

The actual policy operations of the PMC were split into the Advisory Group, responsible for the provision of short-term advice, and, in accordance with the Hunn/Lang recommendations, the Analytical Group, concerned with medium-term policy development. In answer to a question by the Leader of the Opposition, Jim Bolger, during the debate on the Appropriations Bill 1989 (Vote: Prime Minister), the Prime Minister, Geoffrey Palmer, said that the Prime Minister's Department had been strengthened, because 'contestability of advice was the essence of successful policy-making'.

Intellectual expertise was needed in the Prime Minister's Office to contest the advice coming from Treasury. The new analysts would produce information on inflation, balance of payments, and currency. Helen Clark, Deputy Prime Minister, added that the restructuring was to enable the PM 'to fulfil his duties as Prime Minister, as co-ordinator of the Government, and as the person who had to bring together the various strands of policy advice'.[53] In early 1990 about ten people were appointed to the Advisory Group and another ten to the Analytical Group. The Prime Minister's Office, the separate, private, political office recommended by the Hunn/Lang Report, was headed initially by Margaret Wilson, an academic lawyer and former President of the Labour Party, and contained about twenty-seven people, including two trade unionists in order to build better links between unions and the Labour Party.[54]

The distinction between administrative and political support has not always been clearly understood. This has not been a problem where the CO has been concerned, since it was always clearly composed of public servants whose task is to support the procedures and structures of cabinet. There is no doubt, either, that a PM's public relations advisers belong in his or her private Office. But the roles of the different policy analysts, or even the speech writers, are not always clear, at least in part because Department and Office each contain mixtures of private and public sector employees. To illustrate this point, in March 1990 the then Leader of the Opposition, Jim Bolger, challenged the appointment of ten policy analysts to the restructured PMC on three-yearly contracts, arguing that this was unwise given there could be a change of government later that year. The Chief Executive of the PMC, David McDowall, in defence cited Hunn/Lang's distinction between administrative and political functions, saying that the PMC was 'a routine public service department'. Therefore, the analysts would be able to serve any government.[55]

Neither has the distinction been invariably clear in practice. It was reported, for example, that when Geoffrey Palmer was Prime Minister he hired David Slack for the Prime Minister's Office (PMO) to write his speeches. But contributions to speeches also came from other advisers from both the PMO and the PMC, and other ministers and departmental officials.[56] As events have shown, since 1989 the distinction between policy and political advice has continued to be unclear, despite their official, institutional separation. This is primarily because of the increased pressure on prime ministers as chief co-ordinators of government by cabinet. And the more radical the reforms attempted by a government, the more acute becomes the need for a Prime Minister to integrate policy formulation and implementation, and, additionally, mobilize public support for the government's policies.

Advice and Support for the Prime Minister: 1990–93
The new Department of Prime Minister and Cabinet successfully co-ordinated and survived the change of government in 1990. The chief executive, David McDowell, emphasized the neutral and ongoing role of the PMC when, summarizing the second half of 1990, he wrote that the Department must be responsive to the changes wanted by the new Prime Minister 'since it exists primarily to support the Head of Government and Chairman of Cabinet of the day'.[57] Extensive briefing notes were provided for the new Prime Minister, Jim Bolger, describing structures and processes and recommending changes.[58] The initial paragraph is worth quoting in full, not least because it implicitly puts forward a justification for enhanced services to the Prime Minister:

> A number of factors have combined to build up the role of the Prime Minister in New Zealand. The television concentration on the heads of political parties and the Head of Government is one. But there are others. The scope of Government activity has widened. It has grown more complex. And many of the big issues—fostering growth, protecting the environment—are of a multi-sectoral nature. All of this calls for a central political head who can inject coherence into the range of Government policies. In short, the Prime Minister is increasingly required for functional as well as political reasons to be a co-ordinator, an integrator and a mediator on policy issues as well as leader of a political party.[59]

The *Briefing Notes* included advice on altering the cabinet committees, on the relationship between the cabinet committees and officials, and on how to handle the policy agenda and the budgetary process. It was observed that the PMC had remained 'a modest size' of about 50, including the CO (but excluding the recent addition of the 35 Government House staff). In comparison the Australian counterpart was said to have more than 600 people.[60] The separation of 'politics' from 'policy' advice advocated by Hunn and Lang was not always feasible:

> We Public Service policy advisers cannot operate in a total political vacuum, oblivious to the play of political forces around us. For their part the political and media advisers have to take account of what the policy formulators are saying or risk getting the policy substance wrong, running the Prime Minister off the rails or onto a sideline in the process. *So there has to be a degree of integration of politics and policy, a process which must be presided over by the Prime Minister himself.*[61]

The presentation of policy decisions was given as an example. The sentiments of this quotation, made at the very beginning of the new regime, were in 1991 reiterated by an observation from a prominent insider who said that the distinction was 'more theory than reality'. Indeed, there was evidently an active policy of greater integration between the PMO on the ninth floor of the Beehive and the PMC on the eighth.

The PMC between July and December 1991 provided the Prime Minister with 'several hundred advisory and briefing notes on a range of issues before Government', an average of twelve written commentaries per week on the agenda items for cabinet, responses to correspondents, and 200 draft responses to parliamentary questions. Also the Department was chairing the following officials' standing committees: Strategy, Enterprise, Growth and Employment, Social and Family Policy, Environment, Treaty of Waitangi, and External Relations, Defence and Security. It provided the secretariat and liaison for all officials' standing committees. The Department also contributed to the 1991 Budgetary process.[62] The extent to which the PMC had evolved into a central, co-ordinating body, as well as providing policy and tactical advice, is evident.

After Jim Bolger became Prime Minister there were three marked changes, heightening the significance of the PMC as a key arm of cabinet government. First, the Department became larger. By the end of 1991 there were 141 staff members (including the 33 in the External Assessments Bureau and the 34 looking after Government House.[63] Of course the actual policy circles in which the staffers were involved would be much larger still, given the number of consultants employed and the individuals brought in on the various working parties. Second, the distinction between policy and political advice was further blurred, as was shown by the third factor: Jim Bolger used the PMC as a home for three key strategic initiatives: changing social assistance, the health reforms, and enterprise.

The Change Team for Social Assistance, headed by a senior Treasury officer and composed of members from the public and private sectors, was located within the PMC from the beginning of January 1991, and the team in turn employed consultants to advise it. Its purpose was to investigate targeting options across the proposed welfare reforms, and it also contributed to the 1991 Budgetary process. The Convener of the Change Team was accountable to the Prime Minister for the outputs concerning policy advice on targeting, whilst the management responsibility for that output was delegated by the Prime Minister to the Minister of Health. The various health groups housed in the PMC (see Table 7.1) also reported to the Minister of Health, Simon Upton.[64] The National Interim Provider Board, as its name suggested, was a short-lived resident of the Department set up to supervise the changes to the new health providers set out in the 1991 Budget. Spending on health reform consultants alone was in February 1993 reported to have totalled nearly $8 million.[65]

One of the stated outcomes for the group within the PMC set up to co-ordinate and communicate issues relating to the health reforms was 'public awareness of the nature and need for reform', a goal that alone demonstrates that the PMC was not confining itself to non-political activities.[66]

In November 1991 the Prime Minister also established an Enterprise Council as part of the restructuring of the PMC and his Office. Bolger said, 'I want to employ that unit on the high priority task of fostering a constructive and collaborative approach between the State agencies involved in regulating or encouraging private sector development.'[67] The Council operated out of the PMC, serviced by a fourteen-member group (including seconded public servants and private sector contractors) within the Department, but the Council itself was an independent group. The aim of the Council was to provide a direct line of communication between the business sector, ministers and senior officials, and to help formulate the Government's medium- and long-term strategy. The Prime Minister announced at the Council's inception that it was set up 'to develop the relationship between the government and business and union leaders'. He said, 'I want a body that will give me informed advice from the workfront, as opposed to the more theoretical view we tend to receive from traditional advisers in the state sector.'[68] The Council assisted with the formulation of policy proposals as well as making its own suggestions. The range of its work included areas relating to education and training, taxation, research and development, export strategy, and business management.

The Enterprise Council was chaired by the Prime Minister and comprised a range of representatives from top management, and one trade unionist.[69] Large companies were heavily represented; and only one member was a woman. Nevertheless, despite the careful choice of representatives, the views of the Council did not always coincide with those of the Government, especially of the Minister of Finance, Ruth Richardson (1990–93). A sub-group publicly put forward a business incentives package in May 1992, for the proposals only to be equally publicly dismissed by Jim Bolger. According to one report, while some council members intended to have a real input into policies, the non-explicit purpose of the Council was to engage the support of business for government policies rather than to create a body which might challenge the economic agenda.[70] This raises a central problem in hiring *ad hoc* advisory élites: there is a delicate balance to be found for them and their political employers, between support and usefulness in the eyes of each side of this political arrangement.

It seems, therefore, that the three sets of advisers brought into the PMC between 1990 and 1993 were to serve three different purposes. The Enterprise Council existed primarily to enlist practical and symbolic business élite support for the Government's economic policy direction, and secondarily to enable that direction to continue with the help of the advice of the business community. The bodies involved in health were there to side-step the bureaucracy, specifically the Department of Health, and provide leadership and support, and recruit expertise, for the very controversial changes to the health system. The third group, the Change Team for Social Assistance, was probably the only one which had a policy co-ordinating task but of course it was also formed to propose new social policy mechanisms. Thus the PMC did indeed provide a home for different sorts of groups, with differing purposes.

According to a minister interviewed during the 1990–93 Government, the PMC was

> simply a parking place for temporary agencies. . . They've got no connection with the Prime Minister's Department in practical terms, they simply pay their salaries, that's all. . . You want to assemble a very specific team of skills for a short period. You've got a department [Health] which is regarded as being weak, seriously weakened actually, so you need to set up a special team where everybody's got their golden parachutes back to where they've come from. The Prime Minister's Department in theory is supposed to play this co-ordinating role; in my experience they simply get in the way.

This comment illustrates the difficulties inherent in advice agencies of the variety of the PMC. They are rather like upper houses of legislatures: if they have effective powers they challenge other authorities, the ministers in this case; and if they are weak they might as well not exist. Prime ministers need expert advice and a pivotal, personal department; but they have to guard against the suspicion that cabinet government is becoming prime ministerial government.

The Prime Minister's Office
The job description of Jim Bolger's Chief Executive to the Prime Minister accurately indicated the tasks of the PMO. The responsibilities were: office management and administration (including delegation of duties, managing the PM's diary, and financial responsibilities); providing advice to the Prime Minister 'on a wide range of administrative, managerial and political issues as required' and attending advisory committees and meetings; acting as liaison officer between the Prime Minister and the Deputy Prime Minister, the Prime Minister and the other ministers, the Prime Minister and caucus members, the Prime Minister and the Leader of the House and the Whips, the Manager of Ministerial Services and the general public; and travelling with the Prime Minister when required, taking overall responsibility for the PM's

travel arrangements.[71] To give some idea of the people involved, in mid-1993, for example, Bolger appointed to his private office Michael Wall, chief policy adviser, and Rob Eaddy, chief of staff. Wall, with a background in advertising, had worked for National during the 1990 general election campaign, and in the PMO was responsible for Bolger's public image and some of his speeches. He also ran the weekly meetings of the Beehive press secretaries and was on the Communications and Strategy Committee chaired by the Minister of Customs, Murray McCully. Eaddy had a background in defence and defence history, and ran the Bolger office after 1987. He provided the point of contact for back-benchers and dealt with Official Information requests, the appointments diary, sensitive correspondence, and parliamentary tactics. Other important advisers were David Kirk, a medically trained management consultant with a National supporting background, and Wayne Eagleson, former parliamentary research unit director and the 1993 National Party campaign director.[72]

The Prime Minister's Office has become increasingly expensive to run. Just prior to the 1990 general election, with Mike Moore as Prime Minister, the gross annual salary cost was $940,959. In February 1991 Jim Bolger's office cost $808,551, in March 1992 it had cost $977,401, in February 1993 $954,180, and by March 1994 the total cost was $1,111,126. In his 1994 Office were six permanent staff members and 13 working on contract.[73] Increasingly, it seemed, the PMO was responsible for the overall political strategy of the Government, reflecting the heightened salience of political leadership in the age of television on the one hand, and, on the other, the exigencies of policy justification and presentation in an age of radical policy change.

The Private Offices of Ministers

The system of advice and support for ministers has also changed. During the term of the fourth Labour Government the staffing of ministers' offices altered character. Until then, most staff had been supplied from the Public Service, including the press secretaries who came from the Department of Tourism and Publicity. The Labour ministers who came in in 1984, in contrast, recruited their staff from amongst their political supporters, from business acquaintances, from the world of the media, as well as from the public service.[74] The period between 1984 and 1990 likewise saw an expansion in numbers in the ministers' offices, from about five or six in the early 1980s (including secretarial staff and press officers), according to Boston, to an average of eight in 1990, with some ministers having up to twelve.[75] Another change has been that, since 1984, ministers have used their private staffs increasingly for policy formulation, co-ordination, and for monitoring policy implementation.

The cost of the ministers' private offices has risen, like that of the Prime Minister's Office, but to a lesser extent. The total combined annual salary figures for all staff (including the PMO) paid from the Department of Internal Affairs Vote: Ministerial Services, was, shortly before the 1990 general election, $8,398,703. This went down somewhat in the first year of the new National administration but by March 1994 it was up to $8,676,929 (including the PMO and the Parliamentary Under-Secretary staff, but excluding five establishment positions where other Departments were paying the salaries). Bill Birch (Health) ran the most expensive office, costing $601,036 and employing three permanent staff members, three on secondment and five on contract. The allocation of resources, as might be expected, had some relationship to ministerial responsibilities: Jenny Shipley, Philip Burdon, John Falloon, and Wyatt Creech all spent well over the $400,000 mark in servicing their ministries whilst Robert Gray spent under $100,000 and Roger McClay and Murray McCully spent under $200,000. Don McKinnon, Deputy Prime Minister, however, spent a mere $350,742. The ratio between staff on contract and permanent and seconded staff varied, with (excluding the PMO) only two ministers, each with relatively small offices, favouring the contracted over the rest. Three other ministers had half their staff fulfilling contracts.

To give some idea of the backgrounds of the staffers, Bill Birch, in February 1993 Minister of Labour, had in his office two typists supplied by the Department of Internal Affairs, two press officers employed on contract, four private secretaries from the public service, and a further two private secretaries on contract. As can be seen the staff play a variety of roles: the normal office duties of typing and filing: communications, both externally to the public and internally to departments and ministries and, also, other ministers' offices; and the provision of policy advice.[76]

The management function is obviously crucial if a minister is to use time efficiently and effectively and forge good relationships with individuals and bodies beyond the narrow world of the Beehive. A senior minister in the 1990–93 government expressed the view that:

> One has to have access to good management. [My] senior private secretary is an excellent manager, and he and I decide what our priorities are; we do a lot of critical path programming and we actually plan just about every hour of every day. And that's by way of response to trying to get policy developments and doing things which we prioritize as being important.

One of the ministers interviewed had been changing his expectations of the performance of his staff, because

> what's no good . . . whenever I come into this office is for my staff to be descending upon me or simply piling stuff on this table for me to attend to. I'm requiring greater discipline, that they must have the material when it's presented to me, in a form that I can deal with reasonably rapidly. And I'm going to have them here when I'm dealing with it, in fact, so I can question them on it. And if it's badly presented it just takes them longer. And I do that at night. So there's some discipline on them, if they want to get home before midnight.

The departmental advisers are necessary to work with the ministries and departments: 'I asked the Department for somebody really top-line, so the Department didn't have to run up and down the road all the time to give me some special assistance.' Effective ministerial/departmental liaison is not, however, the only task of the seconded public servants; they are also employed because of their institutional knowledge and experience. There was the minister who commented that the individuals seconded from the department were 'really all fired up' on their department's affairs. But

> they don't want to go back because, apart from the sheer chaos, and the political side which they'd never experienced before and [which] they find attractive, they're here because they're all people with certain ambitions. They also now know what the rest of the department is about, and they can look the Secretary [CE] . . . in the eye and match his knowledge.

This minister stressed the importance of having a 'totally harmonious, closely knit team'. Another tactic was to select staffers who are 'not normal run of the mill departmental people', individuals such as an economist who had only been in a department for a short while and had 'never become part of the place. And I knew him actually, just by sheer chance before I got here. But he is really a personal adviser.'

In contrast, the 'outsiders', the staffers employed on contract, tended to fill one of two roles: the specialist policy adviser, or the primarily political adviser. (Sometimes individuals have performed both roles.) An example of the former category was the staffer employed on a contract basis to work with the particular sectors associated with the minister's portfolio 'to try and make them start thinking about where they are, why the real prices have gone down, and what they have to do about becoming prosperous again, because the Government's not going to subsidize them or support them in a sort of direct fashion'.

Press Officers can perform more than one role. For example, a minister who used the seconded officers primarily for liaison used the Press Officer—'more politically motivated'—for political advice. Someone was needed who had 'a political nose' and was 'prepared to see things from a political perspective'. Public servants, in contrast, this minister said, must guard their public service careers. The Press Officer is

> involved in all the portfolio areas, so when the officials come in [the press officers] will be here as well. Sort of an independent monitor, a different point of view. And they don't necessarily get involved in the discussions to any great degree, but we will talk afterwards about how they think, what they think is going on.

McQueen has argued that, on the one hand, the outsiders brought into the private offices of the ministers are people who 'have a commitment to ministerial decisions', but, on the other side, 'loyalty is given to the individual Minister rather than to the Government', and he likened the situation to medieval Europe with loyalties to the barons rather than the king.[77] This comment precisely illustrates how ministers' offices, like the advice and support given to the Prime Minister, have increasingly offered 'personalized' support to their political chiefs.

Advice and Support: Bureaucratization and Personalization

Thus the support systems for the New Zealand cabinet within the intimacy of the Beehive demonstrate the two trends of bureaucratization and personalization. The Cabinet Office, concerned to protect its legitimacy through the traditional, Westminster emphasis upon neutrality of advice and the duty of the permanent public servant towards Prime Minister and cabinet, has become increasingly bureaucratized over the years. The department that serves the Prime Minister, however, shows how it is torn between two contrary tendencies: towards bureaucratization, to provide stable advice and support for prime ministers whatever their political persuasion; and towards personalization, the loyal followers of the ruler. Whereas the PMO is unequivocally political, loyal to party and leader, and the Cabinet Office is equally dutifully faithful to the institutions of cabinet government, the PMC has become both permanent and specialized, at the same time that it has increasingly adopted functions which are temporary, also specialized, and based upon individuals chosen primarily for their loyalty to the Prime Minister of the time. This, of course, overstates the distinction between the two types of formal advice; obviously a variety of relationships is possible in both Department and PMO. For instance, a former speechwriter, not a member of the Prime Minister's own political party, but once a student of that Prime Minister, is said to have emphasized the professional personal relationship that existed between the two of them.[78]

There is no doubt that modern prime ministers, and, indeed, the rest of the cabinet team, need their own Beehive support. The Prime Minister, in particular, as key party spokesperson, policy defender, and policy co-ordinator, needs specialized, institutionalized advice. Whether a strong PMC and CO make for 'prime ministerial' government rather than 'cabinet' government is another question. The evidence since 1975 rather points to the contrary. Although Muldoon undoubtedly employed his Advisory Group to support his policy preferences (despite, often, their advice to the contrary, from all reports), his major strengths were his own bullying personality, his support from party and public, and his key position as Minister of Finance. It can hardly be said that his immediate successors, Lange and Palmer, emphasized prime ministerial authority over that of cabinet, for although at times they both won their policy battles, they had to contend with other strong, ambitious ministers and, indeed, each resigned his leadership position whilst his party was still governing. Moore's tenure was so brief it can hardly be counted; and Bolger's own personal style has been to work closely with senior ministers—government by clique rather than prime ministerial government. Against any tendency towards prime ministerial government in New Zealand must be counted the collectivist, cohesive traditions of the parliamentary parties documented earlier in this work.

It can also be argued that ministers' and prime ministers' advisers challenge the system of accountability of Westminster governments in that they intervene between public servants and ministers in the decision-making process. Much depends upon how roles are construed, territories protected, and boundaries drawn between public servant and adviser. Until the present, the units of advice have been relatively small compared with the resources of the public service, especially in the ministers' private offices. While they remain small, they do not offer a great threat to the power of the public service. But if the present trends continue, of increased bureaucratization on the one hand and personalization on the other, then new conventions of responsiveness and accountability will have to be developed. Moreover, the shift to coalition governments will make more urgent the development of revised notions and practices of accountability.

Other Sources of Policy Advice

Although the focus of this chapter has been upon the government bureaucracy and the Beehive, it should be noted that the New Zealand ministers, including the Prime Minister, also seek and receive advice from a whole range of bodies which are set up by the state for that precise purpose, have some independence, and which are outside the public service.[79] These advisory bodies can be permanent, and some are set up by statute. They fall into two different categories: those which are purely advisory; and those which both provide advice and are policy formulation and implementing bodies in their own right. In the first category there is, for example, the Law Commission; in the second the Securities Commission, and the Human Rights Commission. Other bodies are permanent but their members are part-time. An example has been the Legislation Advisory Committee. Its 1987 report, *Legislative Change: Guidelines on Process and Content*, advised cabinet on how to follow better procedures in preparing legislation, affecting the instruction on consultation in the revised edition of the *Cabinet Office Manual*.[80]

Sometimes Commissions of Inquiry or Royal Commissions are established to advise governments on particular issues. Their advice may or may not be taken: the recommendations of the Royal Commission on Social Policy, for example, were never followed (partly because of the disarray of the then Labour Government over its policy direction). Cabinets may establish Commissions primarily to defuse an issue, to encourage people to believe that action is being taken when all the government wants is for that issue to go away. What all these advisory bodies have in common is their expertise. They are part of the formal structure of advice to ministers, although frequently that advice is *ad hoc*, reflecting their specific purposes and their staffing composition. We know very little about the role played by advisory committees in New Zealand and the policy communities of which they are part.

Then there is the political party from which the cabinet is drawn, both the larger parliamentary party (caucus), and the extra-parliamentary party. This source of advice is permanent, but, unlike the rest of the advice that fits into the category of permanency, it is not bureaucratized. Indeed, it sits rather awkwardly in constitutional terms. This is because, although it can be argued that ministers have the responsibility to seek the advice of the party and respond to its policy viewpoints because those ministers are representing that party in government, it can also be argued that an elected government must represent all people, not just its political supporters. From this perspective the party—caucus even—is merely one special interest among others; governments must represent the public interest. Parties play an important role in setting the policy agenda; they also play their part in formulating policy detail.

A vital source of advice consists of the views of groups and individuals throughout society. A major forum for the representation of views is the select committee system of Parliament. Some legislation explicitly instructs ministers to consult named organizations; but, mostly, whether or not consultation occurs depends upon the ministers themselves and they have always varied in the extent to which they as individuals either listen to or seek the advice of the various interests and pressure groups in New Zealand society. Governments, too, have differed on this. Consultation with those representing different viewpoints is one of the characteristics of a society that is democratic and politically pluralistic. This aspect of the behaviour of cabinets is not well understood, either here or elsewhere, and is the next topic to be discussed.

8

CONSULTATION

Introduction

New Zealand policy-making until the early 1980s had been characterized by exceedingly close relationships between groups and governments. Like all such political arrangements, these were based upon the principle of an exchange relationship: government recognized the legitimacy of group interests (legitimacy increasing with the degree of representativeness of the various interests); and, in turn, the groups recognized the legitimacy of the role of the strong state in the allocation of benefits, thus tacitly also acquiescing with governments' other objectives: maintaining employment and welfare benefits. Groups were given formal representation on quangos; there were regular meetings between groups and bureaucrats; and legislation was drawn up on the basis of consultation with the groups affected by it. It is difficult to imagine in today's New Zealand a minister saying what a previous Minister of Industries and Commerce said in 1951: he would be 'glad if manufacturers would look on him as their minister charged with the task of interpreting government policy to manufacturers and representing manufacturers in Parliament'.[1]

Responsiveness to the demands of groups was part of the role of the cabinet minister in the 1970s. The evidence of the 1970s interviews showed that the representative role was not a separate one, or an alternative for ministers, but part of their overall roles. The representative role fitted fairly easily into the image of the professional politician, trained by parliamentary experience and service in the party and in the major sectional interests— Federated Farmers, employers' associations, trade unions, Chambers of Commerce—before he or she entered Parliament. Interest group representation, moreover, combined far more easily and realistically with the role of the politician cabinet minister than it would with a model of cabinet minister as policy expert and innovator. Partisanship and the pragmatically conceived representation of interests fitted with the sectional bases of the political parties.

With the representative role went the frequently observed accessibility of ministers to groups and individuals, occasioning the criticism that 'the tradition which requires ministers to keep their ears close to the ground invites the danger that earwigs may crawl in'.[2] This criticism was often linked with the tendency of New Zealand ministers overly to concern themselves with administrative details.

Much of the consultation was through *ad hoc* or permanent advisory groups where the representation of the range of interests affected was regarded not only as legitimate but actually desirable. Some networks were brought together in summits: the 1953 National Housing Conference; the 1963–64 Agricultural Development Conference; and the 1968 and 1969 National Development Conference. This latter exercise in summitry was established on a permanent basis and was supported by sector councils.[3]

Even more prevalent in the New Zealand political culture than summitry or jamboree government–group consultation has been the unilateral negotiation. Agriculture has provided the most prolific set of examples of the close relationship that existed between cabinet ministers and sectoral organizations before subsidies were abolished and governments withdrew from their interventionist economic policies.[4] One example will suffice. During the 1960s and early 1970s, despite the relatively poor prices paid for dairy products, dairy farmers maintained their standards of living through increasing their herds whilst keeping labour costs low by mechanization and through product diversification.[5] Export commodity prices of dairy, meat, and wool products were high in the early seventies, only to collapse in 1974 and 1975.[6] By the end of the 1970s farmers' organizations were demanding subsidies so that they could keep up with the inflated wages of others.[7] The Government—first under the Labour PM, Wallace Rowling, and then, after the 1975 election, the new National PM, Robert Muldoon—negotiated with the sectional leaders on schemes to stabilize prices and incomes in order to protect farmers against the fluctuations in export prices. Supported by Reserve Bank credit, schemes were set in place for wool, dairy products, and meat. The principle behind them was that farmers would be paid higher than market prices in lean times and, in return, would be levied when times were good. Minimum prices were fixed at the beginning of each session by a committee composed of equal numbers of Meat Board and government representatives. The funds built up by the levy on wool growers were credited to individual growers and could not be drawn upon without the agreement of the Minister of Finance. Furthermore, the trigger price for wool was set by the Minister of Agriculture in consultation with the Wool Board. The extent of direct government involvement in policy implementation as well as formulation can be seen by those initiatives.

A good example of a single issue, *ad hoc* group was given by a former senior public servant. An advisory committee was appointed by the (National) Minister of Justice to investigate an aspect of penal policy, periodic detention. The committee included: the senior Roman Catholic Chaplain to the Department of Justice; Martyn Finlay, lawyer and President of the New Zealand Labour Party; a District Child Welfare Officer; the Director of Auckland Presbyterian Social Services Association; the Chief Inspector of the Auckland Police; the Vice President of the Labour Party; the President of the Auckland Trades Council; a District Probation Officer; a further, Maori District Probation Officer; and the Secretary of the Auckland and Suburban Local Body Labourers' Union. The chair was a Stipendiary Magistrate.[8] Contemporary ministers do not favour appointing widely representative committees: today the memberships are more narrowly specialized, denoting more restrictive notions of policy communities.

The habit of regular consultation was certainly associated with the interventionist and development goals of most New Zealand governments. Effective policy-making required it, because resources, information, and experience were in the hands of the groups as well as government. Also it might be that the participatory nature of the political culture supported the active, demanding, overlapping pressure groups system that has been one of the characteristics of New Zealand's polity. Representativeness had become a legitimating factor in policy-making. For whatever reasons, New Zealand ministers by habit consulted the pressure groups close to their portfolio, either in a formal or informal setting.

Governments' relationships with the pressure groups, especially the major sectional interests, changed during the 1980s. Public choice theory dictated that governments be wary of heeding the demands of groups which, according to rational choice precepts, inevitably act in their own self interest. It was not only doctrine, however, that was instrumental in making governments wary of group pressures. That most pragmatic of politicians, Robert Muldoon, through the years of his prime ministership, became increasingly critical of the organized interest groups, especially the financial and education sectors.[9] Even Muldoon, however, went through the forms of consultation. In one of his autobiographical works he published a transcript of a meeting he had with the Minister of Labour (Jim Bolger), senior officers from the Prime Minister's Department, Treasury and the Labour Department, and representatives from the Employers' Association, the Federation of Labour, and the Combined State Unions. The topic was the campaign by the unions for a pay increase during the price–wage freeze established on 22 June 1982. The meeting provides an excellent insight into the politics of tripartitism, denoting a clear notion of policy community, and the power relationships therein involved.[10] But the era of institutionalized group–organization consultation was at this time already coming to an end.

The Fourth Labour Government

The belief that ministers must not heed the voices of the agents of persuasion, whether these come from the public service or organized interests (groups and political parties), can be explained by the conjunction of different factors. First, as already indicated, public choice theory, propounded by the Treasury, argued that the 'public interest' could only be successfully pursued if decision-makers avoided being 'captured' by special groups. Capture could be avoided in two complementary ways. First, ministers must provide themselves with alternative views, thus creating policy 'contestability'. Contestable policy cannot, however, emerge from the special interests such as Federated Farmers, the education sector unions, or, indeed, the public service, for these bodies are concerned only with their own, narrowly defined, sectoral interests. Second, when ministers decide to initiate action then they must not delay policy development by consulting those affected by it. Roger Douglas, the most fervent advocate of this latter policy strategy, said in his widely publicized 'Mt Pelerin' speech: 'Implement reform by quantum leaps. Moving step by step lets vested interests mobilise. Big packages can neutralise them.'[11]

The second factor that worked against the new Government's adopting the consultative practices of the past was Labour's own party history. That and ideology worked together to encourage the suspicion of the public service and its practices. In part this came from the long years out of office and, as such, is not an unusual feature of new governments. Labour was wary of the familiar and comfortable networks that had developed between state and groups during the years of National Party dominance. It is worth noting that there were protests by groups between 1972 and 1975 that they were not consulted. Norman Kirk's government, in pursuit of change, chose not to consult with some of the previously highly influential pressure groups.

The need to accumulate sectoral support for policy initiatives, and thus alleviate implementation problems, however, has historically pushed governments back to the meeting table. Cleveland noted that the 1972–75 Labour Government was suspicious of the National Development Conference machinery it inherited from its National predecessor, and reduced it to an advisory committee. In March 1974 the Government announced that the work of the NDC would be done by the Cabinet Committee of Policy and Priorities. Each sector council of the NDC would deal directly with its relevant minister. Thus strategic policy planning would be returned to the elected politicians, the cabinet. But then, according to Cleveland, the Government found that it 'needed to sanctify its economic planning by generating an atmosphere of co-operative discussion and consensus among the pressure groups, the industrial, and other sectors of the community'. Labour held conferences about the problems of the economy in both 1974 and 1975. Cleveland argues that the meetings aired sectional views but failed to 'generate a cohesive spirit of national concern for the realities of economic life in New Zealand'.[12] Leaving aside the extent to which those particular meetings were successful, this example does demonstrate the difficulties of governing when consultation is abandoned, especially when policy changes are being attempted. I return to this theme later.

Third, Labour, compared with National, has had fewer links with the sectional interest groups. In retrospect it is not surprising that it was under Labour that cabinet severed sectional ties; National's roots were more intricately bedded into the community. National has always been the

> more natural political partner of the interest groups that have conducted the quest for state-backed security for individuals: Federated Farmers, the Chambers of Commerce, the Manufacturers and Retailers Federations, at the highest levels, down to the local business association or ratepayers. The National Party has reached easily and comfortably through those networks of influence, across and down into the less formal social networks that link individuals together: the Rotary clubs and sports clubs, for example.[13]

Compared with National, Labour's social links outside the party except for the union movement, and during the 1970s and 1980s women's groups and Maori, have been weak.

Fourth, for the 1984–90 Labour Government, there was the added ingredient of the circumstances under which it took office: a constitutional and economic crisis, and an inherited public service identified with the long years of Robert Muldoon's prime ministership and perceived policy failure. New Zealand, like other liberal democratic states, if not actually ungovernable, had become more difficult to govern. Fiscal crisis and social stress worked together to discredit a public policy shaped by the priorities of organized groups. In retrospect, and with the advantages of hindsight, it is not very surprising that public choice doctrine easily captured the allegiance of key economic decision makers in the new Labour Government.

One note of warning, however: it is simply untrue that the Labour cabinet ceased the practice of consultation. Much depended upon the groups involved and the extent to which the various interests were seen as legitimate. Much, too, depended upon the nature of the issues themselves. There are two influencing factors here. The first of these is political and ideological. All governments regard some policies as largely non-negotiable, whilst other issues, in contrast, are seen as negotiable. Governments are much readier to consult on the latter than the former, although there are exceptions even to this rule. The other factor relates to the characteristics of the issues, for different policies tend to engender different patterns of policy formulation, from the conflictual, class-based issues relating to the redistribution of resources, the sorts of issues which historically have divided the coalition-based parties of dominantly two-party systems (taxes and welfare, for example), to distributional issues (subsidies) and regulatory issues (such as safety regulations).[14] The latter two policy areas have more automatically involved governments in wider consultation than the former. Compare, for example, both the Labour Government's and the 1990 National Government's consultations over the (regulatory) Resource Management Act 1991 with the latter's absence of consultation over cuts to the welfare benefits in 1990–91. In brief, however, when Labour came into power, after a short-lived excursion into corporatist-style consultation with its Economic Summit of 1984,[15] it deliberately reduced the extent of government–group interaction.

The National Government, 1990–93

Non-negotiable issues may or may not be revealed in the debates surrounding general elections. The Labour Government had shown this to be so, for its economic policies of liberalization, commercialization, and privatization were not Manifesto policies, and its National successor followed suit. The overall direction of the new Government's economic policies—monetarist and non-interventionist, and further deregulation of the labour market—was clearly indicated in the 1990 election campaign. This was not to be diverged from in National's first term, as was shown by the Enterprise Council's attempts to alter slightly the Government's general policy direction.[16] Significant details, however, remained to be worked out, such as the pace of continuing deregulation and the problem of how to stimulate employment. But neither the Manifesto nor the debates during the election campaign suggested to the electorate how sweeping the changes to the welfare and health systems would be, and these issues also seemed to be non-negotiable, perhaps even more so than the economic issues.

Whether or not issues were apparently negotiable, did in fact the ministers in Jim Bolger's cabinet consult, and, if so, on what sorts of issues? And how can the policy communities be defined? Chapter Six discussed the role of the caucus committees in the consultative process, but what direct links do ministers have with outside groups? The ministers were therefore asked in interview about their practices of consultation. Of particular interest, given the record of the previous government and the prevalence of the doctrine of public choice, were the attitudes of the ministers towards the notion of 'capture'. Consultation is not only significant for understanding how cabinet government operates; it is also important in understanding the nature of state power in New Zealand, for those who have access to the top decision makers have the best opportunity to influence the policy process. Thus, understanding the consultative process can point us to the relationship between political and economic élites, and the extent to which cabinets are responsive to the needs of those élites, or the needs of the wider community.

Vested Interests and Policy 'Capture'
A minister who had entered Parliament in the last years of the Muldoon period observed:

> Relationships had grown up centred on an interventionist state where there was a minister in charge of your area; he [sic] was supposed to be your mouthpiece, get what he wanted for the self-serving sector out of the kitty, or in the way of privileges or whatever, and they were happy. And, to some extent they saw that minister as the Government, and they judged his performance accordingly. Now the state's not in the business of handing out bits of paper saying you may or may not do things as much as it was, and it's certainly not in the position of shelling out subsidies and all that rubbish, and God forbid we should go back to it.

The 1990s ministers were indeed suspicious of lobby groups seeking audiences with them: 'Consultation coming to you tends to be vested interests . . . in the form of somebody lobbying for things to be changed in a specific way.' It was different when the ministers themselves chose to consult: 'When you're proactive and go the other way, you're talking to people in general who don't actually have a vested interest in what you're doing.' And when discussing the relationship between personal skills and portfolios, a minister said, 'There are some areas where I wouldn't be seen for dust.' Asked for an example, the reply was, 'Education for one. I just couldn't put up with the narrow, selfish, vested interests involved.' Whether or not ministers felt they could consult with interest groups depended to some extent on the policy area concerned; consultation was easier with the industrial and manufacturing sectors than, say, education, because there 'you've got 101 pressure groups with fixed positions . . . I've never been a Minister of Education.'

When discussing the possible shift away from the consensual policy-making patterns of the past to a more adversarial style of government, a senior minister said:

> That's because there's been a somewhat rapid movement in policy. And I think wherever you have a rapid movement you're going to have reaction. . . . And so you have had more—you call it adversarial—but I think you've had more

reactive politics than we've had in the past because of the pace of reform. Now I think we're learning that you can't get ahead too far in terms of public opinion, but you still have to be ahead or otherwise nothing would get done. New Zealanders don't like change.

When asked about the nature of the relationship between government and the individual, the minister explained:

> I think one of the things politically that's wrong in New Zealand is that the debate isn't broad enough. The debate is always led by those who have an interest that isn't likely to be disadvantaged, be they schoolteachers, superannuitants or whatever, and not [about] the long-term sustainability of these programmes we now have, or more particularly the impact that sustaining them will have on the next generation or the one after that, in terms of the amount of debt and the type of country that they'll be able to look forward to.

The minister stressed that the economic environment should be regarded in the same way as the physical environment: 'We have a bad situation here because the debate is captured by those who are directly affected, and nobody speaks up for the people who are children now or the youths, teens or twenties generation.'

Over one-third of the ministers interviewed emphasized the importance of obtaining contestable advice. This may be achieved by using either formally constituted bodies or less formal mechanisms. Evidently, during the formulation of a new, non-mandatory equal opportunities programme, for example, the minister got the public servants to find 'a whole representative range of practitioners . . . and we'll bring them in and brainstorm them about what sort of programmes we should follow'. When asked whether organized groups would be approached to provide representatives, the minister replied that the cabinet would go to a particular individual 'who has been pretty much in the vanguard of it, [a] pretty active practitioner'. The minister would not consult the National Council of Women because that organization believed in legislative remedies for equal opportunities. (One of the first actions of the Government had been to repeal the Pay Equity Act 1990.)

The impression given by the ministers was that consultation in order to achieve policy contestability often happened in an *ad hoc* way: 'I find it very good to talk to New Zealand's business leaders about electricity pricing. . . .' As was shown in the previous chapter, consultation also occurs because of frustration with the quality of policy advice from the departments, and the domination of Treasury advice. An example of *ad hoc* discussions designed to contest or supplant departmental advice was this:

I go out and seek views—I think one of the ways to do it also is in terms of your style of operation. . . . One day next week, I've got a particular problem that's brewed up with businesses [and the minister elucidated]. Now, I've asked for it to be looked at. The policy that came back to me clearly wasn't going to solve the problem, so I said, 'Well, all right, we'll go out and see them.' So these guys are all going to assemble next week, and I'm taking two or three people from here. We'll all sit down and slug it out, and we'll sit down and make some decision. And I think that's one way of overcoming it, to make sure that you're actually forcing your officials to face the people who've got a problem. A lot of the damage I've seen done in this place has come from ministers dealing with officials on a one-to-one basis, and allowing them to really doctor the submissions that are coming to the minister from people outside. I saw it all the time in the select committee process.

The Bolger Government's 'very strong agenda' as 'agents of change' meant that:

It's crucially important for cabinet ministers, and a cabinet generally, to keep a very, very active line of communication with the private sector, and I do. The joyous thing of a deregulated approach to decision making, more of a devolved [approach] [is] you empower so many people. Public policy debate used to be the domain of politicians and the public service, because basically all power was concentrated in central hands. In a deregulated economy, for example, in a society [in which] you expect substantially more power in the hands of the consumer, you have got a very lively public policy debate that's going on out there.

Another minister who acquired a new portfolio (relating to primary industries) found that relationships with industry had broken down:

It took me several months of talking round the table with large groups of people, and making the Department face the industry and vice versa, to get them all back together. . . . It probably brings you to what is the essential thing for survival in this job, and that is understanding human nature. And figuring out what drives people. But the cure to that in the ministerial sense is to be open to contestable advice. I will not accept departmental advice on anything without consulting those affected first. They found that quite irritating at first. They've gotten used to it now, so they actually go off and consult them now. So I just have to ring up and check, or I'll send my staff to do that.

The ministers believed that effective policy formulation requires getting the views of those outside the public service. Indeed, for some, the perceived shortcomings of their official advisers provided the primary reason for expanding their range of contacts. As we saw earlier, public servants were seen as 'captured' by their own policy agendas. But this did not mean that the ministers of the Bolger Government sought the views of the established interest groups as antidotes to public service advice.[17] Rather, advice was generally regarded as more legitimate if it came from those who were involved in the policy areas concerned—the practitioners, the 'experts'— rather than from organized interests.

Nevertheless the interviews showed that established groups were also consulted, although the majority of ministers chose their groups carefully. 'Well you can't stop [the groups]; they keep coming. But you build up a portfolio of contacts who you find congenial.' When I directed the minister's attention to professional associations and pressure groups, the response was, 'Oh yes, oh yes. Well no, when you say "consult", I mean they lobby. But you single out individuals whom you can feel you can trust.' One particular minister had regular meetings with the president of a prominent professional association. Moreover, 'I see anybody who wants to make representations.' Sometimes views were sought out by the minister. Unusually, capture was not voiced by this person as a problem: most of 'the professional societies, the accountants and the lawyers, and the medical association, are very responsible anyway. They're not putting up some daft thing which has no merit. Obviously they've thought the thing through pretty intelligently in the first place.' Asked whether group contacts were used as sources of policy ideas, or as a way of trying out policy alternatives, a minister replied:

> Both. It depends on the groups. Some groups that I trust thoroughly I very much use as policy sounding mechanisms. . . . I always listen to what they've got to put to me. How much I use them for sounding out my thinking on that issue depends on the group. There are some groups I trust thoroughly. [The minister had discussions with groups in a new policy area,] really sharing with them, right at the forefront of my thinking, the different stages and development. . . . [I was] not pretending to share with them my thinking when in fact decisions were made a couple of weeks ago, but genuinely working through aloud with them the problems that I was grappling with.

I asked about 'vested interests': 'Clearly some groups have such vested interests that I get limited value from them.' A group mentioned as trustworthy, the Principals' Association (the education sector was mentioned by several of the ministers), was described thus:

> They've reached the pinnacle of their career. . . . You know, money is not a great problem for them, they're moderately well paid and they're used to working fairly hard. I think their self-interest is limited. They're on employment contracts, they have reasonably limited self-interest but they have a very genuine interest in education, having devoted so much of their life to it. I find them very valuable, whereas—I'd better not name any other groups—there are some groups whose primary interest is the employment

arrangements for their members, and they claim they couch all their representations in terms of [client] advantage, but often it's so plastic, so thin, you can really see that what they're really after is protecting the interests of their members. And why shouldn't a union be interested in protecting the interests of their members?

The minister complained of lacking the ability personally to offer professional input into the policy area, but tried to get out and meet those directly involved.

Discussing time allocation, a minister mentioned sector groups wanting appointments, and meeting groups when travelling around the country:

I certainly try to [consult], but again, one can often get a huge variance of opinion. And if they agree with you they're supportive of you; if they're not they're pretty strident sometimes in opposition, but I think it's important to talk to the various groups—one could almost unkindly call them vested interest groups—but essentially they have an interest in the issue that is being worked on, and I value their input, particularly from an association point of view, or from a social group point of view. In many cases they are much more practically involved and it's important that we listen to them.

It was necessary, however, to filter self-interest from decisions that make sense. 'Nobody has an ownership of good ideas, certainly not within Government nor within caucus or departments.'

Consultation with consumers and clients, especially in the areas of social welfare, was mentioned much more seldom than was consultation with business, although a minister did say, when discussing the problem of the health–welfare interface, that 'we keep forgetting to ask the client groups where they see themselves sitting. And just as an exercise, earlier this year we brought [together] all of the groups affected by the health–welfare interface and talked to them over a day.' Apparently,

There is a huge amount of consultation, much of which is unseen. . . . People will say to a minister like myself, 'You're out of touch.' Now, I just simply don't tell them who I see, because if I say publicly today I'm going to see [person X] or [charitable organization Y], or whoever, there'll be television cameras in that foyer within five minutes. In fact, I have seen all those people on a number of occasions regularly. But I don't actually think it is the public's business. Now, you could say that's politically damaging. . . .

Certain portfolios are by their nature representative (Maori, Pacific Islands, Women's and Youth Affairs): 'In a way I've been sent [to cabinet] to advocate on behalf of [a particular client group], and ministers are only now seeing it important that in certain portfolios you should be advocates for your group rather than enemies of them.' The view that ministers could not advocate groups' interests without being captured by them was 'rubbish'.

> There's a history of the point of view that if you are in any way associated with an industry, have a vested interest, then your opinion is immediately slanted and rubbished. I actually think that it's quite possible for people to have in their heart the interests of their firm or their industry, and the broad interest of the community at the same time. And you only need to have a relatively minor intellectual ability to be able to accomplish that. And the cynicism attributed to it was often used by people to achieve objectives that had just as much vested interest, but from a completely different angle, no involvement.

A similar view was that ministers should communicate between government and groups, for 'if we weren't doing that, what's the point of being here, it's not our government, it's not the National Party's government, it's New Zealand's government'. This associate minister went on to mention a particular client group as a special responsibility: 'I'm getting round the country and I think I've probably met more than half of them so far, to reflect their views to the minister.'

Later, in discussion of another group, the minister observed:

> Of course it's always difficult to represent the views of groups of people when within the group of people there are different views. So what I say is that everybody deserves to have their opinions heard and considered before final decisions are made. Somebody will be disappointed but so long as their views have been heard, that's fine.

Several ministers evidently adopted quite pragmatic, primarily reactive views towards group consultation. It was difficult to learn exactly what they hoped to learn from the process. Sometimes representatives of organized groups were seen quite frequently, once or twice a week for one minister: 'They come to see me, or I go to see them in Auckland or round here in Wellington. They could be trade-related groups, manufacture and exporting related groups.' One colleague, on the other hand, said most groups were seen inside the Beehive, but

> it's a very open door policy in terms of groups who want to come and see me to talk about issues. And I would be very annoyed if any group said that they had not been able to get through to the minister. My staff have been told quite clearly that if anyone's turned down I have to turn them down, so there's a very large range of people go through here.

Again, in another interview, 'Well, the outside world exists very much as far as I'm concerned, it's not just myself and the caucus and the officials. It's what's living outside there, your perception of what's going on.'

In short, although most ministers accepted that they needed to be wary of 'vested interests', group consultation—to gain different ideas, or merely because it was part of the ministerial role—universally occurred. But consultation beyond the public service also was carried out because it helped the processes of policy implementation.

Consultation and Policy Implementation

Although the streamlining of policy implementation was one of the purposes of consultation for most of the ministers, about a third of the ministers interviewed believed, for their different reasons, that gaining the co-operation of society's groups is the principal reason for looking for outside advice. This sort of consultation is to achieve compliance; these ministers were not so much interested in hearing alternative views as in pursuing the politics of persuasion for the purposes of policy feasibility. Like the ministers who sought policy contestability, these ministers preferred to initiate consultation, to choose those with whom they preferred to consult. Again, most respect and legitimacy was granted to the practitioners. The organized interests were perceived as dominating policy debate and alternatives. Thus business people, especially, as the practitioners out in the market-place, played a strong role in the consultative process. The Government's economic policy was 'a programme that relies very heavily on the quality of the private sector response. . . . I'm effectively looking to very high quality action by the private sector, so, I mean it's in my interests to keep a very close dialogue with them.'

A good minister, amongst other capabilities, must have

a clear sense of purpose, and an ability to, in the jargon of this place, drive issues through the system, which requires that you not only take your . . . advisers with you, [but] that you take your cabinet colleagues and your caucus colleagues with you. Plus, if it relates to some area which has an influential lobby group, it pays to be able to take them with you. That's not always possible because you may be in fact implementing a policy they disagree with, and you will never change them.

This minister reported that the Prime Minister had instructed his cabinet to consult widely outside the public service. Ministers need to consult:

A reforming government is a tremendously busy government, and under a lot of pressure. And the tendency of course is to focus inside the office but not reach out. So, if you're reforming, if you're going to succeed, if you look at it constitutionally, I think you're obligated to look outside and get alternate advice. So it's very important that we do, within the capacity of people's hours in the day. In terms of capture there's still the possibility that a minister or ministers will be caught by a particular external pressure group, or a particular department or ministry.

A minister reported that advisory groups had been set up, each with specific focuses. In this case both sectoral interests and practitioners were involved. One group was concerned with industry strategy for the future:

> I tied the various sectors into that, what I'd call the leaders of those sectors, and I put the [head of department] on intentionally, because I felt that he was tangled up with restructuring the Department . . . and that there was a need to get him involved much more in the nature of [the] business and the people. Then I had a conference of a hundred people, brought another layer of people in . . . selected by tortuous negotiation. We tried to pick them from the whole sector.

The minister said, in response to my question, that the conference contained all sorts of people, not just representatives from the sectoral organizations. There had been an attempt to choose the 'leaders . . . people who had influence, people who had experience'.

In another part of the minister's portfolio, also one with which the minister was dissatisfied,

> With the help of the [statutory authority] I set up a small committee, put a few people I knew on it, put a few radicals on it—we even had journalists! Paid them nothing, except gave them lunch or dinner or whatever when they came to Wellington. And they have worked with the industry, produced a marvellous report which I hope to bring into legislation, and we had a conference as well. So we involved the [policy] community, and we had workshops and we did things like that. That's actually changed the mood. And what I'm doing now is behind the scenes. There are strong negotiations going on, I've given them where I'm going, what I want to see happen, which is legislation. I've told them the sort of general objective, and I've said, 'I want you to come to me united if you can because that'll help me get it through caucus and Parliament.'

Thus groups can be utilized to support ministers' own agendas.

Consultation occurred in pursuit of acquiescence:

> I would always attempt to get a consultative consensus in my decisions. Most of the decisions I have made have been received without brutal condemnation. I carefully avoid catching people on the hop. [One industry] was prepared to say [a particular decision] was tough, but they endorsed it. I want to get that qualified endorsement as a rule. It's very important; I don't want people to get caught by surprise . . . people resent having decisions imposed upon them.

Apparently, that minister consulted with specific sectoral groups in preference to the umbrella organizations. A further example was the minister who had business experience and who spoke sympathetically of those who were trying to get their own businesses going. The viewpoint here was that

> We need to get in the place of the organizations that are actually doing these things, and try and incorporate their opinions a little bit more into policy, rather than to continue to divorce ourselves completely from them. Because you can set up policy that is entirely inappropriate for it. . . . I've got a good network in areas I operate in. I know the financial directors of all of New Zealand's leading commercial institutions. I know all the Society of Accountants bigwigs in [the policy area]. And that gives me an overview of that end of the business, but I've also got contacts . . .with very small chartered accountant operations relating to small businesses. . . . I know all the Society of Accountants at a personal level, and we have meals together every now and again, and just chat. I have got quite a lot of people, who I will invite, who I can trust to advise me in total confidence, so that no one in the public would know they'd ever spoken to me.

The interviews provided some evidence, also, that the various groups within the legal system (the Bar Association, the Law Society) were in regular contact with relevant ministers, suggesting that some professional bodies are 'insider groups' as far as ministers are concerned.

Naturally, views about the desirability or otherwise of consultation beyond the public service were bound up with ministers' perceptions of their own roles. Political leadership was seen by one minister as not 'a person having a bright idea and saying "we're going in that direction". Political leadership is actually taking people with you.' Another example was:

> I tend to be a minister who leads the team, by instinct I think. I tell them roughly where I want to go and why. [The government department] was a hopeless outfit when I arrived here. Relationships had broken down with industry. And it took me several months of talking round the table with large groups of people, and making the Department face the industry and vice versa to get them all back together again, and everybody's very excited about it. But they now understand the way it's got to be done, that they have to work together, and the minister will insist, belt them round the ears if they don't.

In order to facilitate policy implementation new structures were being formed within some departments to consult with business interests. One example, composed of private and public sector individuals, had 'tentacles out into the business community'. Thus ministers could learn 'how the businesses are performing, whether or not there are some concerns about them, how you would rectify those, and in general how government policy is working, what kind of effects it's having'. The emphasis was upon proactive consultation. Examples given by ministers included the new Racing Industry Board created to replace the old Racing Authority Board, and the Enterprise Council.

Consultation and the Fourth National Government

There was extensive consultation within the policy communities by the ministers of the 1990–93 cabinet. Indeed, any other finding would indicate that either ministers were being economical with the truth or that government was not occurring; New Zealand's political culture and the complexities of contemporary policy formulation and implementation together work to foster a continuing interchange between groups and political leaders. Besides, as argued by James above, the National Party has close links with many of society's organized interests, especially those related to business (employers rather than employees) and the professions. The National ministers showed in their interviews that individually they had links with a range of groups throughout the economic sector.

But the data here do not only show the extent of consultation. More importantly, the interviews are interesting for the attitudes demonstrated towards the relationship between particular types of interests and government in the New Zealand polity. As critics of pluralist theory have long noted, and as neo-pluralist political theory emphasizes, certain groups are regarded as legitimate in the eyes of our rulers whilst others are not. Not unexpectedly, given the party's own ideological views and the prevalence of the belief amongst members of the economic élite about the functional and moral superiority of the market economy, it was primarily the business interests whose policy perspectives were sought by the ministers.

In part this happened for pragmatic reasons; policy implementation is made difficult if the main sectoral groups are not accommodating. But the patterns of consultation illustrated here show a further characteristic: legitimacy is achieved by 'doing'. Thus the practitioners are heeded; it is their views and co-operation that are sought by ministers, producing what might be called a 'technological' bias in the patterns of consultation. This is reinforced by the support of the ministers of the 1990–93 Bolger Government for the move away from welfare measures and towards increased individual responsibility, a policy goal shared by all ministers, albeit with reservations about the pace of change and the extent to which neo-liberal ideas provide the correct recipe for New Zealand.

Organized groups in general were regarded as less legitimate than the actual 'practitioners', although, from the evidence of the interviews, some of the major sectoral organizations—farming, employment, and manu- facturing—were consulted far more extensively than those groups which argue either as employees or, alternatively, on behalf of the interests of others. The idea of our elected leaders representing citizens' interests in their capacities as clients or consumers was found only in the interviews of a small minority of ministers. Moreover, there was a deep suspicion of some professional associations—educationalists and health professionals, especially—whilst the professional groups such as lawyers and accountants, all of whom have prospered under commercialization and corporatization, and who are predominantly to be found in the private rather than the public sector—were still part of established policy communities.

Overall, the doctrine of 'capture' prevailed, with distinctive biases against public service advice and certain organized interests, and towards others. Respectability is gained through involvement in entrepreneurial, productive, and investment processes, narrowly defined; the influential policy communities, it seems, are those which are based upon and include representatives of certain sectoral interests.

Cabinet, Interests, and Consultation

The shifting patterns demonstrated by the state–group relationship in New Zealand have shown that there is a range of factors that propel cabinet governments towards engagement with groups on the one hand, and disengagement on the other.

The pressures that work against close relationships with groups are as follows. First, the nature of the state itself is significant. The shift from the mixed economy, the interventionist, developmental state, towards economic deregulation and liberalization has radically reduced the extent to which group–government negotiations are necessary. As A. Cawson has argued, overarching changes 'such as the election of a government deeply suspicious of corporatism and eager to achieve a return to the competitive market, or the necessity for adjustment to worldwide recession, can send shockwaves through the elaborate structure of corporatist networks'. This usually results in the breakdown of arrangements at macro-level and 'the displacement of corporatism to meso- and micro-levels where more limited sectoral bargaining might be achieved more readily'.[18]

Second, state structural change in itself changed the composition of the policy communities: the new public sectors shocked established policy-community relationships by changing the institutional and opportunity points of contact. Thus frequency of contact was reduced and patterns of access were changed. Third, political willpower is enabled by an unconstrained and flexible system of state power directed by cabinet, permitting that body some choice of whom to consult; and party ideology and the agenda of government dictate who should be included in the policy communities and who excluded from them. Thus political structure—unfettered cabinet government with single-party government—can work against consultative practices.

There are, however, very strong forces that push governments towards consultation and negotiation. These can be divided into the general and the particular. First, there are the practical requirements of efficiency and implementation. Discussing liberal democracy and the relative powers of preference and corporate groups, Cawson says, 'over the longer term the requirements of policy-making and policy-implementation tend to lead towards mutually supportive and exclusive relationships between the state and organized *producer* interests'.[19] Similarly, interaction is necessary in a non-corporatized but democratic environment, partly to gain the expertise of interest groups but also to ensure effective policy implementation. Second, there is the connected factor that the effective exercise of power in liberal democracies requires at least some policy legitimization. This is particularly important when governments are trying to achieve radical changes. In New Zealand this has been attempted by a constant, sophisticated, public relations exercise, and also by the ministers themselves, communicating with interested groups and key individuals. This can be biased towards powerful corporate economic interests, as we have seen. Deregulated economies free corporate interests from their 'prisoner' status. Autonomy has given economic interests added legitimacy. New Zealand's absorption into the international capitalist economy, and its dependence upon good 'credit ratings' from overseas financial interests, has of course increased the need both to govern in ways that those interests perceive favourably, and to seek to retain legitimacy through the right connections with international financial concerns.

The third general factor that pushes governments towards consultation is policy conflict; the more internal conflict there is within the governing party or parties, the more its components are tempted to seek outside allies. Even in a relatively united government such as that between 1990 and 1993, policy differences resulted in policy consultation. Some disputes are probably endemic to a reforming regime: deregulation, especially of utilities, is inherently divisive.[20] (There will always be conflict about commercially driven operations versus social service responsiveness and continuity and pricing of supplies). There are also the problems of conflicting macro-economic goals (employment versus low inflation, for instance), and continuing argument even within economic élites concerning the extent to which the state should involve itself in activities such as research and development.

There are several factors particular to the New Zealand state that also support consultation and the formation or continuation of policy communities. First, the twin ideological perspectives of trust in the government of business practitioners and distrust of the public service had heightened the respectability of consulting those seen as sympathetic with government goals. Second, the pro-business lobby organizations have been maintaining the pressure on Government to continue neo-liberal economic policies. This was helped by the relationship that exists between industry and the National Party. The irony is that this encourages business–government consultation. Much has been made of the 'good business is in the public interest' argument. Continuing the programme of deregulation and privatization also fosters government dependence upon the expertise of the business and business-associated sectors.

Third, the élite characteristics of the New Zealand state push National cabinets—and to a lesser extent, Labour—towards consultation through the connections of background and social and political engagement. The 1990–93 National caucus was composed of about one-third MPs from business backgrounds and about one-quarter from farming. In cabinet, half of the ministers had agricultural interests, nine had professional backgrounds, and the others had entrepreneurial or corporate business backgrounds.[21] The small scale of the society means that there appears to be an interlocking economic and political élite, yet to be properly researched.

And the normative issues raised by group–government relationships?

The problem is that the doctrine of 'capture' is deeply flawed as an explanatory model of political behaviour. 'Capture' is predicated upon the public choice theory of self-interest as the driving force in political behaviour. As such it is subject to two major criticisms. First, despite its heuristic usefulness, it ignores the empirical evidence showing that motivations such as altruism and civic responsibility are factors in explaining political participation. Second, if self-interest is an accurate portrayal of human nature, then none of us is exempt; nobody and no institution can be the guardian of the public interest. Moreover, leaving aside its empirical aspects, the doctrine of 'capture' is in principle inimical to democratic values because it disparages the value of the participation of groups in the political system.[22]

There is a further democratic problem: when in practice the notion of 'capture' or 'vested interests' is applied selectively to the various groups in society, then it legitimizes the advice of some groups over the advice of others. Whether or not we are all motivated by self-interest, we all have 'interests' in that 'a policy, law or institution is in someone's interest if it increases his [sic] opportunities to get what he wants'.[23] Democratic states cannot respond to all expressed interests, and governments must decide how they are to interpret the 'public interest'. We elect governments precisely for this purpose. There are problems for democracy, however, when the public interest is interpreted to accommodate the goals of those who are in sympathy with government policies and exclude the ideas of others. This touches upon the larger issue of cabinet responsibility and accountability, the topic of the next chapter.

9

TAKING RESPONSIBILITY

Party Government and Political Responsibility

This penultimate chapter returns to two of the constitutional issues discussed in Chapter Two and touched upon in the discussions of cabinet selection and the roles of the ministers. It has been argued that, first, the doctrine of collective cabinet loyalty was as much a mechanism for the retention of political power in Westminster-type systems as it has been a normative ideal. Second, the practice of collective cabinet loyalty in effect has subsumed that of ministerial responsibility in New Zealand cabinet government. The intention of this chapter is to explore these themes more fully.

First I shall discuss ministerial responsibility and, second, collective cabinet responsibility, explaining how New Zealand constitutional and political arrangements facilitate, permit, or inhibit the processes of ministers being made accountable, or, as I prefer to put it, taking responsibility for their political actions. Jeffrey Stanyer has pointed out that accountability requires three components. Actions must be justified, these justifications must be made on specific occasions, and there must be consequences of those actions.[1] This useful clarification will be employed in the following discussion of ministerial responsibility.

Ministerial Responsibility

Ministers individually should have to account for, explain, and defend their decisions, their policies, and their public servants. When ministers take responsibility for the actions of their departments, they are defending the politically neutral governmental bureaucracy.[2] As far as individual ministers are concerned this partly takes place behind closed doors, in cabinet committees, in cabinet itself (as explained in earlier chapters), and in caucus. In all polities accountability mechanisms are partly private; the 'specific occasions' need not necessarily be public and publicized. In democratic terms the privacy of the arguments (and the occasions) would seem to be unsatisfactory. On the other hand, there are some incentives for good (or at least plausible) performance; ministers may not be sacked for ineptitude and error, as I will explain, but they certainly will not be further promoted if their actions work against the collective goals of government authority and continuation in office. Additionally, since the Official Information Act 1982, ministerial decisions have been rather more open to scrutiny. Thus ambition, in theory anyway, provides the incentive for justifiable political behaviour at the individual level. The Prime Minister, especially if the sole cabinet selector, and ministerial colleagues, are the judges of ministerial behaviour in the private forums of political decision making.

The incentives to continue in power and improve one's position in the governing hierarchy carry through to the more important public arenas; it is even worse to perform badly in Parliament, when giving speeches to groups, and when being questioned on television about policies and decisions. Publicity, it has been argued, is an important weapon in the process of ensuring accountability.[3] But taking responsibility, according to Stanyer, needs 'specific occasions'. Here Parliament provides the locus and defines the procedures, through debates and questions to ministers and Prime Minister. Parliament is vital in the process of ministerial responsibility because of its legitimacy as the central, elected institution and the publicity given its deliberations. Nonetheless, despite its authority, Parliament lacks power. Since the nineteenth century it has been dominated by the governing party, which itself is dominated by cabinet. Thus the legislature cannot make ministers resign. The 'consequences' of ministerial actions are left to the dual (and interacting) pressures of public opinion and prime ministerial judgement. Any majority party cabinet (coalition or single party), so long as it can retain its internal solidarity and its own back-bench support, is impervious to parliamentary sanction. Cabinets which do not command a majority of the votes of the legislature may be more vulnerable to the punishing powers of the MPs. Thus, the existence of majority party governments contradicts the practice of ministerial responsibility in so far as it requires resignation as the proper sanction for misconduct and errors of judgement. What, then, has happened to New Zealand ministers who have erred or who have been incompetent?

In general, ministers in the National and Labour parties have been gently punished by a switch of portfolio for their lack of competence. Or else, as happened in 1993, National ministers who have not distinguished themselves in the eyes of the Prime Minister are dropped from cabinet to make room for 'new blood'.[4] As much as anything else, these sorts of changes are designed to signify switches in policy direction or style, and the creation of an invigorated cabinet team.

The tradition in National has generally been for ministers to resign, apparently voluntarily, from Parliament and cabinet. As an under-secretary said during the early 1970s:

> You have certain people who want to retire for age or health or other reasons who feel it is time to pull out. They do it of their own free will. It is recognized in the party that it is good for the party, good for the government, that this happens.

This habit of ministers gracefully retiring from Parliament and cabinet simultaneously has had several consequences for National political leadership in New Zealand. First, it has removed the possibility that those who have gone from cabinet but not from Parliament will stay and give authoritative support to the ministry from the back benches. Second, and conversely, it removes from the back benches the possibility of an experienced nucleus of opposition to the leadership, especially likely if a minister has been dismissed or forced to resign on a matter of principle. Third, it has perpetuated the belief that ministers will not be sacked and that ministers, no matter how incompetent, will at least be able to serve out the parliamentary term. This brings us to the question of what kinds of pressures may have been used to build and reinforce this exterior image of voluntary withdrawal from politics.

The Prime Minister has available various persuasions in the National Party, such as indicating that the power of patronage will be withdrawn in the future if a minister does not retire when the Prime Minister thinks suitable, or promising that a minister who contests the next general election against the Prime Minister's wishes will not be reappointed to the cabinet. The Prime Minister could also in theory threaten to influence the local National Party members and persuade them not to renominate the minister for the next election. Renomination of a sitting member is, however, almost always secured—despite party members liking to feel they are able to withdraw their approval and occasionally doing so. Whether anyone so senior as a minister would be at risk seems unlikely. Alternatively the Prime Minister can simply rely on persuading the minister to do what is best in the party's interest and, accordingly, retire. There is no explicit evidence that any of these alternatives have been practised. Keith Holyoake, when asked about this in interview, said, 'That's my business—the internal affairs of a political family.'

Informal pressures coming from the National Party's expectation that ministers should retire before too long and the existence of a career and an income beyond politics to which to return or to cultivate more intensively have produced a susceptibility to other pressures. External and more overt pressures about ministerial ill-health, and the necessity for cabinet regeneration have come from the media, and, undoubtedly, from the Prime Minister. Thus the hopes of the ambitious are fanned at the same time as open conflict through dismissal is avoided. And a cabinet can carry on loyally protecting an ineffective rump provided that the period for which the team is to continue in office is finite. The short, three-year term thus effectively also inhibits mid-term sackings and radical reshuffles. When Keith Holyoake handed over the prime ministership to John Marshall, however, five ministers announced that, as they planned to retire at the end of the year and not to contest the next general election, they would retire from cabinet immediately and return to the back benches. Whatever the real reasons for these particular retirements, they perpetuated the public image of voluntary retirement from cabinet. The myth was preserved that ministers do not leave because they are incompetent or tired, but because new faces are needed on the Treasury front bench to lead the party for the next election. Dissent, disagreement and inability are all matters for the 'family' to deal with and hide from exterior comment.[5]

One of the problems National prime ministers have, however, in even considering the competence of some of their ministers, is that very often the less able minister is a minister who forms part of the Prime Minister's own political generation and especially loyal group. Oligarchic tendencies within political parties are enhanced by the leaders' need to surround themselves with loyal followers. And the proclivity towards oligarchy and the retention of mediocrity and incompetence is reinforced by the small choice of available talent for cabinet office.

The situation has been rather different in the Labour Party. The uncertainty as to who has the authority to remove ministers from their posts (if that is felt to be necessary) was discussed earlier, and David Lange's problems were outlined. The constraint of institutional smallness is added to the complexity of the interrelationship within the Parliamentary Labour Party between the Prime Minister and caucus, and cabinet and caucus; thus David Lange dismissed, and caucus then reinstated, Roger Douglas. Although Labour prime ministers have sometimes been able to fortify their positions by appealing to the Labour movement, as Savage, Fraser, and Kirk did over various issues, this option was unavailable to Lange because, on the one hand, Roger Douglas had very strong support within cabinet and caucus and, on the other hand, the party was unhappy with the overall direction of Labour Government policy under Lange's leadership. Within the PLP a Prime Minister's authority is circumscribed by the party's belief in the limitations on the extent of leadership powers.

When, during the first and third Labour governments, a Leader was given the opportunity of having a minister or ministers removed by caucus, the Prime Minister discouraged such an outcome. The first case was when Peter Fraser rescued Rex Mason. The second was when Bill Rowling warned the caucus, after the death of Norman Kirk and the election of a new leader and deputy, not to make too many further changes, whereupon no changes were made. At any rate, the tendency has been for caucus to return those ministers

Table 9.1: Reasons for Ministerial Resignations, 1935–93[1]

Personal Reasons	Collective Responsibility Departures
D. G. McMillan, 1941	D. F. Quigley, 1982
W. L. Martin, 1941	R. W. Prebble, 1988
F. Langstone, 1942	R. O. Douglas, 1988
F. W. Doidge, 1951	W. Peters, 1991
W. Sullivan, 1957	
E. B. Corbett, 1957	
H. Watt, 1975	
K. J. Holyoake, 1977	
T. F. Gill, 1980	
T. A. de Cleene, 1988	
M. E. R. Bassett, 1990[2]	
R. O. Douglas, 1990[2]	
C. R. Marshall, 1990[2]	
C. J. Moyle, 1990[2]	
S. J. Rodger, 1990[2]	
R. J. Tizard, 1990[2]	

1. Following G. A. Wood, I have ignored resignations following general elections and when new ministries have been formed.
2. These ministers announced that they would not seek re-election at the 1990 general election, and subsequently they lost their ministerial positions in Geoffrey Palmer's February 1990 cabinet reshuffle.

Source: Wood (ed.), *Supplement to Ministers and Members in the New Zealand Parliament*, Appendix 6, p. 42.

seeking re-election to cabinet posts when there is a 'spill' after the party has been re-elected in power. That is what happened in 1987.

The New Zealand cabinet, therefore, has been remarkable for the relative absence of ministerial dismissals. Indeed, even mid-term resignations, for whatever reason, are rare. Table 9.1 lists all the examples of ministerial resignations under two headings: resignation for personal reasons completely unrelated to either ministerial performance or behaviour (sometimes to take up patronage positions, sometimes for reasons of health, but also out of chagrin—Langstone, de Cleene); and resignations or dismissals because ministers have broken the convention of collective cabinet responsibility. There is no column for ministers who have resigned or who were dismissed on the grounds of ministerial responsibility, since there have been no instances since the resignation of Sir Apirana Ngata in 1934 when a

Commission reported that there was a conflict between Ngata's duties as a minister and his interests.

In Stanyer's terms, although ministers have had to explain their mistakes, and the mistakes of their public servants, in Parliament and in public, they have not had to bear the full consequences for their misdemeanours. The pattern of New Zealand parliamentary politics has worked against the occurrence of public dismissal of cabinet ministers. Cabinet loyalty and cabinet responsibility have been important, not ministerial responsibility. Small size, as usual, has fostered loyalty and conformity, while the tradition of the influential caucus has limited the power and therefore the flexibility of the Prime Minister. As has been shown, the authority handed to the Prime Minister by caucus is strictly limited by the obligation to consult and, more importantly here, to protect. And protection of the choice becomes not only a matter of loyalty to colleagues but also a matter of protecting prime ministerial authority in the National Party by not admitting to mistakes having been made in selection. Labour prime ministers do not have this problem, but, then, they must abide by the choice of ministers made by caucus.

There has been much debate on the problem of ministerial mistakes and responsibility in New Zealand. The discussion of ministerial responsibility became more intense after the implications of the public sector reforms of the fourth Labour Government became evident. The corporatization of trading organizations made ministers only loosely responsible to Parliament for SOE actions. (The SOE boards are responsible to the share-holding ministers, SOE and Finance.) The architects of the reforms justified the changes in terms of improving ministerial responsibility. Roger Douglas said:

> Are the classical principles of ministerial responsibility under the Westminster system compatible with good business management? The answer is undoubtedly no. Requiring ministers to make decisions personally about every little detail of the day-to-day running of a trading department does not make for accountability or for good management.

And he added that under the SOEs ministers would be accountable, but for policy only, through the statement of corporate intent.[6]

Moreover, the distinction between outcomes and outputs, with ministers responsible for the former and public servants for the latter, has also removed ministers from the processes of policy implementation—when mistakes are most likely to be made.

Individual ministerial responsibility can be divided into three different types: personal responsibility, primary responsibility, and vicarious responsibility. John Martin defines personal responsibility as unacceptable ministerial behaviour 'which is *not related* to his or her discharge of ministerial duties'.[7] For instance Cecil Parkinson, a British minister, resigned because of the scandal surrounding an extra-marital affair (although only after it became obvious to the Prime Minister, Margaret Thatcher, that the Conservative Party was sufficiently scandalized to make her support for him impossible to maintain). There has been no known case of a minister resigning on these sorts of grounds in New Zealand. Primary responsibility 'exists when a Minister's actions *related* to his or her ministerial duties are called in question'. Another of Margaret Thatcher's ministers, Lord Carrington, resigned for personal (as well as departmental) misjudgements relating to the invasion by Argentina of the Falklands Islands. Vicarious responsibility 'involves the Minister's accountability for the actions of departmental officers'.[8] The next two sections discuss the latter two types of ministerial responsibility.

Primary Responsibility
In 1954, Dean Eyre, Minister of Industries and Commerce, proposed to travel overseas in connection with his business as an importer. Both the granting of leave and the possible conflict of interest between his public and private activities were criticized. The Prime Minister, Sidney Holland, reacted by exchanging Eyre's portfolios with those of Eric Halstead who was then Minister of Social Security. Holland said that the 'interchange of portfolios between Mr Halstead and Mr Eyre was in no way a result of any defect of administration or personal quality of either Minister'. Holland said that Eyre handed over his portfolios because the questioning of his announced intentions to make the visit made it difficult for him to continue to administer Industries and Commerce and Customs since they both involved contact with the business community. The business leaders, continued Holland, regretted Eyre's departure. And, 'Above all there has been a unanimous assurance that Mr Eyre's personal integrity has not been in question in any way. Members of the Government entirely associate themselves with his position.'[9] There was no admission of wrong by either the Prime Minister or the minister concerned. The matter was treated rather as a miscalculation about what the public would or would not tolerate rather than as a ministerial misdemeanour. Holland said, 'In public administration it is important that the actions of Ministers should not only be right in themselves, but that they should manifestly appear to be so to the man in the street.'[10]

The newspapers criticized the cabinet committee subsequently set up to establish rules about private business. It was rightly felt that the problem should be dealt with by Parliament and not by party in cabinet.[11] John

Marshall reported that, as Attorney-General, he wrote the rules, producing the report which went to a Cabinet committee and then full cabinet, and was then referred to a select committee 'which duly deliberated, changed a word here and there, and confirmed the report', which was unanimously approved by Parliament.[12] The 1956 *Report* declared that there were two basic principles. First, 'A Minister must ensure that no conflict exists, or appears to exist, between his public duty and his private interests.' Second, 'A Minister of the Crown is expected to devote his time and his talents to the carrying out of his public duties.' Guide-lines were set out to ensure these principles were obeyed.[13]

In 1990 new guide-lines were written which limited the conditions under which ministers could either earn outside income or accept gifts or payments. Evidently the revisions were prompted by the payments received by David Lange and Roger Douglas for speaking engagements. In addition to including rules on dealing in shares (which must not relate to their portfolios) and requiring the resignation of company directorships apart from family business, ministers must not accept payment for any appearances related to their portfolios and, also, must seek permission from the Prime Minister to be paid for any outside activity not linked with their portfolios. Except for unpaid party advertising, appearing in advertisements is not allowed. Gifts may only be kept if they are worth less than $500. A yearly schedule of ministers' interests is tabled in Parliament, an important innovation.[14] Note, however, that these are Cabinet Office rules, not statutory requirements. As such the prime sanctions for disobedience are the expressed disapproval of the Prime Minister, and adverse publicity. Geoffrey Palmer was the main instigator of the new rules, but he did not succeed in establishing a register for MPs as well.

When Jim Bolger assumed the prime ministership at the end of 1990, he made some changes. In his words he reinforced 'the premise that ministerial office is expected to be a full-time occupation to which Ministers devote their time and talent'. He broadened the occasions on which ministers were to declare their interests, but did not require ministers to resign their directorships or dispose of their businesses, as long as they refrained from taking an active part in the operation of business and professional activities. The register was made fuller, with the declaration of house ownership as well as commercial properties being required. Trusts as well as shares were to be declared, and business involvement described. However, 'As the existence and public declaration of actual or potential conflict of interests is more important than its monetary value Ministers will not be required to declare the value of the assets on their declaration.'[15]

Have there been cases of ministers acting in ways that might be regarded as producing a conflict of interest since Eyre? Whetu Tirikatene-Sullivan, Minister of Tourism during the third Labour Government, was criticized for appointing a chairperson of the Tourist Hotel Corporation who was also her personal accountant. In this case the criticisms were as much about the inability of the minister to give clear and unambiguous answers to parliamentary questions as about the dubious or unjustified nature of the appointment, since justification could be put forward on the basis of the appointee's qualifications for the job. Despite criticism within and outside the party of her handling of the episode, the minister retained her position, for the Labour Party was rapidly approaching the election of 1975.

Another example was Duncan MacIntyre who was accused of using his influence as Minister of Agriculture and Fisheries to secure a loan from the Marginal Lands Board for his daughter and son-in-law. The Minister of Lands, Venn Young, was also involved.[16] Brookfield discusses the Commission of Inquiry's report and summarizes the issue: unlike the Ngata case, with MacIntyre there was 'no maladministration or impropriety, merely the imprudence, of two Ministers'.[17] Brookfield concludes that public regret should have been expressed, or even resignation offered. In the event, the support of the Prime Minister, Robert Muldoon, deflected pressure for resignation.

A somewhat different, recent example of personal ministerial responsibility was during the Bolger Government. The Minister of Justice, Doug Graham, stated on television (in relation to the revision of the Crimes Act and the different penalties for rape) that rape by a bottle was not as bad for a woman as penile penetration. After a public outcry Graham apologized. In other words, he accepted responsibility for his error—a rare action in New Zealand politics.

Vicarious Responsibility

In 1944, Robert Semple, Minister of Works, was criticized about the unsatisfactory construction of the Fordell and Turakina tunnels. Semple claimed that he was responsible but not to blame, an attitude for which he was criticized.[18] Semple was not penalized in any way for the administrative inefficiencies that had occurred. In effect, cabinet and the prime minister took responsibility.

In December 1954, a murderer and rapist, Horton, serving a life sentence, escaped from Mount Eden Prison when out for the evening to play bowls.[19] After the senior members of the Department of Justice had seen the minister, John Marshall, he released a press statement which said, among other things, that in his view a man with Horton's history ought not to have been allowed out on an outside visit, even if his behaviour had been satisfactory. The prison superintendent at the time defended his action. The media supported the minister's statement and criticized that of the superintendent 'for its alleged aggressiveness'.[20] Horton was later recaptured. After receiving the full report from the department, Marshall issued a press statement saying that: Horton's inclusion in the visiting party was a serious failure in administration; sufficiently explicit directions to cover his and similar cases had not been given to the prison authorities; the permanent head of the department had acknowledged his responsibility in that respect; that Horton's inclusion was also the Superintendent's mistake; and that Marshall regretted the 'alarm and distress which was caused to the public'. He continued that, as minister, he bore responsibility, and 'I have sought to discharge this responsibility by giving a full account of the case and by indicating clearly and as soon as possible the steps which have been taken to avoid such a situation arising again'.[21] When in 1994 there was a similar event concerning an escaped prisoner, the Minister of Justice, Doug Graham, did not accept responsibility for the actions of the public servants.

In 1966 the Minister of Marine, W. J. Scott, charged five directors of Radio Hauraki with defying an order to detain their 'pirate' radio ship, *Tiri*. The magistrate dismissed the charges, finding that the minister had not been properly advised in issuing the detention order in the first place. Like the preceding examples it is difficult to tell the extent to which the minister must assume personal responsibility. In this case there was very little publicity or public criticism of the minister's action, even from the Labour Opposition, perhaps because they themselves were awkwardly placed to criticize since they favoured the public control and ownership of broadcasting. Holyoake removed Broadcasting, but not Marine, from Scott a little later.

Then in 1969 there was a case involving the Tourist and Publicity Department. The Opposition accused the Government of using the information and press section of the department for party political propaganda. The Acting Minister in charge of Publicity, L. R. Adams-Schneider, issued a statement that the article was written by a private citizen. The National Party endeavoured to gloss over the allegations. Norman Kirk demanded the resignation of the responsible minister while the department's General Manager said that the department had erred and he would name the author. A select committee of the House, after untangling the authorship of the paper and the deceiver of the Acting Minister, left the fate of the officers in the hands of the State Services Commission. The ministers—acting and permanent—thus proceeded as though they had been exonerated; the public servants bore the blame. The situation here is also difficult given New Zealand practice. Since the ministers were found to be misled, the most they could be blamed for was not knowing and checking on the work of the department more thoroughly.

Towards the end of the Muldoon administration, an enquiry into the

Maniototo irrigation scheme showed that the Ministry of Works and Development had performed inadequately (in costings and management).[22] The State Services Commission disciplined the public servants deemed responsible. The Minister of Works and Development, Anthony Friedlander, did not accept responsibility for the errors and, of course, declined to resign. Friedlander, thus, did not accept the validity of even the limited notion of taking responsibility by accepting formal responsibility. In this case cabinet itself was also to blame for it had ignored Treasury advice in 1980 that the scheme was becoming too expensive.

In 1986 copies of the Labour Government's budget were distributed, before time, to people who were not entitled to see them. The office of the Minister of Finance, Roger Douglas, was at fault, and the Minister offered the Prime Minister his resignation. David Lange refused it, saying that there was cabinet support for Douglas to retain his position, and that Douglas had behaved properly by accepting responsibility. But it was unnecessary to accept the blame. [23]

In 1987 the Labour Party Minister of Maori Affairs, Koro Wetere, was publicly criticized for his role in a proposed $600 million loan, to be raised in Hawaii. Here the problem was that the Secretary for Maori Affairs had gone ahead with negotiations without cabinet approval or authorization by Treasury or the Minister of Finance (required under the Public Finance Act). The enquiry by the State Services Commission found the Department of Maori Affairs and the Treasury to be at fault for failing to keep the Minister fully informed and satisfactorily advised. Wetere offered to resign his portfolios and his parliamentary seat, 'not because he felt he had done anything wrong but because he thought it was the best way to clear the air'. Geoffrey Palmer continues that cabinet as a whole discussed the matter and refused the resignation offer because it was 'convinced that the Minister had done no wrong which warranted his resignation therefore there was no point in precipitating a by-election'.[24]

In February 1994 the Minister of Housing, Murray McCully, faced with criticisms of a Housing New Zealand 'team-building exercise' (jetboating and ballooning) announced that he had told the Chief Executive that it was 'an inappropriate use of company time, and an insensitive initiative at a time of rent increases, bound to attract [criticism]'.[25] McCully certainly did not take responsibility for the actions of this SOE-like body. Indeed, he gave the impression that the main error was that Housing New Zealand had embarrassed the minister.

A month later an inquiry by the State Services Commission into Treasury's costings of the Labour Party's 1993 election promises reported that Treasury had breached internal guide-lines on political neutrality and impartiality in six out of the seventeen reports on Labour's policies. Don Hunn, who headed the State Services Commission, said that he had made it clear to Murray Horn, Secretary of Treasury, that the failings were serious: 'I do not conduct performance assessments of a chief executive in public but I am sure Dr Horn and I will be discussing this matter further.'[26] The Treasury spokesperson, however, deflected blame to the Treasury staff members who had done the job. Incompetence and dishonesty are of course frequent bedfellows, and it is difficult to say whether the miscostings were errors or over-enthusiasm for the policies of the governing National Party. In either case, however, the miscostings raise issues of accountability. Who, in these circumstances should carry the responsibility? The Labour Party, arguing that the mistakes could have cost the party the election, given the closeness of the 1993 results, interestingly did not try to place the responsibility upon the Minister of Finance. Rather Michael Cullen, the Finance spokesperson, said, 'In the end you can't go headhunting for officials down the line. In the end it is the Secretary of Treasury [who is accountable for the process].'[27] When both Opposition and Government blame the Secretary rather than the minister, one wonders whether the convention of ministerial responsibility has completely disappeared.

But by now it will be plain that New Zealand ministers have never accepted the pure doctrine of vicarious ministerial responsibility which demands that the minister takes the blame as well as the credit for the actions of the administrators, who must remain anonymous and beneath credit or blame. The public sector changes, which have made senior public servants even more patently public figures and separated ministers further from the administrative process, have confirmed this pattern. Collective cabinet responsibility and public knowledge of the identity and policies of many public servants have produced a very different situation in New Zealand from any ideal model of the workings of cabinet government.

In majority party government (if the Prime Minister wishes to), most ministers can be supported through their errors by wrapping around them the cloak of cabinet responsibility and relying on their colleagues' partisanship to support the action. Because credit and blame for performance tend to be interpreted collectively, errors of 'principle', particularly in a society where the press are not very inquisitive or critical, can thus be disguised and reinterpreted. A Prime Minister who forms a government from a series of floating cliques and factions or from a coalition of parties and who must rely on their support may find it actually easier to dismiss a minister for incompetence or a breach of principle. For the Prime Minister can argue that, unless ministers are censured and dismissed in this way, cabinet may lose the support of Parliament.

Contrast the dichotomous position of the legislature dominated by a strongly partisan two-party system as demonstrated in the New Zealand Parliament. In this latter type of situation the majority party can, of course, defeat any motion of no confidence in the government. Given that security, for a Prime Minister to admit ministerial error or wrong-doing in cabinet would be to risk eroding leadership authority. If a National Prime Minister has selected a wrong-doer, this would be tantamount to admitting to poor judgement. To dismiss would thus, in an odd sort of way, lessen the Prime Minister's authority in the New Zealand Parliament. Dismissals by Labour Prime Ministers, as history has shown, are only possible if the minister has lost the support of cabinet and caucus colleagues, as well as that of the Leader. Furthermore, for all Prime Ministers, dismissals create possible insecurity for existing and future cabinet ministers, thereby slackening the bonds of loyalty at present so strong in the legislature. Far better to gamble on the short memory of the electorate at the next general election than to risk one's own immediate position by creating interpersonal doubts and insecurity.

Collective Cabinet Responsibility

The other aspect of cabinet government that might have been expected to have produced some ministerial resignations or removals is disagreement over policy. In fact, however, in neither Labour nor National was a minister dismissed until Derek Quigley lost his place in cabinet in June 1982.

There certainly have been disagreements, many of them fairly public. In National the practice has been to keep the issue as quiet as possible and to allow discussion and argument in cabinet and caucus until the differences are resolved. Ralph Hanan was able to persuade enough of his colleagues in a free vote to vote in the House against capital punishment and to defeat it. Robert Muldoon and others, backed by some powerful interest groups, persuaded enough of their caucus and cabinet colleagues to accept the arguments against the Nelson Cotton Mill, although this case involved the resistance of back-benchers and not the persuasions of a minister. Dissent is acceptable when confined to party circles and not made public. This came out clearly in the interviews, both those of the 1970s and the 1990s.

But there have been cases where ministers have publicly dissented from cabinet policy. Ministers have been identified with contrary viewpoints, although no one until the fourth Labour Government became sufficiently alienated from cabinet and caucus opinion or has felt sufficiently strongly about an issue to resign. Tom Shand, for example, was reported to have differed from most of his cabinet colleagues about economic, labour, and transport matters during the 1960s, but the breach was not sufficient to persuade this very forceful minister to resign. Besides, he probably got his own way frequently enough to make it worthwhile continuing. Later, during the Muldoon period, the Minister of Immigration, Aussie Malcolm, disagreed publicly with cabinet's decision to stop the issuing of permanent residency permits to those Samoans who had been 'overstayers' in New Zealand. Dr Ian Shearer, Minister of Broadcasting, reported that his recommendation to cabinet concerning a third television channel had been overturned.[28] Ben Couch, also one of Muldoon's ministers, disagreed with his colleagues in 1981 over the South African rugby tour of New Zealand. And during the fourth Labour Government ministers constantly disagreed. In the fourth National Government there were also instances of public differences. The Minister of Disarmament and Arms, Doug Graham (also Minister of Justice), spoke of working with multinational defence forces in the United Nations rather than endeavouring to revive the Anzus alliance. The Foreign Minister (and Deputy Prime Minister), in response, supported continuing security arrangements with the USA, and the Minister of Defence supported McKinnon.

How did all these ministers keep their ministerial positions? First, dissent is permissible if it concerns 'conscience' issues. Second, dissent—if not too protracted—is permissible if it does not detract from the authority of the Prime Minister. The following examples (briefly discussed here) illustrate this latter point.

Derek Quigley, Minister for Works and Housing, criticized the Government's economic strategy in a speech to the Young Nationals. Quigley then declined the Prime Minister's request to try to stop the full text from being published in the *Dominion* newspaper.[29] Quigley was told either to apologize to his cabinet colleagues—Bill Birch was reported to be particularly angry—or resign. He chose the latter course.[30] It was clear that Quigley's excursion into public criticism of the direction of government policy was an example of more frequent dissent in cabinet, where he had some support. Quigley's mistake was to criticize the Prime Minister in public.[31] During the fourth Labour Government, under David Lange's prime ministership, Roger Douglas and Richard Prebble failed to support collective cabinet loyalty, and departed from cabinet after they publicly criticized Lange. In all three cases dissent was the product of policy differences and personality conflict. In 1991, Winston Peters was dismissed by Jim Bolger. Peters' place in cabinet was always going to be a risk, since the outspoken Peters had criticized Bolger's leadership even while National was in opposition.[32] But it was difficult not to appoint a popular politician, also the only possible Maori Minister of Maori Affairs. (After the dismissal many Maori leaders demonstrated their displeasure at losing their minister.) Peters spoke against National's economic and social policies, tried to railroad cabinet into accepting his scheme for Maori development, *Ka Awatea*, and compounded these errors by constant criticisms of the leadership. Bolger said that Peters' conduct had been 'inconsistent with continued membership in the Cabinet and inconsistent with the convention of collective responsibility among Cabinet ministers'.[33]

Collective cabinet responsibility is indeed a political device to maintain the power and authority of the New Zealand cabinet, for it is invoked only when a dissenter challenges the authority of the Prime Minister, thus eroding leadership power in the eyes of party and public.

Collective Cabinet Responsibility; the Views of the Ministers, 1990–93
The ministers of the Bolger Government in interview strongly supported the doctrine of collective cabinet responsibility. In this they followed their Labour predecessors. In 1987 David Lange wrote:

> When Cabinet has reached a decision it is the collective decision of all ministers whether present or not and whether agreeing or not. If a minister feels that he [sic] must publicly dissociate himself from a decision of Cabinet which he cannot accept, he must first resign from Cabinet.[34]

In 1991 a National minister said:

> It's hard enough to understand what's going on in your own department and keep abreast of all the various things to do, let alone understand what's going on in Education, Social Welfare, or Inland Revenue. So you have to rely on your fellow ministers. You do your best in cabinet to garner the information and make a decision sensibly. Having done so, or supported the minister, you stand by it. . . . In our system of government, if the cabinet's all over the place and you've got one criticizing the other, then the government will fall.

The general view was that the dismissals and resignations since 1984 did not indicate that collective cabinet responsibility was in disrepute, but rather confirmed that it was being upheld. Indeed, ministers rather gave the impression that they were relieved when Winston Peters was finally dismissed by the Prime Minister. One said in interview shortly afterwards:

> I think you'll find that the cabinet will pull together again . . . he was upsetting all the other ministers. Although Mr Bolger was prepared to let him stay there for as long as he felt it necessary, it really did destabilize ministers who may have held similar—well, not similar views because I don't think anyone holds the same views as Winston—but who had perhaps feelings of disquiet about certain policies . . . but who accepted the cabinet responsibility, the collective responsibility.

When ministers were asked why there had been dismissals and resignations in recent years, they made a number of suggestions. The media was blamed for putting pressure on the system: 'people get isolated from the herd, and having to answer and account or whatever, put under pressure. It's a very intense environment. . . . And the more you say, the more likely you are to get into trouble.' In general, being a politician in the modern world was viewed as more stressful than in the past:

> I think that the processes of being in government in New Zealand have become increasingly difficult. As we have moved from being what was a relatively wealthy nation to a nation that is much less wealthy by comparison with others around the world, then the ability to be able to do things has diminished. So the decisions that have to be made, the competitive decisions [about] where you put resources become much harder for people to have to face up to. Therefore ministers are under much more stress, and from time to time that will evidence itself in there being some breaches of the principle of collective responsibility. But by and large, New Zealand governments have been very good at keeping that particular principle of collective responsibility.

Politics, it was argued, have been more ideological, thus exacerbating stress, and some ministers felt that there had been recently more politicians with 'independent attitudes', perhaps because politicians of today had not gone through the 'discipline' and cohesion of the armed forces or experienced the depression. The 'blind loyalty factor' had gone. The mass media encouraged 'personality politics'. Thus, ministers, as well as seeing themselves as trying to make decisions in a far more difficult era than their predecessors experienced, also felt that there were changes in the aspirants to political office.

One of the interesting questions about collective cabinet loyalty is whether or not it is carried through to caucus meetings of the governing party. Historically, ministers have relied heavily upon their back-bench colleagues for feedback and advice, because MPs, with their 'surgeries' and their local links, have operated in New Zealand politics as the primary vehicles for integrating legislature and executive with the community. Since the 1970s and 1980s, however, governments have increasingly relied on public and private opinion polls and their focused group interviews for policy feedback. It is probably not coincidental that the shift into polling sophistication coincided with what Robert Chapman called the 'fortress cabinet', whereby cabinets could dominate caucus by sheer force of numbers.[35]

The proportion of MPs in a governing party who have executive positions is not, however, a sufficient explanation for the way in which cabinets have increasingly dismissed the views of their back-bench colleagues. The fourth National Government was characterized by back-bench dissent, two MPs leaving the National Party between 1990 and 1993. But the considerable degree of disquiet about the direction of economic and social policy amongst the party's MPs only slightly slowed down the pace of change. The size of caucus is one factor, but this must be seen alongside the degree of unity of the cabinet, and cabinet's own perception of its proper role. And that, as we have seen, has become directed upon policy initiating and formulating. Moreover, back-benchers, even in a large caucus, have conflicting loyalties— whether to look towards their constituents and protect their often marginal seats even at the expense of failing to support their government, or loyalty to support government policy and thus demonstrate their future suitability for ministerial office.

The Bolger ministers seemed to believe that it was the convention that ministers upheld each other in caucus:

> If the cabinet has discussed something and settled on a policy then you are expected to support it not only outside but in the caucus. If you personally feel very strongly about something and you think it was wrong, then I think a minister could stand up in the caucus and say 'I don't agree with this for the following reasons, I'm sorry to say this, I won't say it outside, but I'm telling you because I feel strongly about it'. Nobody gets too excited about that, any more than we get terribly excited if a back-bencher stands up and says 'I don't agree with this, I feel so strongly about it I'm going to cross the floor'. Provided they do that in caucus, then in our party they're free to go. I mean if you did it every week, you might have to start wondering whether you were in the right party. So I think it works reasonably well, but it is most unusual, and not to be encouraged, for a minister to stand up and start weighing into his colleagues who have made a decision. That's not good for unity; it's not good for discipline.

Evidently ministers outside cabinet were equally locked in to this convention. It was acceptable for ministers to disagree when decisions had not been made consensually. Also it was customary for ministers to 'try not to dominate discussions inside caucus'. Nevertheless, 'if the Cabinet can't convince the caucus of what it's doing, then it shouldn't succeed. And the bigger the caucus, the more difficult that is.'

When the Prime Minister chooses the cabinet, then the personal loyalty that is the almost inevitable consequence of patronage helps support the doctrine of both caucus support of cabinet decisions and also collective cabinet loyalty. As an MP said of Keith Holyoake during the 1970s, 'No man will ever appoint a man who's ever opposed him on a matter of substance.' Another said, 'Holyoake values loyalty above all else and rewards loyalty. He's a very loyal man himself.' But also loyalty was 'directed to the team'. Where the power of patronage does not exist, then collective cabinet loyalty is also harder to maintain, as Labour governments have shown. Public policy debate amongst ministers might well be regarded as acceptable, even in a society and legislature which values internal party consensus as much as New Zealand has done, but when policy becomes interwoven with personal rivalries then cabinet government disintegrates.

Taking Responsibility: the New Zealand Cabinet

The absence of a consistent tradition of ministerial responsibility in New Zealand can be seen as a regrettable consequence not only of party government as such—the cabinet's control over Parliament through the possession of a cohesive and loyal party majority—but also of the overriding emphasis in the New Zealand legislative system upon party and cabinet solidarity. Weak ministers and erring ministers are easily defended by the protective fence of collective cabinet responsibility. It is certainly desirable that New Zealand ministers be of better quality than they are. But it would be a help if the few able ministers were less heavily loaded with portfolios, and if it were no longer as necessary to protect the weak from their mistakes.

Resignation, in other words accepting the ultimate consequence of ministerial responsibility, is surely not required in issues of vicarious responsibility, and is unnecessary in very minor, but not major, issues of personal ministerial responsibility. But ministers should be prepared to account for their own errors and for those for whom they are responsible, and accept formal responsibility where necessary. Voters can reward and punish politicians, but they cannot—and should not—reward and punish public servants. Voters deserve a full 'account'. At present there is a disjunction between the prescriptive and descriptive roles of the ministers. Parliament and cabinet, under proportional representation, will have to work to resolve this problem. Conventions will have to be developed that build upon the past but which distinguish between what might be called 'customary'—public explanations and commitments to rectification—and 'exceptional' control measures—ministerial resignation—in the accountability process.

And do cabinets take responsibility for their collective decisions? The results of the triennial elections have shown that voters have frequently punished governments for their errors; and disregard for the convention of the mandate in the last decade has cost governments political power, or at least, as in 1993, cost cabinet the support of a large parliamentary majority. But collective cabinet responsibility is less an accepted constitutional convention than a political convenience—a device to keep the team together and the Prime Minister in office.

The real problem with collective cabinet responsibility in New Zealand is that it has been interpreted as loyalty to one another and the Prime Minister, rather than responsibility to Parliament and public. Thus, as in many other small groups, ministers have made decisions seldom regarding either public (or bureaucratic) opinion or the views of their own political parties. This could be interpreted as 'group think', the phenomenon whereby small groups progressively exclude the views of those who disagree with them.[36] In recent years, the defence against listening to others has been that cabinet is concerned with the 'hard decision' as opposed to seeking 'populist' remedies,[37] a paternalist, self-righteous, and, in the end, self-defeating perspective on the role of cabinet in a representative democracy. The institutional characteristics of the New Zealand political system—small size and the two-party system—reinforce the tendency for politicians to form close links with one another. And the absence of constitutional constraints upon the power of cabinet, outside the triennial election, has permitted cabinets to avoid 'taking responsibility' for their decisions in their pursuit of fulfilling their policy agendas.

10

CONCLUSION:
CABINET AND POLITICAL POWER

With all the social, economic, and political changes that New Zealand has undergone in the past two decades, it is quite astonishing that cabinet itself is still identifiably the same sort of institution that it has always been: the single most important committee of the elected leadership. Of course it has altered, but incrementally rather than radically; if Michael Joseph Savage, New Zealand's first Labour Prime Minister, were to revisit a cabinet meeting he would have no difficulty in recognizing it for what it was. The essential properties of the Westminster system of cabinet government remain. It is much less likely that a former Public Service Permanent Head from the same period would recognize quite so readily the role and responsibilities of a contemporary governmental chief executive.

Nevertheless, the changes to the economy, society, and polity, many of them initiated by the actions of cabinet, have brought tensions and difficulties. The doctrine of collective responsibility has been broken more frequently and with more dramatic effect than since the early years of the two-party system; there have been public disputes about policy alternatives; ministers have been removed from cabinet; and prime ministers have had to manage dissension within their parties and cabinets. The doctrine of ministerial responsibility has been altered, perhaps destroyed, whilst a new version of 'accountability' has developed based upon contractual relationships between ministers and their chief executives. Collective cabinet loyalty has remained, for without it we would not have cabinet government. Collective cabinet responsibility, however, remains a constitutional precept rather than an operating constitutional convention.

The role of the Prime Minister has changed, partly in consequence of the personalization of politics that television has encouraged, but also because there is today renewed emphasis upon the Prime Minister as chief policy co-ordinator. Indeed, although policy co-ordination has been signalled as a major problem for New Zealand cabinets for many years now, the processes of initiating and implementing the dramatic policy changes of the past decades have put an increasing strain on the Prime Minister, as well as upon the institution of cabinet itself, and on the abilities and energies of the ministers. Theoretically, in New Zealand's purest of Westminster systems, with unconstrained, single-party majority governments, prime ministers have had great power. From time to time, prime ministers have indeed exercised their powers fully, even dictatorially. Nevertheless, prime ministers also have had to counter the participatory, majoritarian political culture of the New Zealand Parliament, a product of the interacting factors of small size and party ideologies and traditions. This latter factor has been particularly significant in limiting the powers and authority of Labour prime ministers. Thus we can see the impact of institution and party upon political behaviour.

Whilst the role played by cabinet itself has not changed fundamentally in the last several decades—it has remained the collective, authoritative, decision-making committee of central government—the expectations of the ministers themselves about their own individual roles have altered dramatically. Ministers now see themselves as policy initiators and advocates. Indeed, the evidence of the last two governments is that ministers have perceived themselves as in office to change the relationship between state and individual, making individuals less reliant upon government. Ministers have believed that they are responsible for effecting this transformation of the New Zealand political culture, necessary because of the economic decline from the 1970s onwards. But as the interviews of the ministers of the 1990–93 National Government have shown, the ambitious goals of reforming governments place great stress on those involved. The capacities of cabinet government have been stretched by the demands of radical change, whilst the structural changes made to the state and public sectors have yet to be consolidated. Simultaneously reforming structures and policies is a risky enterprise.

Cabinet government in New Zealand, as elsewhere, illustrates how the prime ministership has become bureaucratized, following quite closely behind the bureaucratization of the cabinet system itself, particularly the cabinet committees. So we now have a Department of Prime Minister and Cabinet on the one hand, and, on the other, increasingly detailed rules about the processes of cabinet.

Other trends that have affected the nature of cabinet government, not directly discussed here but implicit in the new world of public and state sector, are the shifts to managerial and commercial values. These emphasize short-term, contractual, personalized relationships, narrowly defined notions of 'efficiency', and competition between governmental agencies. Cabinet ministers have had to manage the policy process in this changed policy environment.

External consultants have become increasingly used to provide alternative advice in the name of 'contestability'; ministerial and prime ministerial advisers have been expanded in number and importance; and the contributions made by most parts of the public service in the policy formulation process have been reduced whilst the importance of Treasury has expanded. These trends, in turn, have impacted upon the accountability processes, never securely based upon classic notions of Westminster government, and the creations of new policy communities. Hence this cabinet study points towards a changing New Zealand political élite; political power has become increasingly captured by economic élites.

This study of cabinet government in New Zealand has shown that there is constant tension between the need for policy expertise and the demand for representativeness of society's groups and interests. The tension is inherent because, constitutionally, ministers must be drawn from Parliament, with all its social biases in composition: male, non-Maori, middle-class. Cabinets must in a broad sense represent the MPs of the parliamentary parties from which they are drawn. Also, however, this structural characteristic affects the expectations of cabinet governments which, because they are members of directly elected representative bodies, are expected to represent community and party interests from beyond Parliament itself. The party-based incentives towards cabinet consultation with the various interests within society are reinforced by the need to expand the range of expert advice available to ministers and, moreover, ensure effective policy implementation. It is a feature of the New Zealand cabinet that it has had considerable discretion over whom to consult. Nevertheless, governments have increasingly shown that their consultative practices have tended to favour some interests over others. This might help explain why they have also experienced problems both with implementing their policies and gaining public acceptance of them.

The tension between the need to govern expertly and in the public interest, whilst at the same time obeying the imperatives of democratic consultation and representation, is particularly acute in New Zealand. And New Zealand has a history of producing politicians who are accessible and, furthermore, who are expected both to listen to and heed the voices of their constituents. The representative and brokerage roles of ministers, although still aspects of their roles, have lessened in significance as their perceived role of policy formulators and advocates has increased. The interviews of the 1990–93 ministers showed this quite clearly. The tension between performance and representativeness has been additionally strained by two further factors: first, the small pool available for selection or election to cabinet, resulting in mediocre and incompetent ministers; and, second, the policy demands of an increasingly complex, pluralistic, and bicultural society, faced with sweeping social change and a long period of economic decline.

As Parliament becomes a multi-party rather than a dominantly two-party legislature, a consequence of the introduction of proportional representation, coalitions and minority governments will become normal forms of cabinet government. Coalitions will produce new patterns of representation within the political executive, and demand new co-ordinating mechanisms and conventions both between parties and between parties and the public service. As cabinets become more fairly representative of groups such as Maori, women, and, perhaps, those who represent the poorer members of our society, the interests of those groups might be more effectively pursued. Wide consultation, in the pursuit of policy legitimacy and effective policy implementation, might also again become the commonplace practice of New Zealand cabinet government.

The new, multi-party Parliament will, however, still be a relatively small legislature. Although there will be more MPs, the parliamentary parties will still be small and subject to many of the sorts of institutional and cultural factors traced above. Indeed, the expectations concerning intra-party collective decision-making are likely to continue. Furthermore, the small sizes of the parties will continue to limit the choice for selection to cabinet.

So long as coalitions can hold together, practising collective cabinet loyalty, and so long as the governing parties hold the majority of the seats of the House, cabinets will be able to implement their programmes without fundamentally altering the relationship between legislature and executive. In those circumstances cabinet will remain a powerful body. With minority governments (which might also be coalitions), the situation is somewhat different, for then Parliament may become much more important in the policy process, curtailing the power of cabinet. Whether New Zealand is being governed by a majority government coalition or by a minority government dependent upon the acquiescence of MPs outside the governing party for it to continue in office, the tasks of the Prime Minister will increasingly be those of communicator and co-ordinator.

The main argument of this work has been that we cannot understand the nature of cabinet power by focusing solely upon the actions of individual actors. Rather, political behaviour needs to be analysed within the context of the incentives and constraints provided by structure and institutional culture. One of these factors is the electoral system. But the character of single party, majority government in New Zealand has not been entirely the product of the simple plurality, single member constituency electoral system. Other factors have been the absence of other sorts of constitutional constraints upon cabinet government, the small Parliament, the consultative traditions of the parliamentary parties, the incentives for MPs to conform to attain ministerial office, and, increasingly, the impact of the internationalization of the world economy. The introduction of proportional representation to the polity will not affect all these influences upon cabinet government.

Much of political science is concerned with analysing the nature of continuity and change. In addition to considering the impact of political innovation upon cabinet government and power in New Zealand, the future will also need to be understood in the context of structural and cultural continuities.

APPENDIX: THE INTERVIEWS

National Government Interviews, 1991–92

Cabinet Ministers	Date of Interview
W. F. Birch	28.11.91
J. B. Bolger, PM	18.2.92
P. Burdon	20.8.91
W. Cooper	28.8.91
W. B. Creech	8.10.91
P. East	12.10.91
J. Falloon	5.9.91
D. Graham	3.9.91
D. Kidd	26.11.91
J. Luxton	8.10.91
D. McKinnon, Deputy PM	26.11.91
M. McTigue	27.11.91
R. Richardson	3.2.92
J. Shipley	23.10.91
L. Smith	11.2.92
R. Storey	10.10.91
S. Upton	10.10.91

Ministers not in Cabinet	
G. Lee	26.11.91
R. McClay	7.10.91
M. McCully	11.3.92
R. Maxwell	24.10.91
K. O'Regan	4.10.91

Chairs of Caucus Committees	
W. Kyd	2.4.92
J. McLaughlan	12.2.92
R. Meurant	5.3.92

All the ministers except Murray McCully held their appointments from November 1990. When Winston Peters was removed from cabinet in October 1991, Maurice Williamson went from being a minister outside cabinet to full cabinet minister, and McCully became a new minister outside cabinet.

Interview Questions: The Role of the Minister

The questions fell under the following headings. (See below for the methodology.)

1. Skills, background, and expertise required, and definitions of 'good' ministers and effective cabinet participation;
2. Relationships with public servants, including the sorts of issues on which ministers expect to be consulted, perceived role (leadership? manager?) of the minister, obstacles encountered;
3. Impact of public sector changes, including co-ordination issues;
4. Reasons for apparent erosion of collective cabinet responsibility, operation of collective cabinet responsibility;
5. Sources of policy ideas;
6. Relationships/consultation with caucus committees, select committees, National Party electorate committees, and national-level organization;
7. Organization of time, use of advisers in ministerial private offices;
8. Consultation with organized groups;
9. Ministers who are particularly respected and those whose opposition might concern the interviewee;
10. The future: how ministers would like to see New Zealand developing, particularly the relationship between individuals and government.

National Party Interviews, 1971–72

(Ministers or former ministers at time of interview)

Ministers	Date of Interview
L. R. Adams-Schneider	27.8.71 and 1.9.71
P. Allen	1.9.71
D. Carter	13.12.71
L. Gandar	24.8.72
J. Gordon	1.9.71
E. Halstead	21.8.70
A. Highet	25.8.72 and 18.10.72
K. Holyoake	26.8.71
R. Jack	23.8.72
A. McCready	15.10.71
D. MacIntyre	31.8.71
D. McKay	21.10.71
J. Marshall	1.9.71
R. Muldoon	13.3.72 and 31.8.72
H. Pickering	24.8.71
J. Rae	4.12.71
D. Riddiford	24.8.71
D. Seath	19.10.71
N. Shelton	25.8.71
B. Talboys	18.10.71
D. Thomson	31.8.71
H. Walker	31.8.71

plus 24 other National MPs

Labour Party Interviews, 1971–72

(Ministers or former ministers at time of interview)

R. Douglas	13.2.73
W. Fox	24.8.71
P. Holloway	8.7.71
H. G. R. Mason	31.1.72
A. Nordmeyer	1.9.71
P. Skoglund	14.10.71
J. Watt	29.2.72

plus 34 MPs, including N. Kirk (18.8.71), and W. Rowling (17.10.72)

Interview Questions: Political Socialization and Parliamentary Careers

1. Early involvement in politics; involvement in local bodies, interest groups, and party organization;
2. Early experience in Parliament; norms of apprenticeship behaviour;
3. Importance of various parliamentary arenas: debating; caucus and caucus committees; select committees; chairing committees; policy specialization;
4. Relationship between conformist or divergent behaviour and cabinet selection;
5. Selection/election of MPs for non-cabinet official positions;
6. Selection and election of ministers: processes; personal characteristics required; attitudes towards the methods; allocation of portfolios;
7. Seniority, geography and sectionalism in cabinet selection; women and Maori representativeness; problems of marginality of electorates.

Interviewing: Methodology

In the first round of interviews, ministers and many MPs were contacted by letter or telephone while other interviews were arranged by two MPs, a friend and my own MP. No one refused to be interviewed. The conversations were of varying length, a feature of the 1990s interviews also, and, indeed, a characteristic of all political élite interviewing. For the second round of interviews I first wrote to the Prime Minister, Jim Bolger, for his approval, which he granted. All ministers were written to, and follow-up telephone calls were necessary in some cases. Only three ministers either declined to be interviewed or did not respond. The willingness of the politicians in both rounds to be interviewed shows their continued relative accessibility to public and researchers. I took notes for the first round of interviews. By the second round tape-recorders were so commonly used that the politicians seemed to accept that I would be recording the conversations. All respondents were told that their names would not be used without permission. I have used names from the 1970s interviews where those persons have since died.

The interviews were loosely structured around the areas summarized above. As with all interviewing of political élites, the interviews were conducted in a flexible manner. The imposition of a strict interview schedule in these circumstances is counterproductive. First, the interviewer might well impose an inaccurate interpretation upon events and views. Second, a rigid framework does not permit the development of a conversation between interviewee and interviewer that can illuminate political behaviour and values.

NOTES

Chapter One: Introduction

1. For an analysis of the impact of the introduction of MMP upon Parliament and cabinet formation, see P. Harris and E. McLeay, 'The Legislature', in G. R. Hawke (ed.), *Changing Politics? The Electoral Referendum 1993* (Wellington, Institute of Policy Studies, 1993), pp. 103–30.
2. One critic of our constitutional arrangements has proposed a change that would alter this structure; Sir Geoffrey Palmer, a former Labour Prime Minister, has suggested that, because of the combined workload of executive and electorate tasks, ministers should resign from Parliament upon accepting their executive posts: *New Zealand's Constitution in Crisis: Reforming our Political System* (Dunedin, John McIndoe, 1992), pp. 172–4. Jonathan Boston has pointed out that, because the advent of MMP might mean the creation of minority governments from relatively small governing parties, cabinet choice could be expanded by the appointment of some ministers from outside Parliament: see 'The Future of Cabinet Government in New Zealand: The Implications of MMP for the Formation, Organization and Operations of the Cabinet', unpublished paper, Institute for International Research, conference on 'MMP: Changing the Way We Govern' (Wellington, 1994).
3. W. Bagehot, *The English Constitution*, introduced by R. H. S. Crossman (London and Glasgow, Fontana, 1963; first published in 1867), p. 186.
4. On Parliament see: K. Jackson, *The Dilemma of Parliament* (Wellington, Allen and Unwin/Port Nicholson Press, 1987) which includes chapters on the political executive. Cabinet has also been discussed in general political texts and readers. See: J. Boston 'The Cabinet and Policy Making under the Fourth Labour Government' in M. Holland and J. Boston (eds.), *The Fourth Labour Government: Politics and Policy in New Zealand* (Auckland, Oxford University Press, 1990), pp. 62–83; R. Eaddy, 'The Structure and Operations of the Executive' in H. Gold (ed.), *New Zealand Politics in Perspective*, 3rd edn (Auckland, Longman Paul, 1992), pp. 162–73; J. Henderson, 'The Operations of the Executive', in H. Gold (ed.), *New Zealand Politics in Perspective*, 2nd edn (Auckland, Longman Paul, 1989), pp. 94–102; K. Jackson, *New Zealand Politics of Change* (Wellington, Reed Education, 1973); K. Jackson, 'Cabinet and the Prime Minister', in S. Levine (ed.), *Politics in New Zealand* (Sydney, Allen and Unwin, 1978), pp. 63–77; R. Mulgan, *Democracy and Power in New Zealand* (Auckland, Oxford University Press, 1984 and 1989); J. Roberts, 'Cabinet' in A. Robinson (ed.), *Notes on New Zealand Politics* (Political Science Department, Victoria University of Wellington, 1970); and 'Cabinet' in G. A. Wood, *Governing New Zealand* (Auckland, Longman Paul, 1988), pp. 12–24.

5. For an overview which includes a discussion of some of the literature on legislative behaviour see J. J. Mansbridge, 'The Rise and Fall of Self-Interest in the Explanation of Political Life', in J. J. Mansbridge (ed.), *Beyond Self-Interest* (Chicago and London, University of Chicago Press, 1990), pp. 3–22. The classic work based upon rational choice in the analysis of parties and voting was A. Downs, *An Economic Theory of Democracy* (New York, Harper and Row, 1957). W. H. Riker was influential in *The Theory of Political Coalitions* (New Haven and London, Yale University Press, 1962); and see M. Olson on collective action in *The Logic of Collective Action: Public Goods and the Theory of Groups* (Cambridge MA, Harvard University Press, 1965). Major works that affected our understanding of bureaucracies—and the New Zealand Treasury's panaceas for public service failures—are A. Downs, *Inside Bureaucracy* (Boston, Little, Brown, 1967) and W. Niskanen, *Bureaucracy and Representative Government* (Chicago, Aldin-Atherton, 1971). An influential recent revisionist work has been P. Dunleavy, *Democracy, Bureaucracy and Public Choice: Economic Explanations in Political Science* (Hemel Hempstead, Harvester Wheatsheaf, 1991).
6. I. Budge and H. Keman, *Parties and Democracy: Coalition Formation and Government Functioning in Twenty States* (Oxford, Oxford University Press, 1990).
7. E. M. McLeay, *Parliamentary Careers in a Two-Party System: Cabinet Selection in New Zealand*, Ph.D. thesis (University of Auckland, 1978); and 'Selection Versus Election: Choosing Cabinets in New Zealand', in H. D. Clarke and M. M. Czudnowski (eds.), *Political Elites in Anglo-American Democracies* (Dekalb IL, Northern Illinois University Press, 1987), pp. 280–306.
8. An exception is B. Headey, *British Cabinet Ministers: The Roles of Politicians in Executive Office* (London, Allen and Unwin, 1974).
9. The quotations from the 1970s interviews are taken from notes. Although the 1990s transcripts of the taped interviews record the conversations faithfully, including the hesitations, laughs, sighs, repetitions, grammatical errors and problems of syntax that are the common currency of ordinary speech, the quotations here have been very slightly and carefully 'tidied up'. Repetitions, where they are only that, have been omitted without indication in the text. The grammar has occasionally been corrected. Ellipses indicate that brief material has been omitted. Square brackets indicate that, either for clarity or purposes of anonymity, I have interpolated a word or phrase. In order to respect and protect the confidentiality of the interviews, especially the very few women involved, the male and female pronouns have been avoided. This has unfortunately led to clumsy repetitions of phrases such as 'the minister' or 'this minister'.

Chapter Two: Westminster and Wellington: Cabinet and the Constitution

1. A. Lijphart, 'The Demise of the Last Westminster System? Comments on the Report of New Zealand's Royal Commission on the Electoral System', *Electoral Studies*, Vol. 6 (1987), p. 97.
2. Lijphart, 'The Demise of the Last Westminster System?', p. 98. This categorization is based upon Lijphart's fuller development in *Democracies: Patterns of Majoritarian and Consensus Government in Twenty-One Countries* (New Haven, Yale University Press, 1984).

3. A. Lijphart, 'Democratic Political Systems: Types, Cases, Causes, and Consequences', *Journal of Theoretical Politics*, Vol. 1 (1989), pp. 33–48.
4. Royal Commission on the Electoral System, *Report of the Royal Commission on the Electoral System: Towards a Better Democracy* (Wellington, Government Printer, 1986). For a discussion of the impact of MMP upon Parliament and cabinet see Harris and McLeay, 'The Legislature', in Hawke (ed.), *Changing Politics?*, pp. 103–30.
5. MMP, as adopted by New Zealand, provides for a Parliament of 120 MPs, approximately half of whom are elected to represent geographically defined electorates through the first-past-the-post (simple plurality) method of voting. The other half are elected from party lists. Electors have two votes, one for the electorate MP and the other for the party list. The nationwide votes for the latter determine how many seats each party obtains in Parliament, because the list vote is used to compensate parties which are under-represented by the total number of seats they have gained through winning constituencies. Parties must either win an electorate seat or gain five per cent of the nationwide vote in order to qualify for list seats.
6. P. A. Joseph, *Constitutional and Administrative Law in New Zealand* (Sydney, The Law Book Co., 1993), p. 218. There has been a lively academic debate in Australia about 'responsible' government there, stimulated by the dismissal of the Labour Government by the Governor-General in 1975, and by the federal and constitutional features of Australian government. See, for example, the articles in P. Weller and D. Jaensch (eds.), *Responsible Government in Australia* (Richmond, Victoria, Drummond Publishing Co. on behalf of Australian Political Studies Association, 1980).
7. R. S. Parker, 'Responsible Government in Australia', in Weller and Jaensch (eds.), *Responsible Government in Australia*, pp. 11–22. See also in the same volume J. R. Archer, 'The Theory of Responsible Government in Britain and Australia', pp. 23–31. Australia's federal structure, relatively powerful upper house, the constitutional crisis of 1975, and the existence of coalition governments, have all contributed to stimulating debate about whether or not Australia has a Westminster system of government.
8. H. Catt, 'What do Voters Decide?' *Political Science*, Vol. 43 (1991), pp. 30–42.
9. K. Jackson, *The Dilemma of Parliament*, pp. 28–30.
10. Wood, *Governing New Zealand*, pp. 13–14. For a discussion of 'responsibility' in the British context, see A. H. Birch, *Representative and Responsible Government: An Essay on the British Constitution* (London, Allen and Unwin, 1964), esp. pp. 13–22 and 131–70.
11. P. Weller, 'Prime Ministers, Political Leadership and Cabinet Government', *Australian Journal of Public Administration*, Vol. 50 (1991), pp. 131–44; P. Dunleavy and R. Rhodes, 'Core Executive Studies in Britain', *Public Administration*, Vol. 68 (1990), pp. 3–28.
12. Weller, 'Prime Ministers, Political Leadership and Cabinet Government', p. 134.
13. Weller, 'Prime Ministers, Political Leadership and Cabinet Government', p. 135. The emphases are the author's.
14. Weller, 'Prime Ministers, Political Leadership and Cabinet Government', p. 135.
15. See Dunleavy and Rhodes, 'Core Executive Studies in Britain', for a discussion of the six variants of the cabinet/prime ministerial government debate: the monocratic and clique variants of prime ministerial government; and the

cabinet government, ministerial government, segmented decision making, and bureaucratic co-ordination models.

16. Bagehot, *The English Constitution*, p. 220.
17. An exception is A. Gamble who, in 'The Thatcher Decade in Perspective' in P. Dunleavy et al. (eds.), *Developments in British Politics 3* (London, Macmillan, 1990), pp. 333–59, critically observes that at the heart of the Westminster model is the ideal of a sovereign body, Parliament, and behind this is 'the idea of a cohesive and homogeneous British nation which despite internal conflicts and disputes has achieved sufficient consensus on procedures to give the decisions of the Parliament unquestioned legitimacy' (p. 341).
18. Joseph, *Constitutional and Administrative Law in New Zealand*, p. 239, and see pp. 238–67 for a discussion of conventions.
19. Joseph, *Constitutional and Administrative Law in New Zealand*, p. 240; and the Constitution Act 1986.
20. As far as ministers' private interests are concerned, the convention that they must not put themselves in positions where there might be a conflict of interests has been clarified in successive guidelines. See Chapter Nine.
21. Joseph, *Constitutional and Administrative Law in New Zealand*, p. 247.
22. *Standing Orders of the House of Representatives* (Wellington, 1992); Cabinet Office, *Cabinet Office Manual* (Wellington, 1991).
23. See the longer lists, and extracts, in P. Harris and S. Levine et al. (eds.), *The New Zealand Politics Source Book*, 2nd edn (Palmerston North, The Dunmore Press, 1993). The 1992 edition contains the 1956 Electoral Act.
24. Their workings and impact upon the nature of cabinet government are beyond the scope of this book. Some understanding of their effects upon governments can be gained by reading Chapter Six of the *Cabinet Office Manual* (1991).
25. No less than ten per cent of eligible voters must sign a petition requesting a referendum before such a poll can be held.
26. For a list and relevant extracts see Harris and Levine (eds.) *The New Zealand Politics Source Book*, pp. 468–94.
27. S. Dawe, 'Reserve Bank of New Zealand Act', *Reserve Bank of New Zealand Bulletin*, Vol. 53 (March 1990), pp. 33–4. For discussions of the implications of the 1989 legislation see P. Dalziel, 'The Reserve Bank Act: Reflecting Changing Relationships Between State and Economy in the Twentieth Century', in B. Roper and C. Rudd (eds.), *State and Economy in New Zealand* (Auckland, Oxford University Press, 1993), pp. 74–90.
28. Dalziel, 'The Reserve Bank Act', p. 84.
29. In 1994 the Fiscal Responsibility Bill was before Parliament. This aimed to strengthen the Crown's reporting requirements to Parliament and public, to require governments to state clear, medium-term fiscal objectives and achievements with stated areas of fiscal risk, and to 'open the books' on economic and fiscal issues before general elections. As proposed, the legislation would not bind governments to particular policy stances but it would bind them to publish their financial plans. See the (separate) comments by Ruth Richardson and Alan Bollard, 'The Fiscal Responsibility Bill', *Public Sector*, Vol. 17 (March 1994), pp. 10–12.
30. 'Letters Patent Constituting the Office of Governor-General of New Zealand', in Harris and Levine, *New Zealand Politics Source Book*, 2nd edn, pp. 37–8.
31. Joseph, *Constitutional and Administrative Law in New Zealand*, p. 246, fn. 38.

32. K. J. Scott, *The New Zealand Constitution* (Oxford, Clarendon Press, 1962), p. 79. See pp. 80–1 for a description of the meetings of the Executive Council.

33. Scott, *New Zealand Constitution*, pp. 78–9.

34. K. Keith, 'On the Constitution of New Zealand', *Political Science*, Vol. 44 (1992), p. 29. Sir Kenneth also includes the caucus committees as part of the constitution.

35. *Cabinet Office Manual* (1991), 1/3, B6.

36. Scott, *New Zealand Constitution*, p. 97.

37. They were: M. Fagan, Member of the Executive Council (MEC) 1935–1939 (when he became Speaker of the Legislative Council); D. Wilson, MEC 1939–1940 (when he became Minister of Immigration); A. McLagan, MEC 1942 for several months (when he, too, assumed a full portfolio); and W. Polson, MEC 1950 until the end of the year (when the Legislative Council was abolished).

38. P. K. Paikea, MEC from Jan. 1941 until his death in April 1943. E. T. Tirikatene, MEC (representing the Native Race) from May 1943 until Dec. 1947 and then MEC representing the Maori Race from Dec. 1947 until Dec. 1949. (The term 'Maori' replaced 'Native' in 1947.)

39. The three were: J. R. Marshall (Assistant to the Prime Minister), Dec. 1949–Sept. 1951; G. H. Ross, Dec. 1949–Sept. 1957; and W. H. Fortune (Assistant to the Prime Minister), Dec. 1949–Nov. 1954.

40. See Scott, *New Zealand Constitution*, p. 97.

41. 'Constitutional Status and Powers of Associate Ministers and of Acting Ministers', Cabinet Office Circular, CO (90) 9 (17 May 1990). Legal opinion from the Solicitor-General to the Secretary of Cabinet attached. This ruling was included in the 1991, revised version of the *Cabinet Office Manual*, 2/4, E1–4.

42. Scott, *The New Zealand Constitution*, p. 94.

43. Keith, 'On the Constitution of New Zealand', p. 31.

44. P. J. Downey, 'Cabinet and Government', *New Zealand Law Journal* (21 Feb. 1988), pp. 29–30.

45. *Cabinet Office Manual* (1991), 1/2, B1.

46. Cabinet Office, *Cabinet Office Manual* (Wellington, 1979), A 2.13–3.2.

47. *Standing Orders of the House of Representatives*, esp. numbers 307, 309, 313 (on financial matters).

48. *Cabinet Office Manual* (1991), 2/6, G4.

49. *Cabinet Office Manual* (1979), A 2.8–10.

50. A. Morkel, 'The Cabinet Reform', *International Journal of Politics*, Vol. 2 (1972), p. 11. This article summarizes the arguments of those writers who have favoured variously sized cabinets.

51. L. Lipson, *The Politics of Equality* (Chicago, University of Chicago Press, 1948), p. 267.

52. Morkel, 'The Cabinet Reform', p. 13.

53. Until the public sector reforms of the fourth Labour Government a department was 'an organisation which assists a Minister to carry out his official functions. In New Zealand, some departments are constituted by Act of Parliament; others, including some of the oldest, exist only as administrative arrangements. Some have a statutory entity and are able to sue and be sued in their own names; in others, the Permanent Head has been created a corporation sole. But these are not essential characteristics' *Report of the New Zealand Royal Commission of Inquiry on the State Services in New Zealand* (Wellington,

Government Printer, 1962), p. 18. Corporations and boards, constituted by statute, varied in their degrees of financial independence and independence from ministerial control.

54. K. Jackson discusses the history of the Council and the circumstances of its abolition in *The New Zealand Legislative Council* (Dunedin, University of Otago Press, 1972).

55. Jackson, *New Zealand Legislative Council*, p. 124.

56. For the circumstances of the creation of the Maori seats, see W. K. Jackson and G. A. Wood, 'The New Zealand Parliament and Maori Representation', *Historical Studies*, Vol. 11 (1963–65), pp. 383–96, and A. D. Ward, *A Show of Justice: Racial 'Amalgamation' in Nineteenth Century New Zealand* (Canberra, Australian National University Press, 1976), esp. p. 209. For a discussion of the debates surrounding the seats, see E. M. McLeay, 'Political Argument about Representation: The Case of the Maori Seats', *Political Studies*, Vol. 28 (1980), pp. 43–62.

57. L. W. Cook, 'Statistical Populations Calculated', Press release issued by Statistics New Zealand (4 May 1994). The number of Maori who chose to register on the Maori roll increased from 104,414 to 136,708. There were criticisms from many Maori that insufficient time and resources were devoted by the Government to this electoral exercise, given the relatively high proportion of Maori who had been on no electoral register, and Maori took their case to the Court of Appeal. It had been hoped that the number of Maori seats would have gone higher than five.

58. For a plea for research on the variety of factors apart from systemic ones (mainly relating to government formation, coalition creation, portfolio allocation) that may precipitate dissolutions, see J. P. Frendreis et al., 'The Study of Cabinet Dissolutions in Parliamentary Democracies', *Legislative Studies Quarterly*, Vol. 11 (1986), pp. 619–28.

59. Two referendums have been held on the term of Parliament. In both 1967 and 1990 voters decisively rejected a proposed four-year term.

60. See M. Bassett, *Confrontation '51: The 1951 Waterfront Dispute* (Wellington, A. H. and A. W. Reed, 1971), pp. 191–201.

61. N. Roberts, 'Nats, Fat Cats and Democrats: The Opposition Parties Under Labour', in J. Boston and M. Holland (eds.), *The Fourth Labour Government: Radical Politics in New Zealand* (Auckland, Oxford University Press, 1987), p. 40; and B. Gustafson, *The First 50 Years: A History of the National Party* (Auckland, Reed Methuen, 1986), pp. 153–4. For Robert Muldoon's interpretation of events see his work, *Number 38* (Auckland, Reed Methuen, 1986), pp. 156–9.

62. M. Waring, 'The Muldoon Years', in A. Baysting et al. (eds.), *Making Policy Not Tea: Women in Parliament* (Auckland, Oxford University Press, 1993), p. 76.

63. See F. M. Brookfield, 'The Governor-General and the Constitution', in H. Gold (ed.), *New Zealand Politics in Perspective*, 2nd edn, p. 58. Brookfield argues that the preferred interpretation of the extent of the Governor-General's reserved powers on the dissolution issue is that the Governor-General at least has a reserve power not to grant a dissolution. If there are virtually no reserve powers on this, then a Prime Minister defeated both at an election and in Parliament could successfully advise a further dissolution. For a discussion on

the role of the Governor-General under MMP, see Harris and McLeay, 'The Legislature', pp. 108–12.

64. K. Jackson, 'Government Succession in New Zealand', *Journal of Commonwealth and Comparative Studies*, Vol. 15 (1977), p. 152.

65. For example, the Price Freeze Regulations 1982 were implemented under the authority of this Act.

66. After the 1993 general election, however, Parliament was indeed summoned within the required period but for a perfunctory few days only before going into recess.

67. See the *Cabinet Office Manual* (1991), 2/7, G8, 'Briefing for Incoming Ministers', and N 4.1–4 'Changes of Ministers or Government'.

68. *Cabinet Office Manual* (1979), J 2.3D.

69. *Cabinet Office Manual* (Wellington, 1979), amended 1986. See also the *Cabinet Office Manual*, 1991, 6/8–6/13, and Cabinet Office Circular (91) 19, 12 July 1991. There are also rules regarding cabinet papers and the publication of ministerial guidelines.

70. 'Fitzgerald v Muldoon and Others (1976)', in Harris and Levine, *New Zealand Politics Source Book* (2nd edn), pp. 35–6.

71. G. Palmer, *Unbridled Power: An Interpretation of New Zealand's Constitution and Government*, 2nd edn (Auckland, Oxford University Press, 1987), p. 35.

72. B. Kohn, 'Grim reality of the country's dollar crisis', *Evening Post* (4 August 1984), p. 1, reported that, according to the official documents, during the last weeks of the Muldoon administration, 'The Reserve Bank used up all its existing liquid funds and the Treasury began selling medium term bonds to meet the foreign exchange crisis facing the nation during those weeks'. See Muldoon's version in *Number 38*, pp. 169–74.

73. There had been a debate among constitutional lawyers about this. See, for example, P. A. Joseph, 'Ministerial Appointments—Still "The Startling Reality"', *New Zealand Law Journal* (1981), pp. 390–5; and D. G. McGee, '"The Startling Reality" and Ualesi', *New Zealand Law Journal* (1981), pp. 456–7. On the issue of ministerial directions between the dissolution of Parliament and a general election see also 'The Ministerial Direction and the Election Defeat', *Recent Law*, Vol. 11 (1985), pp. 377–84.

74. There have been many criticisms of the pace, quantity, and quality of the legislative process in New Zealand, including the extent to which cabinet can dominate the legislative process. See, for example: Jackson, *The Dilemma of Parliament*, passim; R. Mulgan, 'The Elective Dictatorship in New Zealand', in Gold (ed.), *New Zealand Politics in Perspective*, 3rd edn, pp. 513–32; T. McRae, 'The Reform of Parliamentary Control: A Constitutional and Procedural History of the New Zealand House of Representatives, 1951–1990', MA thesis (Victoria University of Wellington, 1992); and Palmer, *Unbridled Power*, pp. 139–61.

75. G. Skene, 'Parliament: Reassessing its Role', in Gold (ed.), *New Zealand Politics in Perspective*, 3rd edn, p. 254. See also Skene's *New Zealand Parliamentary Committees* (Wellington, Institute of Policy Studies, 1990). See the *Standing Orders of the House of Representatives* for the names and terms of reference for the select committees.

76. M. C. Probine, 'The Public Service and Ministers', *Public Sector*, Vol. 6 (Dec. 1983), p. 22. The author was at the time Chairman of the State Services

Commission which first published the article as a pamphlet. New guidelines will have to be developed under MMP, since more than one party might be in government or supporting it.

77. Probine, 'The Public Service and Ministers', p. 22.

Chapter Three: The Political Parties, Parliament, and Cabinet

1. See E. P. Aimer, 'Travelling Together: Party Identification and Voting in the New Zealand General Election of 1987', *Electoral Studies*, Vol. 8 (1989), pp. 131–42; E. P. Aimer, 'The Changing Party System', in Gold (ed.), *New Zealand Politics in Perspective* (3rd edn), pp. 326–41; and J. Vowles and P. Aimer, *Voters' Vengeance: The 1990 Election in New Zealand and the Fate of the Fourth Labour Government* (Auckland, Auckland University Press, 1993), esp. pp. 9–26. On the 1993 elections, see J. Vowles (ed.), *Double Decision: The 1993 General Election and Referendum* (Wellington, Department of Politics, Victoria University, Occasional Publication No. 6, 1994).

2. S. B. Wolinetz, 'Party System Change: Past, Present and Future', in S. B. Wolinetz (ed.), *Parties and Party Systems in Liberal Democracies* (London, Routledge, 1988), p. 299.

3. *Report of the Royal Commission on the Electoral System, Towards a Better Democracy.*

4. P. Harris, 'Changing New Zealand's Electoral System: The 1992 Referendum', *Representation*, Vol. 31 (1992–93), pp. 53–7.

5. Wolinetz, 'Party System Change', p. 311.

6. New Zealand was not, of course, alone with its poor economic performance.

7. On Maori politics see: L. Cox, *Kotahitanga: The Search for Maori Political Unity* (Auckland, Oxford University Press, 1993); A. Sharp, *Justice and the Maori* (Auckland, Oxford University Press, 1990); A. Sharp, 'The Treaty, the Tribunal and the Law', in Gold (ed.), *New Zealand Politics in Perspective* (3rd edn), pp. 123–42; and R. Walker, 'The Maori People: Their Political Development', in Gold (ed.), *New Zealand Politics in Perspective* (3rd edn), pp. 379–400. On women and politics see: C. Dann, *Up From Under: Women and Liberation in New Zealand, 1970–1985* (Wellington, Allen and Unwin/ Port Nicholson Press, 1985); and R. Du Plessis, 'Women, Politics, and the State', in Roper and Rudd (eds.), *State and Economy in New Zealand*, pp. 210–25.

8. For studies of the fourth Labour Government, see especially: Boston and Holland (eds.), *The Fourth Labour Government: Radical Politics in New Zealand*; Holland and Boston (eds.), *The Fourth Labour Government: Politics and Policy in New Zealand*; J. Boston et al. (eds.), *Reshaping the State: New Zealand's Bureaucratic Revolution* (Auckland, Oxford University Press, 1991); B. Easton (ed.) *The Making of Rogernomics* (Auckland, Auckland University Press, 1989); and J. Kelsey, *A Question of Honour? Labour and the Treaty* (Wellington, Allen and Unwin/Port Nicholson Press, 1990). For an account of the period between 1984 and 1992, see C. James, *New Territory: The Transformation of New Zealand 1984–92* (Wellington, Bridget Williams Books, 1992).

9. This pressure group was established in the 1970s. It is primarily concerned with the politics of ideas, promoting its neo-liberal, monetarist, and managerial

ideas through well-publicized research reports and individual connections with ministers and public servants.

10. B. Easton, 'The Commercialisation of the New Zealand Economy: From Think Big to Privatisation' in Easton (ed.), *The Making of Rogernomics*, p. 115.

11. See especially, J. Boston, 'The Theoretical Underpinnings of Public Sector Restructuring in New Zealand', in Boston et al. (eds.)., *Reshaping the State*, pp. 1–26.

12. See especially, G. Debnam, 'Conflict and Reform in the New Zealand Labour Party, 1984–1992', *Political Science*, Vol. 44 (1992), pp. 42–59 ; and M. Wilson, *Labour in Government, 1984–1987* (Wellington, Allen and Unwin, 1989).

13. See S. Levine and N. Roberts, 'National to Power: Voter Choice in 1990', in Gold (ed.), *New Zealand Politics in Perspective* (3rd edn), pp. 493–511; Vowles and Aimer, *Voters' Vengeance*; and the articles in E. M. McLeay (ed.), *The 1990 General Election: Perspectives on Political Change in New Zealand* (Wellington, Department of Politics, Victoria University, Occasional Publication No. 3, 1991).

14. There has been a vigorous debate on the 'mandate' issue in New Zealand. See Jackson, *The Dilemma of Parliament*, pp. 28–9; Joseph, *Constitutional and Administrative Law in New Zealand*, pp. 450–1; and R. Mulgan, 'The Concept of Mandate in New Zealand Politics', *Political Science*, Vol. 30 (1978), pp. 88–96, 'The Changing Electoral Mandate', in Holland and Boston (eds.), *The Fourth Labour Government: Politics and Policy in New Zealand*, pp. 11–21, and 'The Elective Dictatorship in New Zealand', in Gold (ed.), *New Zealand Politics in Perspective* (3rd edn), pp. 513–32.

15. G. Debnam, 'Adversary Politics in New Zealand: Climate of Stress and Policy Aggressors', *Journal of Commonwealth and Comparative Studies*, Vol. 18 (1990), pp. 1–24. See also S. E. Finer's criticisms of Britain's political system in *Adversary Politics and Electoral Reform* (London, Wigram, 1975).

16. For figures on the composition of the changing parliamentary parties see B. Gustafson, 'The Labour Party', in Gold (ed.), *New Zealand Politics in Perspective* (3rd edn), pp. 273–8; McLeay, 'Selection Versus Election', esp. pp. 290–5; and G. A. Wood, 'The National Party', in Gold (ed.), *New Zealand Politics in Perspective* (3rd edn), esp. pp. 295–6.

17. *Report of the Royal Commission on the Electoral System*, passim, and see A. Phillips, *Engendering Democracy* (Cambridge, Polity Press, 1991).

18. See E. M. McLeay, 'Women's Parliamentary Representation: A Comparative Perspective', in H. Catt and E. M. McLeay (eds.), *Women and Politics in New Zealand* (Wellington, Victoria University Press, 1993), pp. 40–62.

19. W. R. Austin, Awarua 1975–87; M. B. W. Couch, Wairarapa 1975–84; W. R. Peters, Hunua 1978–81, Tauranga 1984– ; L. I. Peters, Tongariro 1990–93.

20. *Christchurch Star-Sun* (4 Dec. 1935), p. 12.

21. *New Zealand Herald* (13 Dec. 1957), p. 15.

22. For statistics and women's names until the 1990 election (inclusive), see G. A. Wood (ed.) *Supplement to Ministers and Members in the New Zealand Parliament 1911–1990* (Dunedin, Tarkwode Press, 1992), pp. 39–40. See also: R. Hill and N. Roberts, 'Success, Swing and Gender: The Performance of Women Candidates for Parliament in New Zealand, 1946–87', *Politics*, Vol. 25 (1990), pp. 62–80; J. McCallum, *Women in the House: Members of Parliament in New Zealand* (Picton, Cape Catley, 1993); J. Wilson, 'The Professionals: A

Study of Women in Parliament', *Political Science*, Vol. 35 (1983), pp. 198–220; and M. Wilson, 'Women and the Labour Party', in M. Clark (ed.), *The Labour Party after 75 Years* (Wellington, Department of Politics, Victoria University, Occasional Publication No. 4, 1992), pp. 35–49.

23. McLeay, 'Women's Parliamentary Representation', pp. 40–62.
24. See especially the conversations with women in Baysting et al. (eds.), *Making Policy Not Tea* , and McCallum, *Women in the House.*
25. *New Zealand Official Yearbook 1993* (Wellington, Department of Statistics, 1993), p. 25.
26. McLeay, 'Parliamentary Careers in a Two-party System'.
27. *New Zealand Herald* (27 Nov. 1954), p. 10.
28. 'Bolger Fields Country Cabinet', *The Dominion* (11 Nov. 1990), p. 16.
29. *New Zealand Official Yearbook 1993*, Table 2.6, p. 16 The sources were the Clerk of the House of Representatives and 1986 census figures.
30. See especially, R. Alley, 'Parliamentary Parties in Office: Government–Backbench Relations', in Levine (ed.), *Politics in New Zealand*, pp. 96–112, and Jackson, *The Dilemma of Parliament*, pp. 43–68.
31. For a theoretical discussion of this point see McLeay, 'Selection Versus Election', esp. pp. 280–3.

Chapter Four: Leadership and Cabinet Selection

1. The stories of how cabinets have been chosen in National and Labour have been pieced together from a range of sources: some secondary sources, newspaper articles, and the interviews, especially of the early 1970s (see Appendix One). Further information on the selections by the National prime ministers might be found from a search through their private papers. Unfortunately that task has had to be left to another researcher.
2. Lipson, *The Politics of Equality*, p. 84.
3. J. B. D. Miller, 'David Syme and Elective Ministries', *Historical Studies*, Vol. 6 (1953), pp. 1–15. David Syme wrote *Representative Government in England: Its Faults and Failings* (London, Kegan Paul, Trench and Co., 1881). As Robert Chapman pointed out to me, in the United States also there was a widespread movement which had greater effects than did the Australasian movements. The arguments used in the United States were widely reprinted in Australia and in New Zealand.
4. Miller, 'David Syme and Elective Ministries', p. 3. These sentiments have most often been expressed in recent years by Winston Peters.
5. Lipson, *Politics of Equality*, pp. 129–31.
6. See: *NZPD*, 183 (1918), p. 1073. In 1920 also there was a debate on the issue in the House, *NZPD*, 186 (1920), esp. pp. 254–69. See A. Mitchell, 'Caucus: The New Zealand Parliamentary Parties', *Journal of Commonwealth Political Studies*, Vol. 6 (1968), p. 28, n. 10.
7. *NZPD*, 186 (1920), pp. 266–7.
8. *NZPD*, 186 (1920), p. 269.
9. E. J. Howard (Christchurch North), *NZPD*, 186 (1920), p. 269.
10. No mention of the caucus using the exhaustive ballot appears in the first set of rules which I could obtain: the 1957 Caucus Rules. The 1964 Caucus Rules stipulated that elections be held in this way and that no one could be elected

without having obtained a clear majority of the votes (Rule 28).

11. Probably the most famous observer of this process was Robert Michels, in his *Political Parties* (Glencoe IL, The Free Press, 1915).

12. *Christchurch Star-Sun* (3 Dec. 1935), p. 12. Present were the Labour and Ratana MPs, two members of the Legislative Council, six from the LP central executive, the head of the Alliance of Labour, an Auckland Labour member, and a party member 'representing the Maoris'.

13. Minutes of the N.Z.L.P. 1935–38, Tuesday 4 Dec. 1935. From a copy of the Minutes taken by a former Labour MP.

14. D. E. McHenry, 'The Origins of Caucus Selection of Cabinet', *Historical Studies*, Vol. 7 (1955), pp. 39–43.

15. See, for example, *Christchurch Star-Sun* (3 Dec. 1945), p. 14. And for the comments of a disappointed aspirant see J. A. Lee, *Simple on a Soap-Box* (Auckland, Collins, 1963), p. 39.

16. Interview, Jan. 1972. This view was also that of another of the MPs present in 1935 and interviewed in 1971. The cabinet was actually constructed by the Leader with Walter Nash and Peter Fraser. I am indebted to the late Professor Keith Sinclair for this information. The evidence from the Nash papers, including lists of possible ministers and the geographical areas they represented (and some lists included Lee) and letters, shows the extent to which the cabinet was jointly constructed.

17. Brown, *The Rise of New Zealand Labour*, p. 188.

18. Minutes of the NZLP 1935–38, 26 May 1936. The MP was D. McMillan.

19. Minutes of the NZLP 1935–38, 3 June 1936. I could find no such rules in the various editions of the *Constitution* and neither, as it has already been shown, did the caucus rules include any such rule. Perhaps both men were arguing from an interpretation of the spirit rather than the letter of the constitution since official positions generally were elected.

20. Minutes of the NZLP 1935–38, 3 and 4 Nov. 1938. The minutes record that, in addition to the PLP members present, there were 7 national executive members and 3 members from the upper house. See Lee's description of the caucus meeting, *Simple on a Soap-Box*, pp. 125–8.

21. Brown, *The Rise of New Zealand Labour*, p. 198. See also the description of this episode by E. N. Olssen, 'John Alexander Lee, the Stormy Petrel: His Ideas, Their Inspiration and Influence and His Attempts to Translate His Ideas into Legislation', unpublished MA thesis (Otago University, 1965), p. 203.

22. Notes of the caucus minutes, 8, 9, 10 and 11 Feb. 1939 compiled by Keith Sinclair. I have lent heavily on these notes in this and the next section.

23. This letter was written to the PLP and later 'leaked' to the press. The letter strongly criticized the government's financial policies and attacked especially Walter Nash, Minister of Finance. It also asked for a return to majority rule in caucus. See Brown, *The Rise of New Zealand Labour*, p. 199. Lee's version is contained in *Simple on a Soap-box*, pp. 139–51.

24. Brown, *The Rise of New Zealand Labour*, p. 200.

25. Brown, *The Rise of New Zealand Labour*, p. 200.

26. See K. Sinclair, *Walter Nash* (Auckland, Auckland University Press and Oxford University Press, 1976), p. 193, for a vivid description. See also B. Gustafson, *From the Cradle to the Grave: A Biography of Michael Joseph Savage* (Auckland, Penguin, 1986), p. 255.

27. Brown, *The Rise of New Zealand Labour*, p. 209, and see R. S. Milne, *Political Parties in New Zealand* (Oxford, Oxford University Press, 1966), p. 145.
28. Sinclair, 'Notes of Caucus Minutes', 4 April 1940.
29. Sinclair, 'Notes of Caucus Minutes', 4 April 1940.
30. Sinclair, 'Notes of Caucus Minutes', 24 May 1940, and *Otago Daily Times* (28 May 1940), p. 6.
31. *Evening Post* (29 Nov. 1940), p. 9. He remained leader until his death in 1950. He was re-elected unanimously in 1943 and again in 1946. 'But "unanimous" re-election may sometimes conceal the fact that there has been a contest, that the selection of the winner has been unanimously endorsed. It has been reported that in 1946 Fraser's re-election was contested unsuccessfully by McLagan before he [Fraser] was re-elected "unanimously". There was no contest in 1949.' —Milne, *Political Parties in New Zealand*, p. 145.
32. For further comment, see W. B. Sutch, *The Quest for Security in New Zealand 1840 to 1966* (Wellington, Oxford University Press, 1966), p. 305.
33. Sinclair notes of caucus minutes, 13, 14, 15 and 16 May, 1947. The press announcement mentioned only Howard's election to cabinet and was combined with the announcements of the elections of the Speaker and Deputy and whips. See the *New Zealand Herald* (14 May 1947), p. 6. It seems that as far as the public was concerned, Howard was elected to fill Sullivan's vacancy. Mason's failure to be re-elected in December 1946 and his subsequent re-election in May 1947 were not generally known. On the latter incident see also T. Skinner, *Man to Man* (Christchurch, Whitcoulls, 1980), pp. 67–8.
34. Sinclair, *Walter Nash*, pp. 292–4.
35. Information given to me by Sinclair, including his notes on the caucus minutes, 5 Dec. 1957. For a fuller account of the 1957 and 1972 elections of cabinet, see McLeay, 'Parliamentary Careers'.
36. It was suggested to me in an interview that perhaps Kirk was sounding out caucus on this and accordingly organized the motion.
37. The *Caucus Rules* were apparently set out in the caucus minute book. Under Walter Nash's leadership, an MP told me, at least one MP did not know of the existence of the rules until told by Nash that a proposed course of action would be against the rules. This MP asked where the rules were and so they were produced. It was not until Rowling became leader in 1974 that MPs were given copies of the (1964) caucus rules.
38. These figures were supplied by MPs interviewed at the time and are confirmed by Michael Bassett, an MP at the time, in his account, *The Third Labour Government* (Palmerston North, The Dunmore Press, 1976), p. 153. Bassett wrote that caucus agreed to give the Prime Minister power to nominate up to five replacements for cabinet. This limitation on the number that the Prime Minister could nominate seems to have been informally agreed upon since it was not included in the formal motion that was passed by caucus. In interview it was reported to me that Kirk said that if there were more than four replacements required he would feel that there would have to be a full re-election of the cabinet. This limitation was not included in the 1976 revised caucus rules.
39. This press-generated dichotomy stuck however. When Labour lost the 1975 election some of the 'traditionalists' blamed the 'technocrats'.
40. The following description was gained from interview information. For a

published account of the leadership and cabinet elections of September 1974, see Bassett, *The Third Labour Government*, pp. 163–72.

41. Bassett writes that Rowling suggested that Walding's notice of motion be dealt with 'though he added that if it passed he hoped there would be no extravagant changes', *The Third Labour Government*, p. 168.

42. Interestingly, the Australian Labor Party acted similarly after the May 1974 federal election. The deputy-leadership was changed, but only the one minister to lose his seat was replaced, and that after intensive lobbying. 'When it came to the other ministerial positions caucus made no changes, partly because certain "tickets" broke down but also because the cabinet voted solidly for itself: 27 out of 96 votes is a solid base to build on.' —G. Hawker, 'Political Review', *The Australian Quarterly*, Vol. 46 (1974), p. 99.

43. *The Dominion* (13 May 1976), p. 3.

44. K. Leonard, 'Election of Party Leaders: Should the Method be Changed?', *Labour Network*, 2 (March/April 1983), p. 1.

45. 'Anderton Lashes Free Marketeers in Party', *Auckland Star* (28 April 1984), p. 3.

46. *Auckland Star* (3 April 1984), p. 1.

47. R. Alley, 'The Powers of the Prime Minister', in Gold (ed.), *New Zealand Politics in Perspective* (2nd edn), p. 107.

48. R. Chapman has pointed out that this manoeuvre might have spread the Douglas influence as much as it contained it. See 'A Political Culture under Pressure: The Struggle to Preserve a Progressive Tax Base for Welfare and the Positive State', *Political Science*, Vol. 44 (1992), p. 7.

49. For insights into this period generally, and a portrayal of David Lange's role and problems as Minister of Education in particular, see H. McQueen, *The Ninth Floor: Inside the Prime Minister's Office—A Political Experience* (Auckland, Penguin Books, 1991).

50. McQueen, *The Ninth Floor*, p. 133.

51. See Chapman, 'A Political Culture under Pressure', for the story of the relationship between Douglas and Lange during their battle over the flat tax and other proposals. Chapman argues that the shift away from progressive taxation signalled a marked change of the political culture itself.

52. See McQueen, *The Ninth Floor*, pp. 171–8.

53. *Strategy*, No. 3 (16 May 1989), p. 2. This news report suggested that Lange's efforts misfired since the April proposals had made it clear that the choice of scenarios was up to cabinet to decide.

54. J. Henderson, 'Labour's Modern Prime Ministers and the Party: A Study of Contrasting Political Styles', in Clark (ed.), *The Labour Party after 75 Years*, p. 109.

55. See the comment by C. James, 'A Botch of a Job', *Management* (March 1990), p. 10.

56. Henderson, 'Labour's Modern Prime Ministers', p. 110.

57. W. H. Oliver, 'Sir Sidney Holland', *Comment* (Spring, 1961), p. 5.

58. Mitchell, 'Caucus: The New Zealand Parliamentary Parties', p. 8.

59. Mitchell, 'Caucus', p. 13.

60. *The Dominion* (8 Dec. 1949), p. 6.

61. Eric Holland, the PM's son, said to me in interview that there was a 'straw poll' whilst others disagreed. Keith Holyoake, Deputy PM at the time, could not remember.

62. K. Jackson, 'Political Leadership and Succession in the New Zealand National Party', in Levine (ed.) *Politics in New Zealand*, p. 164.

63. During my interview with Keith Holyoake he suddenly got out of his chair and moved towards a cupboard which turned out to be a safe with a combination lock. He said he was looking for something which might interest me, and that political scientists would love to get into that cupboard as it contained the cabinet minutes and, also, the cabinet recommendations made by the caucus members. It turned out he was looking for the set of his 'visiting cards' that he used (with John Marshall), with all the different portfolios written on them. He considered about twenty candidates for cabinet, then shuffled the portfolios amongst them. He did not find the cards. See also John Marshall, *Memoirs*, Vol. I (Auckland, Collins, 1989), pp. 1–10, for a description of the making of Holyoake's 1960 cabinet.

64. Keith Holyoake said he did consult caucus. See his interview in Mitchell, *Government by Party* (Christchurch, Whitcombe and Tombs, 1966), p. 107. Two of the MPs I interviewed said not.

65. *New Zealand Herald* (2 Dec. 1966), p. 3.

66. *Auckland Star* (3 Dec. 1966), p. 3.

67. *New Zealand Herald* (13 Dec. 1966), p. 6.

68. *New Zealand Herald* (15 Dec. 1969), p. 3.

69. Mitchell, *Government by Party*, p. 107.

70. *New Zealand Herald* (15 Dec. 1969), p. 3.

71. Mitchell, *Government by Party*, p. 107.

72. On the change of leadership see Jackson, 'Political Leadership and Succession in the National Party', pp. 166–7; and Marshall, *Memoirs*, Vol. II, p. 157.

73. *New Zealand Herald* (10 Feb. 1972), p. 1.

74. See Marshall, *Memoirs*, Vol. II, pp. 213–24; Jackson, 'Government Leadership and Succession in the National Party', pp. 166–79; George Chapman, *The Years of Lightning* (Wellington, A. H. and A. W. Reed, 1980), pp. 82–7; and S. Zavos, *The Real Muldoon* (Wellington, Fourth Estate Books, 1978), pp. 120–38.

75. 'Mr Muldoon describes the procedure as "the Holyoake thing". He will be the sole scrutineer and he will not necessarily be bound by the result, which will be shared only with the new Deputy Prime Minister, Mr Talboys.' *New Zealand Herald* (1 Dec. 1975), p. 1.

76. See Zavos, *The Real Muldoon*, pp. 51–2, for the description of one episode in portfolio allocation.

77. R. D. Muldoon, *My Way* (Wellington, A. H. and A. W. Reed, 1981), pp. 133–5. Muldoon is not reliable on the details. He reports that Les Gandar lost the Rangitikei seat, J. B. Gordon retired because of ill-health, and Peter Wilkinson retired to the back benches for the same reason. Also, however, Muldoon sacked Eric Holland, Minister of Housing, from the cabinet. See B. Gustafson, *The First 50 Years: A History of the National Party* (Auckland, Reed Methuen, 1986), p. 134. Neither Muldoon nor Gustafson mention the other vacancies: the defeat of H. J. Walker and the retirement of H. R. Lapwood. In 1977 Keith Holyoake had retired from cabinet, to be appointed as Governor-General. In a later book Muldoon refers to Eric Holland's ill-health 'although he would have carried on had I wished him to. I did not think it fair to put the additional pressure of Cabinet office on him.' *Number 38* (Auckland, Reed Methuen; 1986), p. 28.

78. Gustafson, *The First 50 Years*, p. 138.
79. Gustafson, *The First 50 Years*, pp. 138–41.
80. *New Zealand Herald* (1 Nov. 1985), p. 1. Muldoon was relegated because he was alleged to have said that the front bench was National's weakest for 25 years.
81. Question to the Prime Minister by Pete Hodgson (Labour: Dunedin North), *NZ Hansard Supplement* (6–27 Dec. 1990), p. 2071.
82. Ministry of Maori Development, *Ka Awatea: A Report of the Ministerial Planning Group, March 1991* (Wellington, 1991).
83. S. Harris, 'Richardson under Threat', *National Business Review* (26 Nov. 1993), p. 3.
84. On the earlier leaders, see Jackson, 'Political Leadership and Succession in the New Zealand National Party'.
85. M. Duverger, *Political Parties: Their Organization and Activity in the Modern State* (University Paperbacks; London, Methuen, 1964), pp. 133–4.

Chapter Five: Making Decisions: Government by Committee

1. Lipson, *The Politics of Equality*, p. 267.
2. J. Boston, 'Reorganizing the Machinery of Government: Objectives and Outcomes', in Boston et al. (eds.) *Reshaping the State*, p. 240.
3. B. Edlin, 'How to Keep Six Cabinet Ministers Busy', *The Independent* (2 Oct. 1992), pp. 24 and 26.
4. See especially M. G. Kerr, 'Establishing the Ministry of Transport: Some Inside Views', unpublished Diploma of Public Administration research paper (Victoria University, 1973).
5. *Report of the Royal Commission of Inquiry on the State Services in New Zealand*, p. 36.
6. *Taranaki Daily News* (11 Dec. 1972), p. 4.
7. *Evening Post* (28 Nov. 1968), p. 15.
8. B. Brown, *The Rise of New Zealand Labour* (Wellington, Price Milburn, 1962), p. 188. Also, Brown points out, the caucus had simply got too large for the scheme to work.
9. *Cabinet Office Manual* (Wellington, 1991), 3 C2 and C3 [capitalization in the original].
10. P. Weller, *First Among Equals: Prime Ministers in Westminster Systems* (Sydney, Allen and Unwin, 1985), p. 110.
11. B. Kohn, 'Grim Reality of the Country's Dollar Crisis', *Evening Post* (4 Aug. 1984), p. 1.
12. Weller, *First Among Equals*, p. 112.
13. *Report of the Department of the Prime Minister and Cabinet, AJHR*, G.48 HY, Appendix I, p. 35.
14. Weller, 'Cabinet Committees in Australia and New Zealand', in T. T. Mackie and B. W. Hogwood (eds.), *Unlocking the Cabinet: Cabinet Structures in Comparative Perspective* (London, Sage, 1985), p. 102.
15. *Cabinet Office Manual* (1991), D3/1, A3.
16. *Cabinet Office Manual* (1991), 4/8–4/9, A47.
17. B. Galvin, 'Change of Government: Impact on the State Sector', *Public Sector*, Vol. 14 (March, 1991), p. 5.

18. A. Mitchell, *Government by Party*, p. 103.
19. S. Verba, *Small Groups and Political Behaviour: A Study of Leadership* (Princeton NJ, Princeton University Press, 1961), p. 29.
20. *Cabinet Office Manual* (1991), 3/1, A1.
21. M. Shroff, 'The Structure and Operations of the Cabinet in Relation to the Budget', in J. N. Nethercote et al. (eds.), *Decision Making in New Zealand Government* (Canberra, Federalism Research Centre, Australian National University, 1993), p. 8.
22. D. McDowell, 'Briefing Notes for Prime Minister' (Department of Prime Minister and Cabinet, Wellington, 1990), p. 18. Emphases in the original.
23. In interview I asked the ministers to outline how they would like the relationship between state and individual to develop in the future. Unfortunately there was too much material generated by the responses to be discussed fully here. Thus this issue will be discussed in a paper on 'The Political Agenda'.
24. P. Weller, 'Cabinet Committees in Australia and New Zealand', in Mackie and Hogwood (eds.), *Unlocking the Cabinet*, p. 87.
25. This includes Tauranga, held by Winston Peters who left the Party during that term of office, and the seats of the two MPs who also left who joined the Liberals. Both Wanganui and Horowhenua were taken by Labour.
26. *Cabinet Office Manual* (Wellington, 1979), D 3.2.
27. *Cabinet Office Manual* (1991), 3/3, C1.
28. B. E. Talboys, 'The Cabinet Committee System', *New Zealand Journal of Public Administration*, Vol. 33 (1970), p. 6.
29. *NZ Hansard Supplement*, Vol. 3 (10 Oct.–19 Dec. 1989), p. 1685.
30. Shroff, 'The Structure and Operations of the Cabinet in Relation to the Budget', p. 3.
31. Jackson, 'Cabinet and the Prime Minister', p. 65.
32. Mitchell, *Government by Party*, pp. 26–7. For some historical background and observations on the Muldoon Government, see Weller, 'Cabinet Committees in Australia and New Zealand', esp. pp. 102–10.
33. P. Hennessy, *Cabinet* (Oxford, Basil Blackwell, 1986), p. 26. For a good overview of the British cabinet, see M. Rush, *The Cabinet and Policy Formation* (Burnt Mill, Harlow, Longman, 1984).
34. Talboys, 'The Cabinet Committee System', p. 2.
35. Talboys, 'The Cabinet Committee System', p. 6.
36. *New Zealand Herald* (29 Feb. 1972), p. 3.
37. T. Garnier et al., *The Hunter and the Hill: New Zealand Politics in the Kirk Years* (Auckland, Cassell, 1978), p. 88.
38. Weller, 'Cabinet Committees in Australia and New Zealand', p. 105.
39. D. J. Mitchell, 'Nelson Cotton Mill: A Case Study in the Politics of Development', unpublished MA thesis (University of Canterbury, 1967), p. 14.
40. *New Zealand Herald* (27 Jan. 1970), p. 1.
41. L. Cleveland, *The Politics of Utopia: New Zealand and its Government* (Wellington, Methuen, 1979), pp. 69–70.
42. Cleveland, *The Politics of Utopia*, p. 70.
43. The Treasury, *Economic Management* (Wellington, Government Printer, 1984), pp. 125–6.
44. A list of the committees in operation in 1986 and their terms of reference is

included in the *Cabinet Office Manual* (1979), amended to Jan. 1987, Appendix V. The 1991 edition of the *Manual*, 3, Appendix 2/1 contains the terms of reference (too full to be repeated here) for each of the committees operating during 1991.

45. R. Long, 'Cabinet Razor Gang to Tackle Deficit', *The Dominion* (10 Nov. 1990), p. 1.

46. Full analysis of the budgetary process is beyond the scope of this work. See: J. Roberts, *Politicians, Public Servants and Public Enterprise* (Wellington, Victoria University Press for the Institute of Policy Studies, 1987), esp. pp. 100–16.

47. J. Goulter, 'No Area Exempt in Government Cutback', *Evening Post* (10 Nov. 1990), p. 1.

48. Shroff, 'The Structure and Operations of the Cabinet in relation to the Budget', pp. 5–6.

49. Shroff, 'The Structure and Operations of the Cabinet in Relation to the Budget', p. 7.

50. This was first called the 'Prime Ministerial Committee on Reform of Social Assistance'. The PM said it was unlikely to continue beyond mid-1991, *NZ Hansard Supplement*, Vol. 8 (26 Feb.–3 April 1991), p. 275.

51. G. Palmer, 'The New Zealand Legislative Machine', *Victoria University of Wellington Law Review*, Vol. 17 (1987), p. 287.

52. Weller, 'Cabinet Committees in Australia and New Zealand', pp. 104–10; Roberts, *Politicians, Public Servants and Public Enterprise*, p. 98; J. Boston, 'The Treasury and the Organisation of Economic Advice: Some International Comparisons', in Easton (ed.), *The Making of Rogernomics*, pp. 73–6; Boston, 'The Cabinet and Policy Making under the Fourth Labour Government', pp. 72–3.

53. *Cabinet Office Manual* (1991), 3/5, D10 and D11.

54. Galvin, 'Change of Government: Impact on the State Sector', p. 5.

55. J. L. Robson, *Sacred Cows and Rogue Elephants: Policy Development in the New Zealand Justice Department* (Wellington, Government Printing Office, 1987), p. 8.

56. J. Bolger, 'The Government's Vision for the Public Service', in State Services Commission, *Proceedings of the Senior Management Conference, 9–11 April 1991* (Wellington, 1991), p. 15.

57. Bolger, 'The Government's Vision for the Public Service', p. 16.

58. J. Aitken, 'Summary', in State Services Commission, *Proceedings of the Senior Management Conference*, p. 23; and Bolger, 'The Government's Vision for the Public Service', p. 18.

59. Aitken, 'Summary', p. 23. (The emphasis is mine.)

60. 'Supporting Paper: Day One, Serving the Collective Interest of Government', *Proceedings of the Senior Management Conference*, p. 25.

61. B. Birch, 'Reflections and Commentary', in State Services Commission, *Proceedings of the Senior Management Conference*, p. 73.

62. Steering Group on State Sector Reforms, *Review of State Sector Reforms* (Wellington, 1991).

Chapter Six: Making Decisions: The Role of the Minister

1. Most of our knowledge comes from policy case-studies where the focus is primarily upon either the policy content itself or the broad policy processes. Case-studies in this important area of cabinet studies are necessary. British ministerial autobiographies have provided important insights, but New Zealand has few equivalent works. There are many important questions that need to be answered on this topic, especially the extent to which ministers have autonomy over the policy areas within their jurisdiction. Unfortunately this chapter cannot answer that question; detailed analysis of the work of ministers needs to be done. For a general study of British ministers, see Headey, *British Cabinet Ministers*.
2. *Cabinet Office Manual* (1991), 3/2 B1.
3. Tourist and Publicity Services Division, 'The Work of Cabinet', Staff Training Paper (Nov. 1972).
4. *Cabinet Office Manual* (1991), 4/1–4/2, A6.
5. Taken from a Table in the *Cabinet Office Manual*, 4/4, A29.
6. See *Cabinet Office Manual* (1991), Chapter 4, Appendix I.
7. G. Palmer, *Unbridled Power*, p. 58. Ministerial recommendations can be rejected. In 1991 one of the recommended board members for the new organization, Housing New Zealand, flew to Wellington to be told at the Airport that cabinet had turned down the recommendation on the grounds of the nominee's past Labour connections.
8. Palmer, *Unbridled Power*, p. 57. See pp. 58–60 for the diaries of two days.
9. Written replies, *Hansard Supplement* (30 March 1993), reported in *The Capital Letter*, Vol. 16, No. 13 (717), p. 2. The Minister of Agriculture's response was that there were many press statements issued from his office (sometimes four or five daily), that he was not prepared to waste his press officer's time counting them, and that 'The honourable member is welcome to visit my office and count them for himself'.
10. Palmer, *Unbridled Power*, p. 57.
11. Figures supplied by the Office of the Clerk of the House.
12. See the 'Executive Summary of Automotive Enquiry Carried out by Government Caucus Sub-Committee on Matters of Concern to the Automotive Industry' (1991). The members were Warren Kyd (chair), Cameron Campion, Hamish Hancock, and Grant Thomas. Pp. 15–18 list the individuals, companies, and groups that made submissions.
13. This committee was composed of, among others, officials from the Ministry of Commerce, Customs, the Prime Minister's Office and Treasury.
14. See: D. J. Levinson, 'Role Personality and Social Structure in the Organizational Setting', in F. I. Greenstein and M. Lerner (eds.), *A Source Book for the Study of Personality and Politics* (Chicago, Markham, 1971). Various typologies have been developed by students of legislative behaviour, some based upon the concept of role. For example, see: H. Eulau et al., 'The Role of the Representative: Some Empirical Observations on the Theory of Edmund Burke', *American Political Science Review*, Vol. 53 (1959), pp. 742–56; M. E. Jewell and S. C. Patterson, *The Legislative Process in the United States* (New York, Random House, 1966); and J. C. Wahlke et al., *The Legislative System: Explorations in Legislative Behavior* (New York, John

Wiley and Sons, 1962). Few if any are suitable for New Zealand; their hypotheses and the categories that result are firmly rooted in the political culture and structures of the United States. With the exception of Headey, *British Cabinet Ministers*, researchers have not used the notion of role to understand how the members of political executives behave. For a further discussion of role, see McLeay, 'Parliamentary Careers in a Two-Party System'.

15. The 1990–93 ministers were also asked about their sources of policy ideas. For reasons of space this aspect has been omitted as a separate issue, although some comments have been used where appropriate.

16. See R. Putnam, *The Comparative Study of Political Elites* (Englewood Cliffs, Prentice-Hall, 1976). Four Labour ministers and eleven National ministers provided the data for this section.

17. B. V. Galvin, 'Some Reflections on the Operation of the Executive', in H. Gold (ed.), *New Zealand Politics in Perspective*, 1st edn (Auckland, Longman Paul, 1985), p. 73. This was a slightly edited version of a talk originally given in 1982.

18. W. Grant, 'Insider Groups, Outsider Groups and Interest Group Strategies in Britain', Working Paper No. 19 (Warwick, University of Warwick, 1978).

19. Mitchell, *Government by Party*, p. 100.

20. Jackson, 'Cabinet and the Prime Minister', pp. 68–9.

21. K. Ovenden, 'Prospect: On the Absence of Political Ideas', in R. Goldstein with R. Alley (eds.), *Labour in Power: Promise and Performance* (Wellington, Price Milburn for New Zealand University Press, 1975), pp. 190–7.

Chapter Seven: Advice and Support

1. A. D. Robinson, quoted in the *Cabinet Office Manual* (1979), A 3.3. See also *Cabinet Office Manual* (1991), 2/1 A3

2. *Cabinet Office Manual* (1979), A 3.1.

3. See R. J. Polaschek, *Government Administration in New Zealand* (Wellington, New Zealand Institute of Public Administration and Oxford University Press, 1958). This contains useful appendices on the growth of agencies and governmental structure. See also the lively discussion in Roberts, *Politicians, Public Servants and Public Enterprise*, pp. 24–37. For a full analysis of the changes made after 1984, see J. Boston et al. (eds.), *Reshaping the State: New Zealand's Bureaucratic Revolution*.

4. Polaschek, *Government Administration in New Zealand* pp. 293–306, and *Report of the New Zealand Royal Commission of Inquiry on the State Services in New Zealand*, p. 18.

5. T. B. Smith, *The New Zealand Bureaucrat* (Wellington, Cheshire, 1974), p. 23. Smith pointed out that in the previous twenty years the central government bureaucracy had not grown rapidly; not, in fact, in proportion with the growth of the labour force, pp. 29–32.

6. See W. B. Sutch, *Local Government in New Zealand: A History of Defeat* (Wellington, Department of Industries and Commerce, 1964).

7. Polaschek, *Government Administration in New Zealand*, p. 25.

8. Polaschek, *Government Administration in New Zealand*, p. 27.

9. Polaschek, *Government Administration in New Zealand*, p. 25.

10. Lipson, *The Politics of Equality*, pp. 404–5.
11. Polaschek, *Government Administration in New Zealand*, p. 36.
12. For a helpful classification and description of government agencies in the early 1970s, see L. Cleveland, 'The Major Agencies of Central Government in New Zealand', in L. Cleveland and A. D. Robinson (eds.), *Readings in New Zealand Government* (Wellington, A. H. and A. W Reed, 1972), pp. 20–64.
13. Among the early critics were Polaschek, *Government Administration in New Zealand* and L. Webb, *Government in New Zealand* (Wellington, Department of Internal Affairs, 1940).
14. Lipson, *The Politics of Equality*, p. 383.
15. J. Boston, 'Reorganizing the Machinery of Government', p. 237. The Treasury briefings are: *Economic Management* and *Government Management* (Wellington, Government Printer, 1987).
16. J. B. Ringer, *An Introduction to New Zealand Government* (Christchurch, Hazard Press, 1991).
17. See B. Edlin, 'Don't Ask the Mandarins about Budget Peeling', *National Business Review* (29 May 1992), p. 18, for some figures. Edlin points out that these redundancies were occurring at the same time as the Government was stating that its top priority was employment.
18. See: J. Boston, 'The Treasury and the Organisation of Economic Advice: Some International Comparisons', in Easton (ed.), *The Making of Rogernomics*, pp. 68–92; J. Boston and E. Cooper, 'The Treasury: Advice, Co-ordination and Control', in Gold (ed.), *New Zealand Politics in Perspective* (2nd edn), pp. 123–44 which outlines Treasury's roles (pp. 124–8); J. Boston, 'The Treasury: Its Role, Philosophy and Influence', in Gold (ed.), *New Zealand Politics in Perspective* (3rd edn), pp. 194–215 for an updating of the earlier piece; and S. Goldfinch and B. Roper, 'Treasury's Role in State Policy Formulation During the Post-War Era', in Roper and Rudd (eds.), *State and Economy in New Zealand*, pp. 50–73.
19. See J. Boston and P. Dalziel (eds.), *The Decent Society? Essays in Response to National's Economic and Social Policies* (Auckland, Oxford University Press, 1992); and J. Kelsey, *Rolling Back the State: Privatisation of Power in Aotearoa/New Zealand* (Wellington, Bridget Williams Books, 1993). Kelsey discusses the Labour and National governments.
20. *Evening Post* (27 Dec. 1983), cited by J. Roberts, 'Ministers, the Cabinet and Public Servants', in Boston and Holland (eds.), *The Fourth Labour Government: Radical Politics in New Zealand*, pp. 100–1. Robertson was responding to David Lange's 1983 statement that, if Labour won the next election, heads of department would be asked where they stood on Labour's policies, and would have to go if they said they would not implement them.
21. John Banks declined on the grounds that he was too busy, and Winston Peters did not answer my letter or respond to my follow-up telephone call.
22. In retrospect these questions were somewhat slanted in the direction of eliciting negative reactions. Thus it is interesting to see that ministers did not invariably attack the public service when they discussed this source of advice in interview.
23. One senior public servant, however, told me in a private conversation that the 'waiting around' was much worse under the Labour Government.
24. G. Scott et al., 'Reform of the Core Public Sector: New Zealand Experience', *Governance*, Vol. 3 (1990), p. 162. The other two conditions were the

consistency of application of the new approach and the degree of support for it among chief executives and ministers (pp. 162–3).

25. J. B. Bolger, *Hansard: Supplement*, 24, Questions for Written Answer (March 1993–May 1993), 6469. The Prime Minister was answering the Leader of the Opposition, Mike Moore.

26. Strategos Consulting Ltd, *New Zealand Police: Resource Management Review 1989* (Government Printer, Wellington, 1989), p. 6.

27. See E. M. McLeay, 'Housing Policy', in Boston and Dalziel (eds.), *The Decent Society?*, p. 183.

28. J. Rivers, 'Advisers Spend Half Budget on Consultants', *Sunday Star-Times* (23 March 1994), p. C10. The name of the consultancy firm was withheld.

29. These observations are largely based upon my experience on the board of the Housing Corporation, particularly between 1990 and 1991. Many of the points raised by senior officials concerning the impact of the new housing structures and policies, ignored or brushed over at the time by ministers, later became problems, as evidenced by the attention given in the media between 1992 and 1993 to evicted families and empty Housing New Zealand accommodation.

30. J. Martin, *Public Service and the Public Servant* (Wellington, State Services Commission, 1991), p. 6. The reference is to J. Roberts, 'The Public Servants and Ministers', *Public Sector*, Vol. 6 (1983), pp. 25–8.

31. Martin, *Public Service and the Public Servant*, p. 18 (emphases in the original). Martin also looks at the duty of public servants towards the public interest.

32. M. Weber, in *From Max Weber: Essays in Sociology*, translated, edited, and introduced by H. H. Gerth and C. Wright Mills (New York, Oxford University Press, 1946), p. 215. (Italics in the original.)

33. Cabinet Office, 'Administrative History', National Archives, AFFD (SNS:11/86).

34. F. Shanahan, 'Cabinet Responsibility for Coordinating Action between Government Departments', National Archives, AFFD, Series 816, Paper 1 (undated).

35. F. Shanahan, 'Memo to Prime Minister', National Archives, AFFD, Series 816, Paper 2 (Dec. 1949).

36. J. Boston, 'Advising the Prime Minister in New Zealand: The Origins, Functions and Evolution of the Prime Minister's Advisory Group', *Politics*, Vol. 23 (1988), p. 9. Boston provides details of names and operations and also draws useful comparisons with the services and resources available to Prime Ministers in other political systems.

37. *Report of the Cabinet Office for the Year Ended 31 March 1989, AJHR*, G.47, pp. 4 and 6. The State Sector Act required an Annual Report, the first ever from the Cabinet Office.

38. Department of the Prime Minister and Cabinet, 'Briefing Notes for Prime Minister' (1990) p. 9.

39. R. D. Muldoon, quoted in V. Wright, 'Muldoon's Fire Brigade', *The New Zealand Listener*, Vol. 87 (26 Nov.–2 Dec. 1977). This article contains much information about the activities and personnel of the Advisory Group.

40. I. B. Johns, 'Efficiency in Government: The Changing Role of the Central Administrative Agencies 1962–78', *Public Sector* Research Paper, Vol. 1, No. 2 (April 1979), p. 144.

41. Johns, 'Efficiency in Government', p. 145.

42. Boston, 'Advising the Prime Minister in New Zealand', p. 11.
43. Boston, 'Advising the Prime Minister in New Zealand', pp. 16–17. Boston provides a range of examples of the activities of the Group.   •
44. J. Boston, 'The Cabinet and Policy Making', in Holland and Boston (eds.), *The Fourth Labour Government: Politics and Policy in New Zealand* (2nd edn), p. 76.
45. See M. McLaughlin, 'Lange's Lot', *The New Zealand Listener* (10 Dec. 1988), pp. 18–20.
46. *Report of the Prime Minister's Office for the Year Ended 31 March 1989, AJHR*, G.48, pp. 7–8.
47. McQueen, *The Ninth Floor*, p. 50. He adds that Lange was reluctant to request cabinet to grant him more resources (p.51).
48. N. Sallee, 'The Touchy Question of the Eighth Floor Think Tank', *National Business Review* (11 Nov. 1985), p. 13. The article contains some interesting comments from David Lange and John Henderson on the 'political' role of the Group.
49. D. Hunn and H. Lang, 'Review of the Prime Minister's Office and Cabinet Office' (Wellington, State Services Commission, 1989). The authors also recommended that the Opposition parties be granted funds to provide them with high-quality advice, thus helping them with their constitutional roles. In May 1993 the office of the Leader of the Opposition (Labour) was granted $656,000, and the Alliance Leader was granted $54,700. These sums were additional to those granted to MPs in the Parliamentary Services Commission Vote. See M. Munro, 'The Minders', *The Dominion* (21 May 1993), p. 9.
50. Hunn and Lang, 'Review of the Prime Minister's Office and Cabinet Office', p. 9.
51. Hunn and Lang, 'Review of the Prime Minister's Office and Cabinet Office', p. 7.
52. J. Goulter, 'Palmer Applies the Oilcan to Wheels of Government', *The Evening Post* (9 Sept. 1989), p. 8.
53. *NZPD* 9 Nov. 1989, p. 13492.
54. S. Kilroy, 'Unionists join PM's Office as advisers', *The Dominion* (1 Nov. 1989), p. 2.
55. R. Long, 'Uncertain future for PM's new staff', *The Dominion* (1 March 1990), p. 1.
56. M. Munro, 'Second-Guessing the Prime Minister', *The Dominion* (26 Dec. 1989), p. 9.
57. *Report of the Department of Prime Minister and Cabinet for the Period 1 July to 31 Dec. 1990, AJHR*, G.48 HY, p. 4.
58. Department of the Prime Minister and Cabinet, 'Briefing Notes for Prime Minister' (28 Oct. 1990).
59. Department of the Prime Minister and Cabinet, 'Briefing Notes for Prime Minister', p. 1.
60. Department of the Prime Minister and Cabinet, 'Briefing Notes for Prime Minister'. p. 4.
61. Department of the Prime Minister and Cabinet, 'Briefing Notes for Prime Minister', p. 2 (emphases in the original).
62. *Report of the Department of the Prime Minister and Cabinet for the period 1 July 1991–31 Dec. 1991, AJHR*, G.48 HY, pp. 9–10.

63. *Report of the Department of the Prime Minister and Cabinet for Period 1 July–31 Dec.*, p. 32.
64. See J. Boston, 'Grand Designs and Unpleasant Realities: The Fate of the National Government's Proposals for the Integrated Targeting of Social Assistance', *Political Science*, Vol. 46 (July 1994), pp. 1–21, for a discussion of the change process and its problems. The *Report of the Department of the Prime Minister and Cabinet for the Period 1 July 1991–31 Dec. 1991*, *AJHR*, G.48 HY, p. 8, gives the accountabilities.
65. F. Ross, 'Nearly $8m Spent on Health Care Consultants', *The Dominion* (10 Feb. 1993), p. 1. The source was figures supplied by the PMC to a parliamentary select committee. The breakdown was: consultants' advice, $2.4 million; advice on new health structures, including advice of structural and ownership issues from CS First Boston, $1.07 million; search for regional health authority (4) and crown health enterprise heads (14) heads, $859,094.12. The staffing of the PMC more than doubled.
66. *Report of the Department of the Prime Minister and Cabinet for Period 1 July 1991–31 Dec. 1991*, p. 19.
67. J. Bolger, 'The Government's Vision for the Public Service', p. 16.
68. Press statement issued by the Office of the Prime Minister, 'Prime Minister Announces Enterprise Council Members' (11 November 1991).
69. The membership in November 1991 was: John Anderson, Chief Executive (CE), National Bank; Michael Barnett, CE, Auckland Regional Chamber of Commerce and Industry; Tom Burns, Chair and Managing Director (MD), Ameritech and Bell Atlantic NZ Ltd; Rick Christie, CE, NZ Trade Development Board; Ken Douglas, President, NZ Council of Trade Unions; Hugh Fletcher, CE, Fletcher Challenge Ltd; Norman Geary, Chair, NZ Tourism Board; Bruce Hancox, Chair, Brierley Investments Ltd; Graeme Marsh, Group MD, Donaghys Ltd; Douglas Myers, CE, Lion Nathan Ltd; Gary Paykel, MD and CE, Fisher and Paykel Ltd.; Wendy Pye, President, Wendy Pye Books Ltd; David Richwhite, Director, Fay Richwhite and Company Ltd; and Dryden Spring, Chair, NZ Dairy Board.
70. F. O'Sullivan, 'Bolger drops curtain on incentive play by commercial glitterati', *National Business Review* (15 May 1992), p. 9.
71. Answer by Jim Bolger, PM, to a question asked by Pete Hodgson (Dunedin North), *Hansard Supplement* (23 Oct.–26 December 1991), pp. 3639–40.
72. M. Munro, 'The Minders', *The Dominion* (19 May 1993), p. 9. See, too, N. Legat, 'Say it Again, Jim', *Metro* (June 1992), pp. 56–63.
73. These figures were kindly supplied by Pete Hodgson, MP for Dunedin North, who obtained them using parliamentary questions during the period 1990 to 1994. The statistics are from the Minister of Internal Affairs.
74. McQueen, *The Ninth Floor*, p. 66.
75. Boston, 'The Cabinet and Policy Making', p. 77.
76. For profiles of some of the press secretaries see M. Munro, 'The Minders', *The Dominion* (20 May 1993), p. 9.
77. McQueen, *The Ninth Floor*, p. 66.
78. Munro, 'Second-Guessing the Prime Minister', referring to Geoffrey Palmer's speechwriter, David Slack.
79. See Legislation Advisory Committee, *Public Advisory Bodies: A Discussion Paper* (Wellington, September 1990). This proposes principles and methods to

guide the 'creation, operation and control' of these bodies (p.1). The Committee lists 110 public advisory bodies operating in 1989, twenty-four of which operated under a statute or a regulation (pp. 17–19). 'All the other bodies in the list have been established either under a Minister's common law power to set up advisory committees, or under a Minister's general statutory power to do so' (p. 20).

80. Report by the Legislation Advisory Committee, *Legislative Change: Guidelines on Process and Content* (August 1987). The Report was requested by the Minister of Justice, Geoffrey Palmer, and the committee was chaired by G. R. Laking.

Chapter Eight: Consultation

1. A. Mitchell, *Politics and People in New Zealand* (Christchurch, Whitcombe and Tombs, 1969), p. 48, quoting J. T. Watt in the *New Zealand Manufacturer*. On pressure group activities generally, see L. Cleveland, *The Anatomy of Influence* (Wellington, Hicks Smith and Sons, 1972).

2. Lipson, *The Politics of Equality*, p. 284.

3. See: J. Gould, *The Rake's Progress? The New Zealand Economy Since 1945* (Auckland, Hodder and Stoughton, 1982), esp. pp. 88–113; E. M. McLeay, 'The State in New Zealand', in Gold (ed.), *New Zealand Politics in Perspective* (3rd edn), esp. pp. 434–8; and Mitchell, *Politics and People in New Zealand*.

4. The example of agriculture is used effectively by Mulgan, *Democracy and Power in New Zealand* (2nd edn).

5. The payout per kilogram of butterfat, for example, 'barely doubled between 1945/46 and 1973/74 while the consumer price index rose almost fourfold', Gould, *The Rake's Progress?*, p. 99.

6. Gould, *The Rake's Progress?*, p. 131.

7. Cleveland, *The Politics of Utopia*, p. 62. Most of the rest of this paragraph has been drawn from this work.

8. Robson, *Sacred Cows*, p. 174.

9. On Muldoon's views of the educational pressure groups, see his *Number 38*, p. 28.

10. Muldoon, *Number 38*, pp. 117–45.

11. R. Douglas, 'The Politics of Successful Structural Reform', Paper delivered to Mt Pelerin Society (31 Nov. 1989), p. 10.

12. Cleveland, *The Politics of Utopia*, p. 61, and Gould, *The Rake's Progress?*, p. 137.

13. C. James, *The Quiet Revolution* (Wellington, Allen and Unwin/Port Nicholson Press, 1986), p. 17.

14. For a New Zealand application, see A. J. Kellow, 'Politicians Versus Bureaucrats: Who Makes Public Policy?' in Gold (ed.), *New Zealand Politics in Perspective* (2nd edn), pp. 145–70. T. Lowi's seminal article was, 'American Business, Public Policy, Case Studies, and Political Theory', *World Politics*, Vol. 16 (1964), pp. 677–715. Lowi further developed his typology in a series of articles.

15. See W. H. Oliver, 'The Labour Caucus and Economic Policy Formation, 1981–1984', in Easton (ed.), *The Making of Rogernomics*, pp. 11–52. See also: P. Harris, 'Pressure Groups and Protest', in Gold (ed.), *New Zealand Politics in*

Perspective (2nd edn), pp. 295–311; K. du Fresne, 'Lobbying: New Zealand Style', in Gold (ed.), *New Zealand Politics in Perspective* (2nd edn), pp. 312–19; B. Roper, 'The Political Activism of Business and the Emergence of the New Right in New Zealand, 1975–1987', *Political Science*, Vol. 44 (1992), pp. 1–23; and J. Vowles, 'Business, Unions and the State: Organising Economic Interests in New Zealand', in Gold (ed.), *New Zealand Politics in Perspective* (3rd edn.), pp. 342–65. Some works that examine recent group–government relationships in New Zealand are: J. Deeks and N. Perry (eds.), *Controlling Interests: Business, the State and Society in New Zealand* (Auckland, Auckland University Press, 1992); and Roper and Rudd (eds.), *State and Economy in New Zealand*, especially R. Bremer, 'Federated Farmers and the State', pp. 108–27, R. Mulgan, 'A Pluralist Analysis of the New Zealand State', pp. 128–46, B. Roper, 'A Level Playing Field? Business Political Activism and State Policy Formulation', pp. 147–71, and P. Walsh, 'The State and Industrial Relations in New Zealand', pp. 172–91.

16. See also P. Dalziel, 'National's Economic Strategy', in Boston and Dalziel (eds.), *The Decent Society?*, pp. 19–38.

17. The major business lobby groups are: the Business Roundtable (with at least $1.2 million budget for its policy platforms); the Chambers of Commerce and Industry; the Employers' Federation; Federated Farmers; the Manufacturers' Association; the Merchants' Association; and the Tourist Industry Federation. The umbrella organization for the unions is the New Zealand Council of Trade Unions. See Vowles, 'Business, Unions and the State'. The major state-sponsored groups are the various primary industry producer boards (meat, dairy, apple and pear), repeatedly attacked by the Business Roundtable.

18. A. Cawson, 'Is there a Corporatist Theory of the State?' in G. Duncan (ed.), *Democracy and the Capitalist State* (Cambridge, Cambridge University Press, 1989), p. 250. I am not here suggesting that New Zealand once had a properly corporatist state. See McLeay, 'The State in New Zealand', pp. 435–8.

19. Cawson, 'Is There a Corporatist Theory of the State?', p. 241 (author's own emphasis).

20. E. McCoy, 'Deregulation: Public Utilities and New Zealand Economic Reform', in B. Head and E. McCoy (eds.), *Deregulation or Better Regulation?* (Melbourne, Macmillan, 1991), p. 52.

21. Vowles, 'Business, Unions and the State'.

22. R. Mulgan, 'Comment: The Principles of Rogernomics', *Public Sector*, Vol. 15 (March 1992), pp. 16–17.

23. B. M. Barry and W. J. Rees, 'The Public Interest', *Proceedings of the Aristotelian Society: Supplement*, Vol. 58 (1964), p. 4.

Chapter Nine: Taking Responsibility

1. J. Stanyer, 'Divided Responsibilities: Accountability in Decentralized Government', *Public Administration Bulletin*, Vol. 17 (1974), pp. 14–30.

2. For a good exposition, see G. A. Wood, 'Should Tony Friedlander Resign?' *Auckland Star* (1 March 1984).

3. N. Johnson, 'Accountability, Control and Complexity: Moving Beyond Ministerial Responsibility', in A. Barker (ed.), *Quangos in Britain* (London, Macmillan, 1982), p. 215.

4. See Chapter Four. Rob Storey was not reappointed. Ruth Richardson chose not to accept another portfolio.

5. One minister, Norman Shelton, made it clear that, although he intended to retire from Parliament, he did not wish to leave cabinet prematurely. See *New Zealand Herald* (12 Feb. 1972), p. 2.

6. G. Lawson, quoting R. Douglas, 'Politicians, Public Servants and Public Enterprise: Revolution in Executive Power', *Public Sector*, Vol. 10 (1987), p. 9. See the following criticisms: S. J. Davies, 'State-Owned Enterprises Act: Accountability of State Enterprises and Responsibility of Ministers', *Public Sector*, Vol. 10 (1987), pp. 2–5; and J. Martin, 'The Buck Stops Where?' *Evening Post* (9 July 1992), p. 7. Joseph, *Constitutional and Administrative Law in New Zealand*, pp. 307–10, provides useful examples. For a defence, see Palmer, *Unbridled Power*, pp. 82–90.

7. The definitions are from Martin, *Public Service and the Public Servant*, pp. 26–7 (author's own emphases).

8. The Edwina Curry episode is also interesting for it was clear that her statement about salmonella in eggs was acceptable to the PM and her immediate colleagues. She lost her position to appease the farming lobbies. See A. Doig, 'The Resignation of Edwina Curry: A Word Too Far', *Parliamentary Affairs*, Vol. 42 (1989), pp. 317–29. See also a recent publication: D. Woodhouse, *Ministers and Parliamentary Accountability in Theory and Practice* (Oxford, Clarendon Press, 1994).

9. *New Zealand Herald* (21 March 1956), p. 10.

10. *Evening Post* (22 Feb. 1956) quoted by Scott, The *New Zealand Constitution*, p. 123.

11. *New Zealand Herald* (21 Mar. 1956), p. 10. And see Scott's criticisms, *The New Zealand Constitution*, p. 123.

12. Marshall, *Memoirs*, Vol. I, p. 245.

13. Ministers' Private Interests Committee, 'Report', *AJHR*, 1956, Vol. 4, I.17.

14. *Cabinet Office Manual* (Wellington, 1991), 2/10, H.

15. J. B. Bolger, *NZ Hansard: Supplement*, Vol. 8 (26 Feb.–3 April, 1991), pp. 202–3.

16. See F. M. Brookfield, 'The Marginal Lands Board Affair', *New Zealand Law Journal*, Part I (17 March 1981), pp. 96–104, and Part II (7 April 1981), pp. 124–8.

17. Brookfield, 'The Marginal Lands Board Affair', Part II, p. 125.

18. See the discussion of this in Scott, *The New Zealand Constitution*, pp. 124–31, where the author compares Semple's attitude with John Marshall's concerning the Horton escape (see below).

19. See Robson, *Sacred Cows and Rogue Elephants*, pp. 67–75; and Marshall, *Memoirs*, Vol. I, pp. 226–7.

20. Robson, *Sacred Cows and Rogue Elephants*, p. 70.

21. Robson, *Sacred Cows and Rogue Elephants*, pp. 71–2. See the author's discussion of the debate concerning whether or not Marshall should have resigned and protected his public servants from public criticism.

22. See G. Watson, 'Ministerial Responsibility and the Maniototo Irrigation Scheme', *Otago Law Review*, Vol. 6, No. 1, pp. 158–74; and Roberts, *Politicians, Public Servants and Public Enterprise*, pp. 48–50.

23. See Palmer, *Unbridled Power*, pp. 49–52 for copies of the exchange of letters.

24. Palmer, *Unbridled Power*, p. 55.
25. *The Dominion* (10 Feb. 1994).
26. B. Edwards, 'Treasury Head Won't Quit Despite Mistakes', *Evening Post* (28 March 1994), p. 1. Labour costed its policies at about $180 million, a private consultancy firm at $315 million, and Treasury at $1.4 billion.
27. Edwards, 'Treasury Head Won't Quit Despite Mistakes', p. 1.
28. B. Lagan, 'Cabinet Dissenters Escape Unpunished', *The Dominion* (1 Nov. 1982), p. 2.
29. See R. Long and B. Lagan, 'Quigley: The Man Who Wouldn't be Gagged', *The Dominion* (15 June 1982), pp. 1 and 2.
30. See Muldoon, *Number 38*, p. 147, for his argument that Quigley resigned rather than was dismissed.
31. It seems that the dispute had also reached into the upper levels of the National Party extra-parliamentary organization. See R. Long, 'Clash Preceded Quigley Sacking', *The Dominion* (16 June 1982), p. 1. For a discussion of the constitutional aspects, see P. A. Joseph, 'The Honourable D. F. Quigley's Resignation: Strictly Political—Not Constitutional', *Canterbury Law Review*, Vol. 1 (1982), pp. 428–36.
32. See M. Munro, 'Fearless and Outspoken Loner Pays the Price', *The Dominion* (3 Oct. 1991), p. 8.
33. R. Long, 'Peters Vows to Overturn Richardson's Policies', *The Dominion* (3 Oct. 1991), p. 1.
34. Letter from D. Lange to P. W. Wood (29 April 1987), included with copies of other responses in Wood, 'The Doctrine of Ministerial Responsibility', unpublished research paper for B.Laws (University of Canterbury, 1988), pp. 68–9.
35. R. Chapman, 'Political Culture: The Purposes of Party and the Current Challenge', in Gold (ed.), *New Zealand Politics in Perspective* (2nd edn), pp. 14–32.
36. I. L. Janis, *Groupthink: Psychological Studies of Policy Decisions and Fiascoes* (Boston, Houghton Mifflin, 1982); and Janis, *Crucial Decisions: Leadership in Policymaking and Crisis Management* (New York, The Free Press, 1989).
37. Interview with a minister, 1991.

BIBLIOGRAPHY

Aimer, E. P., 'Travelling Together: Party Identification and Voting in the New Zealand General Election of 1987', *Electoral Studies*, Vol. 8 (1989), pp. 131–42
——, 'The Changing Party System', in Gold (ed.), *New Zealand Politics in Perspective* (3rd edn, 1992), pp. 326–41
Aitken, J., 'Summary', in State Services Commission, *Proceedings of the Senior Management Conference, 9–11 April 1991* (Wellington, 1991)
Alley, R, 'Parliamentary Parties in Office: Government-Backbench Relations', in Levine (ed.), *Politics in New Zealand* (1978), pp. 96–112
——, 'The Powers of the Prime Minister', in Gold (ed.), *New Zealand Politics in Perspective* (2nd edn, 1989), pp. 103–22
Appendices to the Journals of the House of Representatives [*AJHR*]
Archer, J. R., 'The Theory of Responsible Government in Britain and Australia', in P. Weller and D. Jaensch (eds.), *Responsible Government in Australia*, pp. 23–31
Bagehot, W. *The English Constitution*, introduced by R. H. S. Crossman (London and Glasgow, Fontana, 1963; first published in 1867)
Barry, B. M. and W. J. Rees, 'The Public Interest', *Proceedings of the Aristotelian Society. Supplement*, Vol. 58 (1964), pp. 1–38
Bassett, M., *Confrontation '51: The 1951 Waterfront Dispute* (Wellington, A. H. and A. W. Reed, 1971)
——, *The Third Labour Government* (Palmerston North, The Dunmore Press, 1976)
Baysting, A. et al., (eds.), *Making Policy Not Tea: Women in Parliament* (Auckland, Oxford University Press, 1993)
Birch, A. H., *Representative and Responsible Government: An Essay on the British Constitution* (London, Allen and Unwin, 1964)
Birch, B., 'Reflections and Commentary', in State Services Commission, *Proceedings of the Senior Management Conference, 9–11 April 1991* (Wellington, 1991)
Bolger, J., 'The Government's Vision for the Public Service', in State Services Commission, *Proceedings of the Senior Management Conference, 9–11 April 1991* (Wellington, 1991)
Bollard, A., 'The Fiscal Responsibility Bill', *Public Sector*, Vol. 17 (March 1994), pp. 10–12
Boston, J., 'Advising the Prime Minister in New Zealand: The Origins, Functions and Evolution of the Prime Minister's Advisory Group', *Politics*, Vol. 23 (1988), pp. 8–20
——, 'The Case for a Department of Prime Minister and Cabinet', *Public Sector*, Vol. 12 (1989), pp. 7–11
——, 'The Treasury and the Organisation of Economic Advice: Some International Comparisons', in Easton (ed.), *The Making of Rogernomics* (1989), pp. 68–91
——, 'The Cabinet and Policy Making under the Fourth Labour Government', in

Holland and Boston (eds.), *The Fourth Labour Government: Politics and Policy in New Zealand* (1990), pp. 62–83

——, 'The Theoretical Underpinnings of Public Sector Restructuring in New Zealand', in Boston et al. (eds.)., *Reshaping the State* (1991), pp. 1–26

——, 'Reorganizing the Machinery of Government: Objectives and Outcomes', in Boston et al. (eds.) *Reshaping the State* (1991), pp. 233–67

——, 'The Future of Cabinet Government in New Zealand: The Implications of MMP for the Formation, Organization and Operations of the Cabinet', unpublished paper; Institute for International Research, conference on 'MMP: Changing the Way We Govern' (Wellington, 1994)

——, 'Grand Designs and Unpleasant Realities: The Fate of the National Government's Proposals for the Integrated Targeting of Social Assistance', *Political Science*, Vol. 46 (1994), pp. 1–21

——, and E. Cooper, 'The Treasury: Advice, Co-ordination and Control', in Gold (ed.), *New Zealand Politics in Perspective*, (2nd edn, 1989), pp. 123–44

——, and P. Dalziel (eds.), *The Decent Society? Essays in Response to National's Economic and Social Policies* (Auckland, Oxford University Press, 1992)

——, and M. Holland (eds.), *The Fourth Labour Government: Radical Politics in New Zealand* (Auckland, Oxford University Press, 1987)

——, et al. (eds.), *Reshaping the State: New Zealand's Bureaucratic Revolution* (Auckland, Oxford University Press, 1991)

Bremer, R., 'Federated Farmers and the State', in Roper and Rudd (eds.), *State and Economy in New Zealand* (1993), pp. 108–27

Brookfield, F. M., 'The Marginal Lands Board Affair', *New Zealand Law Journal*, Part One (17 March 1981), pp. 96–104, and Part Two (7 April 1981), pp. 124–8

Brown, B., *The Rise of New Zealand Labour* (Wellington, Price Milburn, 1962)

Budge, I., and H. Keman, *Parties and Democracy: Coalition Formation and Government Functioning in Twenty States* (Oxford, Oxford University Press, 1990)

Cabinet Office, 'Administrative History', National Archives, AFFD, (SNS:11/86)

——, *Cabinet Office Manual* (Wellington, 1979)

——, *Cabinet Office Manual* (Wellington, 1991)

——, 'Constitutional Status and Powers of Associate Ministers and of Acting Ministers', Cabinet Office Circular, CO (90) 9 (17 May 1990)

——, 'Report of the Cabinet Office for the Year Ended 31 March 1989', *AJHR*, G.47

Catt, H., 'What do Voters Decide?' *Political Science*, Vol. 43 (1991), pp. 30–42

Cawson, A., 'Is there a Corporatist Theory of the State?' in G. Duncan (ed.), *Democracy and the Capitalist State* (Cambridge, Cambridge University Press, 1989), pp. 233–52

Chapman, G., *The Years of Lightning* (Wellington, A. H. and A. W. Reed, 1980)

Chapman, R., 'Political Culture: The Purposes of Party and the Current Challenge', in Gold (ed.), *New Zealand Politics in Perspective* (2nd edn, 1989), pp. 14–32

——, 'A Political Culture under Pressure: The Struggle to Preserve a Progressive Tax Base for Welfare and the Positive State', *Political Science*, Vol. 44 (1992), pp. 1–27

Clark, M. (ed.), *The Labour Party after 75 Years* (Wellington, Department of Politics, Victoria University, Occasional Publication No. 4, 1992)

Cleveland, L., 'The Major Agencies of Central Government in New Zealand', in Cleveland and Robinson (eds.), *Readings in New Zealand Government*

(Wellington, A. H. and A. W. Reed, 1972), pp. 20–64

——, *The Anatomy of Influence* (Wellington, Hicks Smith and Sons, 1972)

——, *The Politics of Utopia: New Zealand and its Government* (Wellington, Methuen, 1979)

Cook, L. W., 'Statistical Populations Calculated', Press release issued by Statistics New Zealand (4 May 1994)

Cox, L., *Kotahitanga: The Search for Maori Political Unity* (Auckland, Oxford University Press, 1993)

Dalziel, P., 'National's Economic Strategy', in Boston and Dalziel (eds.), *The Decent Society?* (1992), pp. 19–38

——, 'The Reserve Bank Act: Reflecting Relationships Between State and Economy in the Twentieth Century', in Roper and Rudd (eds.), *State and Economy in New Zealand* (1993), pp. 74–90

Dann, C., *Up From Under: Women and Liberation in New Zealand, 1970–1985* (Wellington, Allen and Unwin/Port Nicholson Press, 1985)

Davies, S. J., 'State-Owned Enterprises Act: Accountability of State Enterprises and Responsibility of Ministers', *Public Sector*, Vol. 10 (1987), pp. 2–5

Dawe, S., 'Reserve Bank of New Zealand Act', *Reserve Bank of New Zealand Bulletin*, Vol. 53 (March 1990), pp. 33–4

Debnam, G., 'Adversary Politics in New Zealand: Climate of Stress and Policy Aggressors', *Journal of Commonwealth and Comparative Studies*, Vol. 18 (1990), pp. 1–24

——, 'Conflict and Reform in the New Zealand Labour Party, 1984–1992', *Political Science*, Vol. 44 (1992), pp. 42–59

Deeks, J., and N. Perry (eds.), *Controlling Interests: Business, the State and Society in New Zealand* (Auckland, Auckland University Press, 1992)

Department of the Prime Minister and Cabinet, 'Briefing Notes for Prime Minister, 28 October 1990' (Wellington, 1990)

——, 'Report of the Department of the Prime Minister and Cabinet for the Period 1 July to 31 Dec. 1990', *AJHR*, G.48 HY

——, 'Report of the Department of the Prime Minister and Cabinet for the Period 1 July 1991–31 Dec. 1991', *AJHR*, G.48 HY

Doig, A., 'The Resignation of Edwina Curry: A Word Too Far', *Parliamentary Affairs*, Vol. 42 (1989), pp. 317–29

Douglas, R., 'The Politics of Successful Structural Reform', Paper delivered to Mt Pelerin Society (31 Nov. 1989)

Downey, P. J., 'Cabinet and Government', *New Zealand Law Journal* (21 Feb. 1988), pp. 29–30

Downs, A., *An Economic Theory of Democracy* (New York, Harper and Row, 1957)

——, *Inside Bureaucracy* (Boston, Little, Brown, 1967)

Du Fresne, K., 'Lobbying: New Zealand Style', in Gold (ed.), *New Zealand Politics in Perspective* (2nd edn, 1989), pp. 312–19

Dunleavy, P., *Democracy, Bureaucracy and Public Choice: Economic Explanations in Political Science* (Hemel Hempstead, Harvester Wheatsheaf, 1991)

——, and R. Rhodes, 'Core Executive Studies in Britain', *Public Administration*, Vol. 68 (1990), pp. 3–28

Du Plessis, R., 'Women, Politics and the State', in Roper and Rudd (eds.), *State and Economy in New Zealand* (1993), pp. 210–25

Duverger, M., *Political Parties: Their Organization and Activity in the Modern*

State, translated by Barbara and Robert North (University Paperbacks; London, Methuen, 1964)

Eaddy, R., 'The Structure and Operations of the Executive' in Gold (ed.), *New Zealand Politics in Perspective* (3rd edn, 1992), pp. 162–73

Easton, B., 'The Commercialisation of the New Zealand Economy: From Think Big to Privatisation' in Easton (ed.), *The Making of Rogernomics* (1989), pp. 114–31

——(ed.), *The Making of Rogernomics* (Auckland, Auckland University Press, 1989)

Edlin, B., 'How to Keep Six Cabinet Ministers Busy', *The Independent* (2 Oct. 1992), pp. 24 and 26

——, 'Don't Ask the Mandarins about Budget Peeling', *National Business Review* (29 May 1992), p. 18

Edwards, B., 'Treasury Head Won't Quit Despite Mistakes', *Evening Post*, 28 March 1994

Eulau H, et al., 'The Role of the Representative: Some Empirical Observations on the Theory of Edmund Burke', *American Political Science Review*, Vol. 53 (1959), pp. 742–56

Finer, S. E., *Adversary Politics and Electoral Reform* (London, Wigram, 1975)

Frendreis, J. P. et al., 'The Study of Cabinet Dissolutions in Parliamentary Democracies', *Legislative Studies Quarterly*, Vol. 11 (1986), pp. 619–28

Galvin, B. V., 'Some Reflections on the Operation of the Executive', in Gold (ed.), *New Zealand Politics in Perspective* (1st edn, 1985), pp. 66–83

——, 'Change of Government: Impact on the State Sector', *Public Sector*, Vol. 14 (March, 1991), pp. 4–6

Gamble, A., 'The Thatcher Decade in Perspective' in P. Dunleavy, A. Gamble, and G. Peele (eds.), *Developments in British Politics 3* (London, Macmillan, 1990), pp. 333–58

Garnier, T., B. Kohn, and P. Booth, *The Hunter and the Hill: New Zealand Politics in the Kirk Years* (Auckland, Cassell, 1978)

Gold, H. (ed.), *New Zealand Politics in Perspective*, 1st edn (Auckland, Longman Paul, 1985)

—— (ed.), *New Zealand Politics in Perspective*, 2nd edn (Auckland, Longman Paul, 1989)

—— (ed.), *New Zealand Politics in Perspective*, 3rd edn (Auckland, Longman Paul, 1992)

Goldfinch, S. and B. Roper, 'Treasury's Role in State Policy Formulation During the Post-War Era', in Roper and Rudd (eds.), *State and Economy in New Zealand* (1993), pp. 50–73

Gould, J., *The Rake's Progress? The New Zealand Economy Since 1945* (Auckland, Hodder and Stoughton, 1982)

Goulter, J., 'Palmer Applies the Oilcan to Wheels of Government', *Evening Post* (9 Sept. 1989), p. 8

——, 'No Area Exempt in Government Cutback', *Evening Post* (10 Nov. 1990)

Grant, W., 'Insider Groups, Outsider Groups and Interest Group Strategies in Britain', Working Paper No. 19 (Warwick, University of Warwick, 1978)

Gustafson, B., *The First 50 Years: A History of the National Party* (Auckland, Reed Methuen, 1986)

——, *From the Cradle to the Grave: A Biography of Michael Joseph Savage* (Auckland, Penguin, 1986)

——, 'The Labour Party', in Gold (ed.), *New Zealand Politics in Perspective* (3rd edn, 1992), pp. 263–88

Harris, P., 'Pressure Groups and Protest', in Gold (ed.), *New Zealand Politics in Perspective* (2nd edn, 1989), pp. 295–311

——, 'Changing New Zealand's Electoral System: The 1992 Referendum', *Representation*, Vol. 31 (1992–93), pp. 53–7

——, and E. M. McLeay, 'The Legislature', in G. R. Hawke (ed.), *Changing Politics? The Electoral Referendum 1993* (1993), pp. 103–30

——, and S. Levine et al. (eds.), *The New Zealand Politics Source Book*, 2nd edn (Palmerston North, The Dunmore Press, 1993)

Harris, S., 'Richardson under Threat', *National Business Review* (26 Nov. 1993), p. 3

Hawke, G. R. (ed.), *Changing Politics? The Electoral Referendum 1993* (Wellington, Institute of Policy Studies, 1993)

Hawker, G., 'Political Review', *The Australian Quarterly*, Vol. 46 (1974), pp. 94–103

Headey, B., *British Cabinet Ministers: The Roles of Politicians in Executive Office* (London, Allen and Unwin, 1974)

Henderson, J., 'The Operations of the Executive', in Gold (ed.), *New Zealand Politics in Perspective* (2nd edn, 1989), pp. 94–102

——, 'Labour's Modern Prime Ministers and the Party: A Study of Contrasting Political Styles', in Clark (ed.), *The Labour Party after 75 Years* (1992), pp. 98–117

Hennessy, P., *Cabinet* (Oxford, Basil Blackwell, 1986)

Hill, R. and N. Roberts, 'Success, Swing and Gender: The Performance of Women Candidates for Parliament in New Zealand, 1946–87', *Politics*, Vol. 25 (1990), pp. 62–80

Holland, M. and J. Boston (eds.), *The Fourth Labour Government: Politics and Policy in New Zealand* (Auckland, Oxford University Press, 1990)

Hunn, D. and H. Lang, 'Review of the Prime Minister's Office and Cabinet Office' (Wellington, State Services Commission, 1989)

Jackson, K., *The New Zealand Legislative Council* (Dunedin, University of Otago Press, 1972)

——, *New Zealand Politics of Change* (Wellington, Reed Education, 1973)

——, 'Government Succession in New Zealand', *Journal of Commonwealth and Comparative Studies*, Vol. 15 (1977), pp. 151–69

——, 'Cabinet and the Prime Minister', in Levine (ed.), *Politics in New Zealand* (1978), pp. 63–77

——, 'Political Leadership and Succession in the New Zealand National Party', in Levine (ed.), *Politics in New Zealand* (1978), pp. 161–81

——, *The Dilemma of Parliament* (Wellington, Allen and Unwin/Port Nicholson Press, 1987)

——, and G. A. Wood, 'The New Zealand Parliament and Maori Representation', *Historical Studies*, Vol. 11 (1963–65), pp. 383–96

James, C., *The Quiet Revolution* (Wellington, Allen and Unwin/Port Nicholson Press, 1986)

——, 'A Botch of a Job', *Management* (March 1990), pp. 9–10

——, *New Territory: The Transformation of New Zealand 1984–92* (Wellington, Bridget Williams Books, 1992)

Janis, I. L., *Groupthink: Psychological Studies of Policy Decisions and Fiascoes* (Boston, Houghton Mifflin, 1982)

——, *Crucial Decisions: Leadership in Policymaking and Crisis Management* (New York, The Free Press, 1989)

Jewell, M. E. and S. C. Patterson, *The Legislative Process in the United States* (New York, Random House, 1966)

Johns, I. B., 'Efficiency in Government: The Changing Role of the Central Administrative Agencies 1962–78', *Public Sector*, Research Paper, Vol. 1, No. 2 (April 1979), pp. 139–49

Johnson, N., 'Accountability, Control and Complexity: Moving Beyond Ministerial Responsibility', in A. Barker (ed.), *Quangos in Britain* (London, Macmillan, 1982), pp. 206–18

Joseph, P. A., 'Ministerial Appointments—Still "The Startling Reality"', *New Zealand Law Journal* (1981), pp. 390–5

——, 'The Honourable D. F. Quigley's Resignation: Strictly Political—Not Constitutional', *Canterbury Law Review*, Vol. 1 (1982), pp. 428–36

——, *Constitutional and Administrative Law in New Zealand* (Sydney, The Law Book Co., 1993)

Keith, K., 'On the Constitution of New Zealand', *Political Science*, Vol. 44 (1992), pp. 28–34

Kellow, A. J., 'Politicians Versus Bureaucrats: Who Makes Public Policy?' in Gold (ed.), *New Zealand Politics in Perspective* (2nd edn, 1989), pp. 145–70

Kelsey, J., *A Question of Honour? Labour and the Treaty* (Wellington, Allen and Unwin/Port Nicholson Press, 1990)

——, *Rolling Back the State: Privatisation of Power in Aotearoa/New Zealand* (Wellington, Bridget Williams Books, 1993)

Kerr, M. G., 'Establishing the Ministry of Transport: Some Inside Views', unpublished Diploma of Public Administration research paper (Victoria University, 1973)

Kilroy, S. 'Unionists join PM's Office as advisers', *Dominion* (1 Nov. 1989), p. 2.

Kohn, B., 'Grim Reality of the Country's Dollar Crisis', *Evening Post* (4 Aug. 1984), p. 1

Lagan, B., 'Cabinet Dissenters Escape Unpunished', *Dominion* (1 Nov. 1982), p. 2

Lawson, G., 'Politicians, Public Servants and Public Enterprise: Revolution in Executive Power', *Public Sector*, Vol. 10 (1987), pp. 8–12

Lee, J. A., *Simple on a Soap-Box* (Auckland, Collins Publishers, 1963)

Legat, N., 'Say it Again, Jim', *Metro* (June 1992), pp. 56–63

Legislation Advisory Committee, *Legislative Change: Guidelines on Process and Content* (August 1987)

——, *Public Advisory Bodies: A Discussion Paper* (Wellington, September 1990)

Leonard, K., 'Election of Party Leaders: Should the Method be Changed?', *Labour Network*, 2 (March/April 1983).

Levine, S. (ed.), *Politics in New Zealand* (Sydney, Allen and Unwin, 1978)

——, and N. Roberts, 'National to Power: Voter Choice in 1990', in Gold (ed.), *New Zealand Politics in Perspective* (3rd edn, 1992), pp. 493–511

Levinson, D. J., 'Role Personality and Social Structure in the Organizational Setting', in F. I. Greenstein and M. Lerner (eds.), *A Source Book for the Study of Personality and Politics* (Chicago, Markham, 1971), pp. 61–74

Lijphart, A., *Democracies: Patterns of Majoritarian and Consensus Government in*

Twenty-One Countries (New Haven, Yale University Press, 1984)

——, 'The Demise of the Last Westminster System? Comments on the Report of New Zealand's Royal Commission on the Electoral System', *Electoral Studies*, Vol. 6 (1987), pp. 97–114

——, 'Democratic Political Systems: Types, Cases, Causes, and Consequences', *Journal of Theoretical Politics*, Vol. 1 (1989), pp. 33–48

Lipson, L., *The Politics of Equality: New Zealand's Adventures in Democracy* (Chicago, University of Chicago Press, 1948)

Long, R., 'Clash Preceded Quigley Sacking', *Dominion* (16 June 1982), p. 1

——, 'Uncertain future for PM's new staff', *Dominion* (1 March 1990), p. 1

——, 'Cabinet Razor Gang to Tackle Deficit', *Dominion*, (10 Nov. 1990), p. 1

——, 'Peters Vows to Overturn Richardson's Policies', *Dominion* (3 Oct. 1991), p. 1

—— and B. Lagan, 'Quigley: The Man Who Wouldn't be Gagged', *Dominion* (15 June 1982), pp. 1 and 2

Lowi, T., 'American Business, Public Policy, Case Studies, and Political Theory', *World Politics*, Vol. 16 (1964), pp. 677–715

Macintosh, J. P., *The British Cabinet*, 3rd edn (London, Stevens and Sons, 1968)

Mansbridge, J. J., 'The Rise and Fall of Self-Interest in the Explanation of Political Life', in J. J. Mansbridge (ed.),*Beyond Self-Interest* (Chicago and London, University of Chicago Press, 1990), pp. 3–22

Marsh, D. and R. A. W. Rhodes, *Policy Networks in British Government* (Oxford, Clarendon Press, 1992)

Marshall, J., *Memoirs*, 2 vols. (Auckland, Collins, 1983, 1989)

Martin, J., *Public Service and the Public Servant* (Wellington, State Services Commission, 1991)

——, 'The Buck Stops Where?' *Evening Post* (9 July 1992), p. 7

McCallum, J., *Women in the House: Members of Parliament in New Zealand* (Picton, Cape Catley, 1993)

McCoy, E., 'Deregulation: Public Utilities and New Zealand Economic Reform', in B. Head and E. McCoy (eds.), *Deregulation or Better Regulation?* (Melbourne, Macmillan, 1991), pp. 57–68

McDowell, D., 'Briefing Notes for Prime Minister' (Department of Prime Minister and Cabinet, 1990)

McGee, D. G., '"The Startling Reality" and Ualesi',*New Zealand Law Journal* (1981), pp. 456–7

McHenry, D. E., 'The Origins of Caucus Selection of Cabinet', *Historical Studies*, Vol. 7 (1955), pp. 39–43

McLeay, E. M., 'Parliamentary Careers in a Two-Party System; Cabinet Selection in New Zealand', Ph.D. thesis (University of Auckland, 1978)

——, 'Political Argument about Representation: The Case of the Maori Seats', *Political Studies*, Vol. 28 (1980), pp. 43–62

——, 'Selection Versus Election: Choosing Cabinets in New Zealand', in H. D. Clarke and M. M. Czudnowski (eds.), *Political Elites in Anglo-American Democracies* (Dekalb IL, Northern Illinois University Press, 1987), pp. 280–306

—— (ed.), *The 1990 General Election: Perspectives on Political Change in New Zealand* (Wellington, Department of Politics, Victoria University, Occasional Publication No. 3, 1991)

——, 'Housing Policy', in Boston and Dalziel (eds.), *The Decent Society?* (1992), pp. 169–85

——, 'The State in New Zealand', in Gold (ed.), *New Zealand Politics in Perspective* (3rd edn, 1992), pp. 427–49

——, 'Women's Parliamentary Representation: A Comparative Perspective', in H. Catt and E. M. McLeay (eds.), *Women and Politics in New Zealand* (Wellington, Victoria University Press, 1993), pp. 40–62

McLaughlin, M., 'Lange's Lot', *The New Zealand Listener* (10 Dec. 1988), pp. 18–20

McQueen, H., *The Ninth Floor: Inside the Prime Minister's Office—a Political Experience* (Auckland, Penguin Books, 1991)

McRae, T. 'The Reform of Parliamentary Control: A Constitutional and Procedural History of the New Zealand House of Representatives, 1951–1990', unpublished MA thesis (Victoria University of Wellington, 1992)

Michels, R., *Political Parties* (Glencoe IL, The Free Press, 1915)

Miller, J. B. D., 'David Syme and Elective Ministries', *Historical Studies*, Vol. 6 (1953), pp. 1–15

Milne, R. S., *Political Parties in New Zealand* (Oxford, Oxford University Press, 1966)

Ministers' Private Interests Committee, 'Report', *AJHR*, 1956, Vol. 4, I.17

Ministry of Maori Development, *Ka Awatea: A Report of the Ministerial Planning Group, March 1991* (Wellington, 1991)

Mitchell, A., *Government by Party* (Christchurch, Whitcombe and Tombs, 1966)

——, 'Caucus: The New Zealand Parliamentary Parties', *Journal of Commonwealth Political Studies*, Vol. 6 (1968), pp. 3–33

——, *Politics and People in New Zealand* (Christchurch, Whitcombe and Tombs, 1969)

Mitchell, D. J., 'Nelson Cotton Mill: A Case Study in the Politics of Development', unpublished MA thesis (University of Canterbury, 1967)

Morkel, A., 'The Cabinet Reform', *International Journal of Politics*, Vol. 2 (1972), pp. 10–50

Muldoon, R. D., *My Way* (Wellington, A. H. and A. W. Reed, 1981)

——, *Number 38* (Auckland, Reed Methuen, 1986)

Mulgan, R., 'The Concept of Mandate in New Zealand Politics', *Political Science*, Vol. 30 (1978), pp. 88–96

——, *Democracy and Power in New Zealand* (Auckland, Oxford University Press, 1984)

——, *Democracy and Power in New Zealand*, 2nd edn (Auckland, Oxford University Press, 1989)

——, 'The Changing Electoral Mandate', in Holland and Boston (eds.), *The Fourth Labour Government* (1990), pp. 11–21

——, 'Comment: The Principles of Rogernomics', *Public Sector*, Vol. 15 (March 1992), pp. 16–17

——, 'The Elective Dictatorship in New Zealand', in Gold (ed.), *New Zealand Politics in Perspective* (3rd edn., 1992), pp. 513–32

——, 'A Pluralist Analysis of the New Zealand State', in Roper and Rudd (eds.), *State and Economy in New Zealand* (1993), pp. 129–46

Munro, M., 'Second-Guessing the Prime Minister', *Dominion* (26 Dec. 1989), p. 9

——, 'Fearless and Outspoken Loner Pays the Price', *Dominion* (3 Oct. 1991), p. 8

——, 'The Minders', *Dominion* (19 and 21 May 1993), p. 9.

New Zealand House of Representatives, *Standing Orders of the House of Representatives* (Wellington, 1992)

New Zealand Labour Party, *Caucus Rules*

New Zealand Labour Party, 'Minutes of the N.Z.L.P. 1935'

New Zealand National Party, 'Executive Summary of Automotive Enquiry Carried out by Government Caucus Sub-Committee on Matters of Concern to the Automotive Industry' (1991)

New Zealand Parliamentary Debates [*NZPD*]

New Zealand Official Yearbook 1993 (Wellington, Department of Statistics, 1993)

Niskanen, W., *Bureaucracy and Representative Government* (Chicago, Aldin-Atherton, 1971)

O'Farrell, P. J., *Harry Holland: Militant Socialist* (Canberra, Australian National University, 1964)

Office of the Prime Minister, 'Prime Minister Announces Enterprise Council Members' (11 November 1991)

——, 'Report of the Prime Minister's Office for the Year Ended 31 March 1989', *AJHR*, G.48

Oliver, W. H., 'Sir Sidney Holland', *Comment* (Spring, 1961), pp. 4–6

——, 'The Labour Caucus and Economic Policy Formation, 1981-1984', in Easton (ed.), *The Making of Rogernomics* (1989), pp. 11–52

Olson, M., *The Logic of Collective Action: Public Goods and the Theory of Groups* (Cambridge MA, Harvard University Press, 1965)

Olssen, E. N., 'John Alexander Lee, the Stormy Petrel: His Ideas, Their Inspiration and Influence and His Attempts to Translate His Ideas into Legislation', unpublished MA thesis (Otago University, 1965)

Ovenden, K., 'Prospect: On the Absence of Political Ideas', in R. Goldstein with R. Alley (eds.), *Labour in Power: Promise and Performance*, (Wellington, Price Milburn for New Zealand University Press, 1975), pp. 190–7

O'Sullivan, F., 'Bolger drops curtain on incentive play by commercial glitterati', *National Business Review* (15 May 1992), p. 9

Palmer, G., 'The New Zealand Legislative Machine', *Victoria University of Wellington Law Review*, Vol. 17 (1987), pp. 285–306

——, *Unbridled Power: An Interpretation of New Zealand's Constitution and Government*, 2nd edn (Auckland, Oxford University Press, 1987)

——, *New Zealand's Constitution in Crisis: Reforming our Political System* (Dunedin, John McIndoe, 1992)

Parker, R. S., 'Responsible Government in Australia', in P. Weller and D. Jaensch (eds.), in *Responsible Government in Australia* (1980), pp. 11–22

Phillips, A., *Engendering Democracy* (Cambridge, Polity Press, 1991)

Polaschek, R. J., *Government Administration in New Zealand* (Wellington, New Zealand Institute of Public Administration and Oxford University Press, 1958)

Probine, M. C., 'The Public Service and Ministers' *Public Sector*, Vol. 6 (1983), pp. 21–4

Putnam, R., *The Comparative Study of Political Elites* (Englewood Cliffs, Prentice-Hall, 1976)

Richardson, R., 'The Fiscal Responsibility Bill', *Public Sector*, Vol. 17 (March 1994), pp. 10–12

Riker, W. H., *The Theory of Political Coalitions* (New Haven and London, Yale University Press, 1962)

Ringer, J. B., *An Introduction to New Zealand Government* (Christchurch, Hazard Press, 1991)

Rivers, J., 'Advisers Spend Half Budget on Consultants', *Sunday Star-Times* (23 March 1994), p. C10

Roberts, J., 'Cabinet' in A. Robinson (ed.), *Notes on New Zealand Politics* (1970)

——, *Politicians, Public Servants and Public Enterprise: Restructuring the New Zealand Government Executive* (Wellington, Victoria University Press for the Institute of Policy Studies, 1987)

——, 'Ministers, the Cabinet and Public Servants', in Boston and Holland (eds.), *The Fourth Labour Government: Radical Politics in New Zealand* (1987), pp. 89–110

——, 'The Public Servants and Ministers', *Public Sector*, Vol. 6 (1983), pp. 25–8

Roberts, N., 'Nats, Fat Cats and Democrats: The Opposition Parties Under Labour', in Boston and Holland (eds.), *The Fourth Labour Government: Radical Politics in New Zealand* (1987), pp. 36–53

Robinson, A. (ed.), *Notes on New Zealand Politics* (Political Science Department, Victoria University of Wellington, 1970)

Robson, J. L., *Sacred Cows and Rogue Elephants: Policy Development in the New Zealand Justice Department* (Wellington, Government Printing Office, 1987)

Roper, B., 'The Political Activism of Business and the Emergence of the New Right in New Zealand, 1975–1987', *Political Science*, Vol. 44 (1992), pp. 1–23

——, 'A Level Playing Field? Business Political Activism and State Policy Formulation', in Roper and Rudd (eds.), *State and Economy in New Zealand* (1993), pp. 147–71

——, and C. Rudd (eds.), *State and Economy in New Zealand* (Auckland, Oxford University Press, 1993)

Ross, F., 'Nearly $8m Spent on Health Care Consultants', *Dominion* (10 Feb. 1993), p. 1

Royal Commission on the Electoral System, *Report of the Royal Commission on the Electoral System: Towards a Better Democracy* (Wellington, Government Printer, 1986)

Royal Commission of Inquiry on the State Services in New Zealand, *Report of the NZ Royal Commission of Inquiry on the State Services in New Zealand* (Wellington, Government Printer, 1962)

Rush, M., *The Cabinet and Policy Formation* (Burnt Mill, Harlow, Longman, 1984)

Sallee, N., 'The Touchy Question of the Eighth Floor Think Tank', *National Business Review* (11 November 1985), p. 13

Scholefield, G. H. (ed.), *New Zealand Parliamentary Record: 1840–1949* (Wellington, Government Printer, 1950)

Scott, G. et al., 'Reform of the Core Public Sector: New Zealand Experience', *Governance*, Vol. 3 (1990), pp. 138–67

Scott, K. J., *The New Zealand Constitution* (Oxford, Clarendon Press, 1962)

Shanahan, F., 'Cabinet Responsibility for Coordinating Action between Government Departments', National Archives, AFFD, Series 816, Paper 1 (undated)

——, 'Memo to Prime Minister', National Archives, AFFD, Series 816, Paper 2 (Dec. 1949)

Sharp, A., *Justice and the Maori* (Auckland, Oxford University Press, 1990)

——, 'The Treaty, the Tribunal and the Law', in Gold (ed.), *New Zealand Politics in Perspective* (3rd edn, 1992), pp. 123–42

Shroff, M., 'The Structure and Operations of the Cabinet in Relation to the Budget', in J. N. Nethercote, B. Gilligan and C. Walsh (eds.), *Decision Making in New*

Zealand Government (Canberra, Federalism Research Centre, Australian National University, 1993), pp. 1–9

Sinclair, K., *Walter Nash* (Auckland, Auckland University Press and Oxford University Press, 1976)

Skene, G. 'Parliament: Reassessing its Role', in Gold (ed.), *New Zealand Politics in Perspective*, 3rd edn, pp. 247–62

Skinner, T., *Man to Man* (Christchurch, Whitcoulls, 1980)

Smith, T. B., *The New Zealand Bureaucrat* (Wellington, Cheshire, 1974)

Stanyer, J., 'Divided Responsibilities: Accountability in Decentralized Government', *Public Administration Bulletin*, Vol. 17 (1974), pp. 14–30

State Services Commission, *Proceedings of the Senior Management Conference, 9–11 April 1991* (Wellington, 1991)

Steering Group on State Sector Reforms, *Review of State Sector Reforms* (Wellington, 1991)

Strategos Consulting Ltd, *New Zealand Police: Resource Management Review 1989* (Government Printer, Wellington, 1989)

Sutch, W. B., *Local Government in New Zealand: A History of Defeat* (Wellington, Department of Industries and Commerce, 1964)

——, *The Quest for Security in New Zealand 1840 to 1966* (Wellington, Oxford University Press, 1966)

Syme, D., *Representative Government in England: Its Faults and Failings* (London, Kegan Paul, Trench and Co., 1881)

Talboys, B. E., 'The Cabinet Committee System', *New Zealand Journal of Public Administration*, Vol. 33 (1970), pp. 1–7

Tourist and Publicity Services Division, 'The Work of Cabinet', Staff Training Paper (Nov. 1972)

Treasury, *Economic Management* (Wellington, Government Printer, 1984)

Treasury, *Government Management* (Wellington, Government Printer, 1987)

Verba, S., *Small Groups and Political Behaviour: A Study of Leadership* (Princeton NJ, Princeton University Press, 1961)

Vowles, J., 'Business, Unions and the State: Organising Economic Interests in New Zealand', in Gold (ed.), *New Zealand Politics in Perspective* (3rd edn, 1992), pp. 342–65

—— (ed.), *Double Decision: The 1993 General Election and Referendum* (Wellington, Department of Politics, Victoria University, Occasional Publication No. 6, 1994)

——, and P. Aimer, *Voters' Vengeance: The 1990 Election in New Zealand and the Fate of the Fourth Labour Government* (Auckland, Auckland University Press, 1993)

Wahlke, J. C., et al., *The Legislative System: Explorations in Legislative Behavior* (New York, John Wiley and Sons, 1962)

Walker, R., 'The Maori People: Their Political Development', in Gold (ed.), *New Zealand Politics in Perspective* (3rd edn, 1992), pp. 379–400

Walsh, P., 'The State and Industrial Relations in New Zealand', in Roper and Rudd (eds.), *State and Economy in New Zealand* (1993), pp. 172–91

Ward, A. D., *A Show of Justice: Racial 'Amalgamation' in Nineteenth Century New Zealand* (Canberra, Australian National University Press, 1976)

Waring, M., 'The Muldoon Years', in A. Baysting et al. (eds.), *Making Policy Not Tea* (1993), pp. 75–83

Watson, G., 'Ministerial Responsibility and the Maniototo Irrigation Scheme', *Otago Law Review*, Vol. 6, No. 1, pp. 158–74

Webb, L., *Government in New Zealand* (Wellington, Department of Internal Affairs, 1940)

Weber, M., *From Max Weber: Essays in Sociology*, translated, edited, and introduced by H. H. Gerth and C. Wright Mills (New York, Oxford University Press, 1946)

Weller, P., *First Among Equals: Prime Ministers in Westminster Systems* (Sydney, Allen and Unwin, 1985)

——, 'Cabinet Committees in Australia and New Zealand', in T. T. Mackie and B. W. Hogwood (eds.), *Unlocking the Cabinet: Cabinet Structures in Comparative Perspective* (London, Sage, 1985), pp. 86–113

——, 'Prime Ministers, Political Leadership and Cabinet Government', *Australian Journal of Public Administration*, Vol. 50 (1991), pp. 131–44

——, and D. Jaensch (eds.), *Responsible Government in Australia* (Richmond, Victoria, Drummond Publishing Co. on behalf of Australian Political Studies Association, 1980)

Wilson, J., 'The Professionals: A Study of Women in Parliament', *Political Science*, Vol. 35 (1983), pp. 198–220

Wilson, M., *Labour in Government, 1984–1987* (Wellington, Allen and Unwin, 1989)

——, 'Women and the Labour Party', in Clark (ed.), *The Labour Party after 75 Years* (1992), pp. 35–49

Wolinetz, S. B., 'Party System Change: Past, Present and Future', in S. B. Wolinetz (ed.), *Parties and Party Systems in Liberal Democracies* (London, Routledge, 1988), pp. 296–320

Wood, G. A., 'Should Tony Friedlander Resign?' *Auckland Star* (1 March 1984)

——, *Governing New Zealand* (Auckland, Longman Paul, 1988)

——, 'The National Party', in Gold (ed.), *New Zealand Politics in Perspective* (3rd edn, 1992), pp. 289–309

—— (ed.), *Supplement to Ministers and Members in the New Zealand Parliament 1911–1990* (Dunedin, Tarkwode Press, 1992)

Wood, P. W., 'The Doctrine of Ministerial Responsibility', unpublished research paper for B.Laws (University of Canterbury, 1988), pp. 68–9

Woodhouse, D., *Ministers and Parliamentary Accountability in Theory and Practice* (Oxford, Clarendon Press, 1994)

Wright, V., 'Muldoon's Fire Brigade', *The New Zealand Listener*, Vol. 87 (26 Nov.–2 Dec. 1977), pp. 14–18

Zavos, S., *The Real Muldoon* (Wellington, Fourth Estate Books, 1978)

INDEX